OFF- HOLLYWOOD

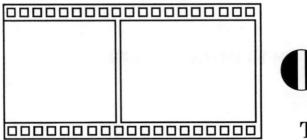

OFF-

The Making

DAVID ROSEN

BASED ON A STUDY
ORIGINALLY COMMISSIONED BY
THE SUNDANCE INSTITUTE AND
THE INDEPENDENT FEATURE PROJECT

HOLLYWOOD:

and Marketing of Independent Films

with Peter Hamilton

GROVE WEIDENFELD

NEW YORK

The production and distribution of independent films is by no means an exact science. This study does not purport to be a comprehensive or objective analysis, but attempts to shed light on the mystifying process of producing, distributing, and marketing independent films. The study does not represent the views of the Sundance Institute and the Independent Feature Project (which commissioned the study), David Rosen, or any other person or entity. Rather, it expresses the differing, and sometimes conflicting, views of the principals involved in the various film groups that participated in the study. The methodology used in compiling the study described in the Introduction was designed to ensure the greatest accuracy possible. Accordingly, any error or omission of fact is wholly unintentional.

Published by Grove Weidenfeld
A division of Grove Press, Inc.
841 Broadway
New York, NY 10003-4793

Published in Canada by General Publishing Company, Ltd.

Library of Congress Cataloging-in-Publication Data

Rosen, David (David M.)
Off-Hollywood.

"Based on a study originally commissioned by the Sundance Institute and the Independent Feature Project."
1. Motion pictures—United States—Production and direction.   2. Motion pictures—United States—Distribution.   3. Motion picture industry—United States.
I. Hamilton, Peter.   II. Title.   III. Title: Independent films.
PN1995.9.P7R64   1989   384′.8′0973   89-7597
ISBN 0-8021-3187-5 (pa)

Manufactured in the United States of America

Printed on acid-free paper

Designed by Irving Perkins Associates

First Edition 1990

1   2   3   4   5   6   7   8   9   10

To Jessica, Dara, Madeline, Irma, and Bill

*a unique family that proves love is a conscious commitment
and not merely an accident of birth*

Acknowledgments

THE film business, not unlike the movies shown on the silver screen, is a world of illusion. This book is an attempt to demystify a small but significant part of that world. Such an undertaking could only have been accomplished with the active cooperation of dozens of film-makers, distributors, exhibitors, and friends of independent filmmaking. I would like to extend my deepest appreciation to all those who not only provided information, much of it of a traditionally proprietary nature, but also generously offered their insights into the complexities of the world of American specialty film.

First and foremost, I would like to thank the two sponsoring organizations of this study: the Sundance Institute, especially Jivan Tabibian, whose vision shaped the study, and Michelle Satter, whose leadership and tireless effort assured its completion; and the Independent Feature Project, particularly Sandra Schulberg, who set the rigorous standards that I hope have been met. I would also like to thank the Benton Foundation, Orion Classics, the American Film

Marketing Association, and the Bydale Foundation for their generous support, without which this project could not have been realized.

My deepest personal appreciation is extended to Peter Hamilton. He collaborated on this project from its inception and took responsibility for developing several case studies. His counsel and friendship have been invaluable.

The following filmmakers, distributors, and other principal players actively assisted in the preparation of the individual film profiles:

The Ballad of Gregorio Cortez: Tom Bower, Moctesuma Esparza, Robert Hoffman, Edward James Olmos, and Robert Young

Cold Feet: Ira Deutchman, Sara Risher, and Bruce vanDusen

Eating Raoul: Jane Alsobrook, Paul Bartel, Anne Kimmel, and Ed Schuman

El Norte: Jesse Beaton, Cary Brokaw, Ira Deutchman, Amir Malin, Greg Nava, Bill Quigley, and Anna Thomas

The Good Fight: Noel Buchner, Janet Cole, Karen Cooper, Mary Dore, Sam Sills, and Fran Spielman

Heartland: Richard Pearce, Jerome Pickman, and Annick Smith

Hollywood Shuffle: Eamonn Bowles, Leonie de Picciotto, and Robert Townsend

My Dinner with Andre: George W. George, Andre Gregory, Jeff Lipsky, Louis Malle, Wallace Shawn, and Dan Talbot

Old Enough: Mark Balsam, Michael Barker, Tom Bernard, Dina Silver, and Marisa Silver

Return of the Secaucus Seven: Ben Barenholtz, Randy Finley, Sam Kitt, Jeff Nelson, Mel Novikoff, Maggie Renzi, and John Sayles

Stand and Deliver: Larry Bershon, Robert Hoffman, Ramon Menendez, Tom Musca, Edward James Olmos, and D. Barry Reardon

The Weavers: Wasn't That a Time!: Michael Barker, Tom Bernard, Jim Brown, Ira Deutchman, Fred Hellerman, Harold Leventhal, Nathaniel Kwit, and George Stoney

Wild Style: Charles Ahearn, Janet Cole, Peter Elson, and Fran Spielman

I would especially like to thank Michael Barker, Tom Bernard, Ira Deutchman, and Sam Kitt for their generous guidance, enthusiasm, and support throughout the project. Irwin Young, Herb Hauser, the late Steve Seifert, Melody Korenbrod, and Steve Block generously provided valuable background information.

The following advisors assisted the project: Charles Benton, Ralph Donnelly, Jeff Dowd, Lindsay Law, Terry Lawler, Tim Ney, Amy Robinson, Jonas Rosenfeld, Carolyn Sachs, Nancy Sher, Ray Silver, and Larry Sugar.

A debt of gratitude is owed to those who helped prepare the appendices: Sam Kitt and Ira Deutchman for the theatrical distribution flow charts; Michael Barker, Tom Bernard, Jeff Lipsky, and Larry Roth for the discussion of media buying; Karen Arikian for the contact reference list; and Heather Welty and Sam Kitt for the glossary.

Gail Harper helped revise the original manuscript and performed valuable research. Tony Safford and Donald Smith provided extensive editorial advice. All ad material is used with the permission of the individual distribution company or filmmaker. I am particularly indebted to my colleagues at LINK Resources for their encouragement and patience.

Thanks to Mitchell Rose for sticking with the project and Walter Bode, my editor, for his patience awaiting delivery of the final manuscript.

I would also like to express appreciation to my daughters Dara and Jessie, who have accompanied me throughout their childhoods to specialty film showings—though sometimes less than willingly. Their responses have always been reliable in picking the winners!

Finally, Peter and I would like to dedicate this book to the late Leo Dratfield, who not only selflessly provided us with invaluable guidance during the long process of completing this book, but extended the same generosity and support to innumerable independent filmmakers.

David Rosen
April 1990

Contents

When the movie opened, serendipity took over.

—*Aljean Harmetz*

Preface

THE initial concept for *Off-Hollywood* first emerged at a conference on "Distribution, Marketing, and Exhibition of Specialized Films in the 1980s," sponsored by the Sundance Institute in June 1981.

Charles Benton, president of Public Media, Inc., and a conference participant, expressed his conviction that there was a need for a history of the distribution and marketing of independent films. Such a study could serve as a valuable educational tool for filmmakers, producers, and professionals who both make and sell these films. His initiative, inspiration, and support through the Benton Foundation was the catalyst for this project. Mr. Benton recommended that the three major organizations that support independent film—the Sundance Institute, the Independent Feature Project, and the American Film Institute—collaborate in producing the study.

The original personnel assigned to the project included Michelle Satter of the Sundance Institute, Michael Goldberg of the Independent Feature Project, and Nancy Sher of the American Film Institute.

Sundance and the IFP continued the work begun by the three founding organizations. Nancy Sher, then director of development at IFP, worked with Sam Kitt, then IFP market director, to ensure the project's completion. The project had a long history. Early and subsequent key supporters and contributors are acknowledged.

Our initial hope was that this study would increase the understanding of the making and marketing of specialty films, and benefit an ever-expanding community that we respect, admire, and upon which we rely. The positive response to, and continued demand for, the book have far exceeded our expectations and have led to this new publication by Grove Weidenfeld, with two additional case studies. We are grateful for the praise *Off-Hollywood* has received from filmmakers and other industry professionals, and we are delighted that it has become recommended or required reading in several independent and university film courses.

Both the Sundance Institute and the Independent Feature Project are committed to providing information and opportunities for independent filmmakers. We hope this book continues to be a source of knowledge and inspiration for those involved in the world of independent cinema.

Michelle Satter   Nancy Sher
The Sundance Institute   The Independent Feature Project

```
□□□□□□□□□□□□□□□□□□□
```

Introduction

```
□□□□□□□□□□□□□□□□□□□
```

THIS book consists of case-history profiles of eleven narrative and two documentary "independent" feature films and confirms a simple premise about the specialty film business: because no two films are alike, either as works of art or as commercial ventures, there is no "right way" to make or market one. This is not to say, however, that there aren't wrong ways. We hope that this book will help filmmakers and others interested in independent film to avoid the pitfalls that have plagued some of the projects described herein.

The term "specialty" refers to a set of characteristics shared by all the films analyzed here—and many others not included in this study. Specialty films—by definition feature-length, in that they are intended to have a life in theatrical exhibition—reflect the personal vision of the filmmakers, who retain complete control over their projects. Therefore, such films are usually produced and distributed outside the Hollywood studio system. However unique, specialty films share a common humanism and are neither racist, sexist, nor exploitative; this is a key difference between specialty films and independently produced, low-budget genre films. A relatively low production budget is also characteristic of specialty films. (The examples here range from $60,000 for *Return of the Secaucus Seven* to over $1 million for *The Ballad of Gregorio Cortez* and *Stand and Deliver*; but these films were all produced several years ago. Currently, the average "negative cost" of a studio film is $20 million, so any film under about $5 million is considered low-budget.)

The films profiled in this book were produced and theatrically released from the early to late 1980s, a unique moment in American film history. It was a period characterized by a wonderfully naïve, almost self-deceptive euphoria. While this historical context is analyzed more rigorously in the Conclusion, four factors contributed to the remarkable success of independent films during this period: (1) the greater demand for visual entertainment, driven by the increase in the number of movie-theater screens, the rapid adoption of homevideo and the expansion of cable television; (2) the increased availability of capital (from investors as well as consumers) derived from the "Reagan revolution" of debt-based affluence; (3) the maturation of the baby-boom generation, a group with more sophisticated filmgoing tastes as well as disposable time and income for movie attendance; and (4) the proliferation of numerous quasi-commercial filmmakers and independent distributors throughout the country to take advantage of this unique opportunity.

As the 1980s come to an end, the old order is regaining hegemony. The Hollywood studios, through integration with exhibition chains and ancillary distribution arms, are rationalizing production to meet more stabilized demand. In addition, further shifts in demographics and economic contraction (forcing a cutback in both consumer spending and leisure time) are contributing to a decline in movie attendance. Thus, the situation specialty filmmakers find themselves in today is far different from that experienced during the formative period chronicled in this book.

All thirteen films analyzed in this book were carefully chosen to reflect the vagaries, vicissitudes, and varieties of experience encountered within the specialty film marketplace. As all were commercially distributed, self-distributed films were thereby excluded. To ensure a representative sample we used the following criteria:

- That there be a mix of narrative and documentary films.
- That financing come from one or more of a variety of sources, including federal and public television grants, presales, limited partnerships, personal loans, and private investors.
- That films be included whose distribution was handled variously by studio classics divisions, major studios, and by both small and relatively large independent distributors.
- That different marketing and distribution strategies be reflected, as well as a range of results achieved, in terms of the level of both critical response and financial performance.

In addition, each film had to have completed its principal theatrical release and ancillary market distribution. Finally, and perhaps most critical, we chose films whose makers and distributors we could rely upon to cooperate actively in providing information. This book is intended to illustrate a variety of experiences in the specialty film business rather than serve as a comprehensive or objective analysis of the field. Many films significant to the evolution of the specialty market were excluded because the principals were either unavailable or unwilling to provide needed information.

The methodology consisted mainly of extensive interviews with the principals involved in each film. The interviews and resulting reports basically followed the film's life-history: development (including concept genesis, scripting, and financing), production, the distribution deal (the process of obtaining it and its terms), the marketing campaign (overall strategy, promotion and publicity, and the ad and trailer), the theatrical release (strategy, opening run, and national rollout), the film's performance in ancillary markets (i.e., homevideo, pay cable, nontheatrical, broadcast television, and foreign release). Further, we asked filmmakers and distributors to fill out a separate "performance report" detailing financing, revenues, campaign costs, release playdates, and ancillary sales figures. (Not all participants did this.) Finally, secondary sources such as reviews, feature articles, unpublished reports, and third-party experts were consulted.

After gathering preliminary information, a draft report on each film was prepared. It was circulated for comments to the principals as well as to an advisory group composed of representatives from the Sundance Institute, the Independent Feature Project (IFP), and outside independent filmmakers and distributors. We then revised and recirculated each report to the principals and review group for final corrections. Principals for each film did not involve themselves equally fully in the research process, nor was equally complete or comparable information always available on each film. While all the profiles share a high level of candor, they are—much like the films themselves—unique. As a serendipitous rather than intentional result, however, each profile has a distinct emphasis, addressing more completely some particular aspect of the production or marketing process. Each profile, incomplete in itself, is like one in a series of colored overlays that can be placed one atop the next so that a fuller picture emerges.

The book was originally published by the Sundance Institute and the IFP for the January 1987 U.S. Film Festival in Park City, Utah. Subsequently, Grove Press accepted the work for commercial release and the existing information was updated as much as possible. Original case studies for two additional films, *Hollywood Shuffle* and *Stand and Deliver*, were prepared exclusively for this publication.

I must say, as a final word, that at times the preparation of this book called to mind Akira Kurosawa's *Rashomon*. The most difficult task was not simply reconstructing the actual historical events, but rather reconciling conflicting views on the meaning of those events. Each of our sources had different perspectives on the process, some of whom spoke passionately but off-the-record about some touchy aspect of the story. In some cases we were able, on further inquiry, to arrive at a consensus of interpretation. In others, we made our own determinations from the testimony received. In still other instances, we decided to forgo the attempt at reconciliation and to present the differing opinions. Conflict may be a verity of the film business, and what is more important, the genuine sincerity of the conflicting views often merits appreciation. Such differences may in fact help to illuminate the process of making and marketing films like these.

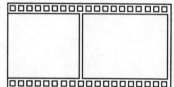

THE BALLAD OF GREGORIO CORTEZ

(August 1983)

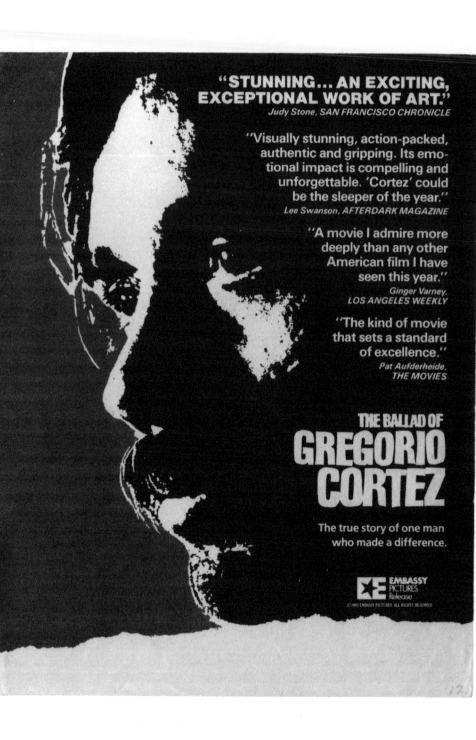

PRINCIPALS	*Director*	Robert M. Young
	Producers	Moctesuma Esparza and Michael Hausman
	Writers	Victor Villasenor, adapted by Robert Young
	Principal cast	Edward James Olmos, Tom Bower
	Producers' reps	Robert Hoffman, Edward James Olmos, and Tom Bower
DISTRIBUTORS	*Theatrical*	Embassy Pictures
		Gregorio Cortez Distribution
	Homevideo	Embassy Home Entertainment
	Pay cable	Embassy Home Entertainment
	Nontheatrical	Films Incorporated
	Broadcast	PBS/"American Playhouse"
	Foreign	Embassy Pictures
THEATRICAL	*Opening date*	August 1983
	Total playdates	600 (c)
	Box-office gross	$909,000*
	Gross film rental	429,000
	Total distributor costs	
	Guarantee	500,000
	Publicity	837,000
	Prints	84,000
ANCILLARY	*Homevideo*	$350,000
	Pay cable	55,000
	Nontheatrical	118,000
	Foreign	300,000
PARTICIPANTS CONTACTED		Robert Young
		Moctesuma Esparza
		Edward James Olmos
		Tom Bower
		Robert Hoffman
		Irwin Young
		Lindsay Law

*All figures combine Embassy and Gregorio Distribution releases.

c = Approximate.

Note: This report is indebted to Robert Hoffman's unpublished article "The Marketing of *The Ballad of Gregorio Cortez*: A Grassroots Approach."

FILM SYNOPSIS

Gregorio Cortez, a Mexican-American farmer in turn-of-the-century Texas, is visited by a sheriff who questions him in connection with a horse theft. A deputy translates (Cortez does not speak English), but doesn't understand the distinction made in Spanish between "horse" and "mare." The sheriff becomes convinced that Cortez is guilty, attempts to arrest Cortez, and pulls his six-gun whereupon Cortez's brother approaches him questioningly. After the sheriff wantonly shoots Cortez's brother, Cortez pulls his gun from behind his back and kills the sheriff.

Leaving a terrified wife and son behind, Cortez flees, becoming the object of the most massive manhunt in Texas history. Led by the Texas Rangers, the posse eventually swells to 600 men. Miraculously eluding capture for eleven days, Cortez leads them on a chase covering hundreds of miles. This saga of flight and pursuit was followed closely on the front pages of newspapers across the country (aided by the recent introduction of the telephone) and became the subject of a Chicano folk ballad that is still part of the border repertoire.

With racial tensions high in the border territory, vigilance on the part of the local authorities is required to protect Cortez from a huge lynch mob that tries to storm the jail. He is eventually brought to trial, where the tragic misunderstanding is ultimately revealed, and he is sentenced to fifty years for manslaughter.

DEVELOPMENT

Genesis · The Ballad of Gregorio Cortez was developed by producer Moctesuma Esparza under the aegis of the National Council of La Raza (NCLR), a public advocacy group, as part of a five-part film series based on the literature and history of Americans of Hispanic

4

ancestry. *Cortez*, the first in the series to be produced, is based on the historical study *With His Pistol in His Hand* by Dr. Americo Paredes. *The Milagro Beanfield War* is the second film of the series and was a joint venture of Moctesuma Esparza Productions and Wildwood Enterprises. It was directed by Robert Redford and released by Universal Pictures in 1988.

Esparza undertook what became a three-year development process because of the deep personal connection he felt with the film's subject matter and the political and social message it expressed. Like the wrongly accused hero of the film, Esparza had been wrongly indicted by a Los Angeles grand jury in connection with his political activities in the late 1960s. He believed in the potential impact of a narrative film that dealt with the racial and cultural issues underlying such incidents. Esparza was committed to making a film that could speak to a broad multiethnic, multilanguage audience about cultural misunderstanding, and also to making a film that was a project *of* the Chicano community, not *for* it.

The screenplay was developed and written by Victor Villasenor with the support of a National Endowment for the Humanities (NEH) grant. Working with the actors Edward James Olmos and Tom Bower to develop their own dialogue, director Robert M. Young wrote the shooting script. The film's unusual structure features flashbacks and multiple points of view, mirroring the story's theme of culturally based misunderstanding.

Financing · Of the $1,305,000 raised for the project, $1,174,000 went toward film production and the balance toward script development for the other films in the proposed series and overhead for NCLR. Funding sources were:

National Endowment for the Humanities:	
Outright grant	$450,000
Matching grant	150,000
Corporation for Public Broadcasting	540,000
"American Playhouse"	100,000
ZDF (German television)	65,000

The profit participants included La Raza, NEH, the Corporation for Public Broadcasting (CPB), Young, Villasenor, coproducer Michael

Hausman, Paredes, and Olmos. As Olmos has observed, "The major 'investment' in this film was the time and energy of those of us who believed in it—it was a labor of love, from start to finish."

Anticipating an audience · Esparza felt strongly that the film would have a broad appeal, that its compelling protagonist could permit cross-ethnic viewer identification. However, no market research was undertaken to ascertain the makeup of the film's potential audience. The public subsidy from NEH, CPB, and "American Playhouse" proved a cushion against marketplace exigencies, allowing the film to go forward based on its inherent dramatic and social merits and on the belief that it would find an audience.

PRODUCTION

The preproduction phase lasted from the receipt of funding in June 1981 to the commencement of principal photography and location work in October of that year. During this phase, three critical issues were addressed: (1) the selection of the principal cast and crew; (2) the decision to shoot so as to allow for 35mm blowup for theatrical release, as opposed to producing the film exclusively for a public television airing; and (3) the decision to use a dual-language approach without employing subtitles.

Esparza's decision to have Olmos play the role of Gregorio Cortez and Olmos's request to have Young direct the film both proved critical to producing the film as well as marketing it.

Esparza, who wanted to see *Cortez* as a theatrical release, was committed to getting the film made, even if only as a television production. Olmos, who subsequently had a lead role in the top-rated weekly NBC series "Miami Vice," had earlier starred in *Zoot Suit* and more recently in *Stand and Deliver* (see case study). He saw the project from the beginning as a theatrical piece. Young, whose films include *Nothing But a Man, Short Eyes, Alambrista!, One-Trick Pony, Extremities, Dominick and Eugene*, and *Triumph of the Spirit*, agreed with Olmos on this, and stipulated that the film be made for theatrical release before agreeing to direct it. Young recommended Michael Hausman as line producer and Esparza agreed. Hausman's background as a producer is extensive, ranging from *Heartland* (see case study) to *Amadeus*.

Although the existing funding contracts with NEH, CPB, and "American Playhouse" were based on the assumption that *Cortez* was to be a television film, Esparza enthusiastically agreed to Young's conditions, undertaking to deal with the budgetary increases and extensive renegotiations required by the decision to produce the film for theatrical release. One set of difficult and time-consuming negotiations involved going back to the Screen Actors Guild (SAG) and the craft unions to secure new agreements regarding compensation and royalty fees. This unique situation involved long negotiation, but the new contracts allowed *Cortez* to avoid the serious guild problems experienced by other independents like *Heartland*, *El Norte* (see case studies), and *Testament*, for which renegotiations were done after-the-fact.

Esparza's second renegotiation, with the Public Broadcasting System (PBS), was to secure a theatrical "window" following the broadcast. As Lindsay Law of "American Playhouse" pointed out, the question about *Cortez* arose at a time when PBS was deeply divided over the question of whether federally funded television projects should be allowed a commercial life. With the strong support of "American Playhouse," Esparza reached an agreement with PBS for an unprecedented two-year window—six months to secure a theatrical distributor and eighteen months for the release.

Dealing with the film's use of both English and Spanish dialogue was at once an artistic and a commercial concern. Because the historical story of Gregorio Cortez hinges on a tragedy arising from language and cultural barriers, the filmmakers decided that the film should not use subtitles. They felt that the audience's experience of what was said would parallel the experience of the characters. If this unusual technique worked as they hoped, strengthening the audience's appreciation of the tragic story, it would help sell the film. If, however, audiences were alienated or unable to follow the narrative easily, it would clearly damage the film's possible performance. Their decision was a major risk.

Production involved five weeks of principal photography, from October to November of 1981, and one week of second-unit shooting. The film was shot in super-16mm on location in three states, involving a cast that included 1,500 extras in full period costume—an extremely ambitious scale of production for a low-budget film.

To gain authenticity, the principal location was shifted in preproduction from New Mexico to the Texas area where Cortez had actually lived. Despite this and the higher guild scales, the film came in only 9 percent over its original budget. (Contractually, CPB would not allow for a contingency line.)

Editing took seven weeks and was completed early in June 1982. Processing was done at the DuArt Labs, as was the 35mm blowup. The costs of the blowup were deferred until the signing of a theatrical distribution deal.

DISTRIBUTION DEAL

·

Making the deal · On June 29, 1982, *The Ballad of Gregorio Cortez* was broadcast on the first season of "American Playhouse." This public-television exposure led to resistance from every theatrical distributor. *Cortez* had violated one of the cardinal conventions of the film business; it was no longer a "virgin property" for theatrical release.

But the filmmakers remained committed to a theatrical release. Olmos and fellow featured actor Tom Bower had attended the first Sundance Institute summer workshop in June 1981. There they met Jeff Dowd, who had worked with the Seattle-based exhibitor/distributor Randy Finley and had pioneered innovative and successful "grassroots" promotional outreach strategies patterned on 1960s political organizing techniques. Olmos was convinced that this approach could work effectively for *Cortez* in the context of a market-by-market national release.

A condition of the guild contracts required that the film open theatrically *prior* to its first television airing. So, three weeks before the "American Playhouse" broadcast, Olmos organized a theatrical premiere in San Antonio, Texas. NCLR committed $5,000 to cover the cost of "four-walling" one screen of a local Santico multiplex theater for a one-week run. Esparza Productions underwrote the travel costs for the principals to undertake the release.

NCLR supplied posters and the Santico chain provided promotional material. Olmos stood in front of the auditorium calling attention to himself and the film by handing out leaflets and talking to people headed for other screenings within the complex. (*Cortez* was up against *Conan*, *Superman II*, and a Disney rerelease!) Many recognized Olmos as "El Pachuco" from his earlier film, *Zoot Suit*. The night before the film was to open, DuArt's president, Irwin Young, arrived in San Antonio with the first untimed answer print. At the first screening on June 4, the audience consisted of only two paying customers. However, Olmos's efforts paid off: word-of-mouth spread, so that by week's end the film was drawing 250 people per screening, and NCLR recouped its investment.

Following the two national PBS airings (one of which earned PBS the second highest ratings of the year), Olmos moved to duplicate the San Antonio experience in Los Angeles. He knew that the only way to secure a distribution deal was to demonstrate that the film could generate positive press attention and draw an audience. Esparza paid the four-walling charges for a six-week Saturday morning run at the Los Feliz Theater, and Olmos underwrote a three-week run at the Beverly Hills Music Hall. During these nine consecutive Saturdays beginning in September 1982, *Cortez* caught the imagination of the Los Angeles film community. Building on two key *Los Angeles Times* pieces—an editorial praising Gregorio Cortez as a role model for Latino youth and a feature article by arts editor Charles Champlin— the film was playing to capacity audiences by the end of the run, amassing a total of about 5,000 viewers.

Champlin was especially important to the success of *Cortez*. He invited Olmos, Bower, and Young to screen the film for his USC Film School class. In attendance were *L.A. Weekly* reporter Ginger Varney, who subsequently wrote a very supportive piece, and Ross LaManna, who was then with Embassy Pictures. Through LaManna, the film-makers were able to make their way up the Embassy ladder. Directly after viewing *Cortez*, studio president Jerry Perenchio rose and stated emphatically, "I want that film!" Hearing of this unusual acquisition, studio chairman Norman Lear asked to see *Cortez*, and the filmmakers obliged with a private screening in his home.

Terms of the deal · The Embassy* executives were all extremely committed to *Cortez*. But based on the San Antonio and Los Angeles successes, the principals began to wonder whether it was best to continue to self-distribute the film or to accept a studio deal. In the end, Esparza convinced the group to go with Embassy.

Embassy first asked for a five-year window, but CPB would agree to only two years. After five months of negotiations, Esparza received an agreement for a three-and-a-half-year window, with the additional year and a half secured from CPB in exchange for two other films to substitute for the additional *Cortez* broadcasts on "American Playhouse" over the full period. With Young's help, and at a cost of $85,000 for the rights, Esparza provided PBS with Young's *Nothing But a Man* and Robert Duvall's *Tomorrow*. Esparza also had to buy back some foreign sales rights from Affinity Enterprises as Embassy insisted upon having nearly complete world-wide rights for all markets.

For *The Ballad of Gregorio Cortez*, Embassy offered the filmmakers a package consisting of a $500,000 guarantee and 50 percent of the net profits after deducting the film's purchase price, the costs of prints and ads, and an administrative fee of 30 percent of the gross film rental. At this writing, no profits have been reported.

Perhaps the most novel aspect of the deal was Embassy's willingness to hire Olmos and his team to continue grassroots promotional efforts to assist in marketing *Cortez*.

MARKETING CAMPAIGN

Strategy · "The *Cortez* group," which Embassy hired as a separate marketing unit, included Olmos, Bower, specialty film consultant Rob Hoffman, and four field representatives—Daniel Haro, a civil rights attorney; Rosemarie Morales, a political fundraiser; Kirk Whisler,

*Embassy was subsequently sold to Coca-Cola and is now part of Columbia Pictures Entertainment. Columbia, in turn, was acquired by the Sony Corporation.

publisher of *Caminos* magazine; and Kaija Olmos, special assistant during the entire project.

The *Cortez* group was in an awkward position. While they had a relatively free hand to develop their grassroots campaign, they were still responsible to the overall corporate structure at Embassy. All final decisions regarding the trailer and ad, opening, national release, and other issues ultimately rested in the hands of the marketing and distribution departments to whom the *Cortez* group reported.

The period in which the *Cortez* group functioned at Embassy, from March 1983 to February 1984, turned out to be a very volatile one. Embassy's marketing division had itself been restructured just two weeks prior to their arrival, due to the recent merger of Embassy and Avco Pictures. A series of additional corporate shakeups was to follow over the next few months. First, and most significant, Norman Lear left Embassy Pictures and returned to Embassy Television. Second, new heads of production and distribution were brought in. Third, about 150 employees were laid off and many pictures slated for release were shelved. Fourth, the Latino division that Lear had established was abolished. Lastly, the company adopted an approach characterized by greater cost consciousness and corporate accountability.

Even in this turbulent environment, the *Cortez* group, to its surprise, continued to receive generous support from David Weitzner, the senior marketing vice-president, and his staff. The group was initially given an eight-month contract and an overall fee of $85,000, which included salaries, travel, and other expenses. After the film opened, the contract was extended another three months and the financial package was increased to a total of $120,000.

The group's marketing goal was simple yet ambitious: to cultivate as many cities within the top forty markets as possible during the original eight-month contract period. Their strategy aimed at building a solid base of critical support through festivals, reviews, feature articles, and similar activities; and creating a grassroots following among the specialized audiences targeted as promising the strongest support for the film.

Ultimately, according to Bower and Hoffman, they felt they had succeeded in six markets, had "seeded" another fourteen, and had failed to reach another twenty-four because of a lack of time.

The Ballad of Gregorio Cortez was acclaimed at a number of important film festivals, including Telluride and Mill Valley in the U.S., as well as festivals in South Africa and the Soviet Union. The experience at Telluride illustrates how clever and aggressive the *Cortez* group could be in pushing for visibility. Due to the first PBS broadcast, Telluride director Bill Pence had great reservations about screening the film. However, Hoffman proposed that the festival sponsor a special tribute to Irwin Young, president of DuArt Labs. Pence incorporated the idea by dedicating the tenth annual festival to American independent films and to Irwin Young for his lifelong contribution to the field. (Four of the films shown at the festival were processed at DuArt.) This device enabled the *Cortez* group to secure a spot for their film. The fact that the film's director, Bob Young, is Irwin's brother strengthened its presence at the festival.

Cortez was extremely well received at Telluride, drawing the largest turnout in the festival's history up to that time. A similar tribute to Bob Young was organized at the Mill Valley Film Festival, along with a retrospective of his films.

To reach special audiences, Edward James Olmos began making personal appearances at screenings of the film, almost a year before the Embassy deal was signed, in conjunction with his nationwide civic work with community leaders and organizations. A product of the East Los Angeles barrio, Olmos had been helping the disadvantaged young to escape the drugs, violence, and crime that sent many of his childhood friends to early deaths or to prison. He showed the film at Hispanic community centers, schools, and juvenile detention centers, and discussed the importance of promoting cross-cultural understanding and providing both a positive image and a sense of cultural heritage for American Hispanics.

Once the *Cortez* group was formed, its members also contacted local and national organizations for which the film would have special meaning or appeal. For example, endorsements were secured from such organizations as the California Court Interpreters Association, whose members' profession involves ensuring due process for non-English-speaking defendants; the American Historical Association, which proclaimed the film to be one of the most, if not *the* most, accurate depictions of turn-of-the-century life; and the National Council of Teachers of English.

While these efforts were under way, Embassy unilaterally decided to test-market the film in two representative cities. They selected San Francisco to test the response of the "art" market, and El Paso to test the Spanish-speaking audience. These test markets, which served essentially as the film's opening engagements, will be discussed in the next section.

Promotion and publicity · Promotional activities grew out of the film's basic marketing campaign. The *Cortez* group organized extensive speaking engagements among community groups in the ten top markets in which Embassy initially planned to launch the film. They also identified key critics and tried to arouse their interest in the film. In some markets, like San Francisco and Seattle, they were able to gain valuable critical support; elsewhere, in Boston and New York for example, important critics were uninterested.

Throughout this period and even afterward, when they were self-distributing the film (see below), the *Cortez* group worked with Embassy's Century City staff and its branch representatives, which proved an invaluable resource, providing contacts with local exhibitors and the press and bringing the benefit of their experience to the promotional efforts. Michele Reese, head of field promotion, who believed in the efficacy of grassroots promotional techniques, was especially helpful.

Overall, Embassy's approach to advertising and promotion was very much the standard mass-marketing one, stressing high visibility through a big budget and rapid "rollout." The *Cortez* group realized that this standard Hollywood method prohibited tailoring the marketing efforts to the regional particularities of the audiences.

Embassy's reported advertising and promotional budget for *The Ballad of Gregorio Cortez*, totaling $828,000, breaks down as follows:

Creative	$112,000
Publicity	210,000
Promotion	106,000
Screenings	70,000
Co-op ads	330,000

Trailer and ad · Embassy subcontracted the trailer and ad to independent production companies. The trailer was cut by the Los

Angeles production house Kaleidoscope. The filmmakers feel that the Kaleidoscope producers and editors not only accepted their input, but believed in the film enough to make an exceptionally well-crafted trailer.

Some criticized the image used for the ad. Esparza feels it suggested a tone that was too somber. Others within the *Cortez* group feel that by depicting only Gregorio Cortez, it suggested a typically hero-oriented Western, rather than emphasizing the universality of the story.

Embassy did not have the graphic image of the ad ready until one week before the opening, and it wasn't until three weeks after the opening that Embassy had the "slick" available. The makeshift image used for both the "one-sheet" and the slick was essentially a blowup of a poster La Raza had supplied for the earlier San Antonio four-wall opening.

Finally, difficulties were encountered with another element of the ad campaign—the film's title. When originally conceived, the project was titled *The True Story of Gregorio Cortez*. Director Young found this title problematic in that the film doesn't show the "true" story of Cortez, but the way in which cultural barriers created conflicting versions of the events, precluding a single objective viewpoint. Producer Esparza had reservations about the final title, fearing that it was inaccessible to the average viewer and would reinforce the audience's stereotypes and prejudices in identifying the film as a Chicano Western. Olmos felt, however, that the title wasn't of key importance since what would sell the film in any event was word-of-mouth.

THEATRICAL RELEASE

Strategy · Two competing release plans were developed simultaneously, reflecting the inherent conflict between Embassy's traditional studio launch strategy and that of the *Cortez* group. The studio's original distribution plan called for New York City and Los Angeles openings in late September 1983, followed by a staggered rollout over the next four weeks to ten major markets until a total of fifty prints were in circulation. Opposing this plan, the *Cortez* group sought a slower, more focused, region-by-region release. Further consideration of this matter was put to rest when Embassy moved unilaterally on its plan, beginning with test-marketing in San Francisco and El Paso in August.

Opening run · After indirectly learning of Embassy's decision to test-market the film, the *Cortez* group launched an intensive promotional campaign for the San Francisco run. Working closely with Embassy's local branch office and field representative Sharon Lydic of Jack Wodell and Associates, they targeted Bay Area independent filmmakers and Hispanic community groups for special outreach. Tom Bower, who apart from his role in *Cortez* had starred in John Hanson's *Wildrose*, then being edited in Berkeley, helped draw local filmmakers to "opinion-maker" prescreenings. Screenings were also organized for local Chicano groups and the press. The Bob Young tribute and retrospective at the Mill Valley Film Festival, which occurred at this time, also helped greatly in generating word-of-mouth for the San Francisco run of *Cortez*.

One of many innovative schemes remembered fondly by the *Cortez* group involved a stunt they pulled at one of the final Embassy-sponsored preview screenings at the Four Star Theater. Without telling anyone at Embassy, the group printed and distributed 3,000 tickets for the 300-seat theater. Embassy management was, in Hoffman's words, "freaked out" by the gimmick and the street happening that ensued. Those who couldn't get in were entertained by mariachis, street jugglers, fire eaters, and local activists, after having been calmed by the charismatic Olmos's consummate crowd-handling skills. It was a promotional coup that created tremendous word-of-mouth for the film.

Cortez's San Francisco run lasted four months. The first- and second-week grosses were $22,000 and $21,500, spectacular for a small theater. The success in San Francisco led Embassy to move the film to Berkeley and then into a nineteen-city regional "breakout" over a single weekend. This scale of exposure was too much for the *Cortez* group to handle, and subsequent box-office performance was inconsistent.

In Santa Cruz it was booked into a local UA theater instead of the local art house. Those most likely to support the film didn't go, thinking *Cortez* was just another Western. In San Jose, the local theater was in the midst of a labor strike and even though the town's mayor had issued a proclamation supporting the film, the filmmakers wouldn't cross the picket line to make promotional appearances. In all, *Gregorio Cortez* grossed $500,000 in the Bay Area.

The El Paso opening occurred one week after San Francisco's and was Embassy's opportunity to test a Spanish-language print campaign among Hispanic audiences. But the opening split the efforts of the *Cortez* group. While the others stayed in the Bay Area, Olmos and Danny Haro, a well-known Southwest civil rights attorney and the group's field representative, coordinated community outreach. Despite the fact that El Paso was in the grip of a major recession with a 40 percent unemployment rate, the film did excellent business, outperforming Chevy Chase's *Vacation*.

National playoff · Embassy proceeded with its wide release plan despite the objections of the *Cortez* group. With the support of Embassy's marketing staff, the group argued for a gradual, market-by-market release, which would allow them to undertake the intensive kinds of promotional techniques that had proven so successful in San Francisco. Embassy's new distribution head, while not disputing the group's arguments about the effectiveness of their approach for *Cortez*, preferred to go with a rapid rollout, even though it might hurt the film's potential. Embassy was losing interest in being in the business of specialized film distribution.

Olmos vividly recalls this critical juncture:

> We felt trapped. This had been my original fear about signing with a major studio. They were willing to sabotage the film, despite their investment in it, in favor of business as usual. We should have done it our own way without their money.

To no one's surprise, *Cortez* did poorly in most major markets, leading Embassy to cut its losses by pulling the film from circulation.

The New York booking illustrates the problems that rushed timing and inadequate grassroots promotion can cause for specialty films. Embassy was anxious to roll the film out rapidly, yet during the busy autumn release period, theater availability was tight. Ralph Donnelly, the head of Cinema Five Theaters, offered to take *Cortez* at his Cinema I theater, a prestigious East Side art house, if it would open in six days' time. Embassy agreed, even though it gave them—and the *Cortez* group—very little time to undertake the advance work necessary for an effective opening.

In anticipation of the opening, the *Cortez* group had visited New York in April 1983 and again in August for some preliminary seed work. Lillian Jimenez, then of the Film Fund, assisted by having *Cortez* featured at the Latino Film and Video Festival. The group also held a well-attended and enthusiastic screening for opinion-makers at the Sutton Theater. However, even with this valuable groundwork, the time constraints imposed by Embassy's surprise announcement of a mid-October opening severely limited the group's ability to promote the New York run. These dates also coincided with the New York Film Festival, which undercut both audience attendance and press coverage.

As it was, the press attention *Cortez* did receive in New York was mixed. Pablo Guzman of the *Village Voice* strongly supported the film, while Janet Maslin of the *New York Times* panned it. The filmmakers feel that the earlier television broadcast negatively affected the seriousness with which Maslin approached *Cortez*, and that her arriving ten minutes late to the press screening, thus missing the scene at the core of the story, had an unfortunate impact on her judgment. Donnelly, among others, complained about this in a letter to the *Times*.

Box-office grosses at the Cinema I during the film's first four weeks were $11,102; $8,630; $7,260; and $5,477.

The Los Angeles run was also disappointing, producing only $250,000 in box-office receipts. According to the *Cortez* group, this was the first instance of a film performing better in San Francisco than in Los Angeles. The film opened at Mann's Fine Arts Theatre, which negotiated a four-week exclusive run from Embassy, thus preventing the desired simultaneous opening in a Chicano theater in East Los Angeles. A run in the barrios was ultimately precluded when the Pacific and Metropolitan theater chains, reputed to exert near-monopoly control of the Spanish-language movie houses in East Los Angeles, demanded a $20,000 guarantee plus the cost of advertising for a two-week engagement. The *Los Angeles Times*, because of Champlin's extensive earlier coverage, chose to bury its positive review on a back page.

Both exhibitor and critical interest in Boston were low after the so-so run in New York. In Texas, *Cortez* was placed in the wrong theater and without the proper promotional support. One of the more surprising aspects of the national release was that, except for San Diego, the closer the film was exhibited to the U.S.-Mexican border, the smaller the audience was; response was generally stronger the farther north it played.

While in distribution at Embassy Pictures, the box-office gross was $805,000; gross film rental was $400,000. These revenues were offset by total advertising and publicity expenses of $828,000 and print costs of an additional $84,000 for the forty-one prints in circulation. Having invested a total of $1.5 million in the film (including the advance), Embassy withdrew it from active theatrical distribution after three months in national release.

Following this move by Embassy, the *Cortez* group decided to option a subdistribution deal. As the group had put so much time into the distribution process and developed important contacts in cities throughout the country, they felt they could successfully market the film on their own.

A subdistribution company, Gregorio Cortez Distribution (GCD), independent of both Embassy Pictures and Moctesuma Esparza Productions, was set up at Lion's Gate Studios in Los Angeles under the patronage of Robert Chester and Hal Harrison. The company was made up of Olmos, Bower, Hoffman, Haro, and Greg Friedkin.

Continued theatrical distribution by GCD was concurrent with the film's release in ancillary markets—pay-cable sales, homevideo release through Embassy Home Entertainment, and Films Incorporated's pursuit of the nontheatrical market. GCD's deal with Embassy called for a licensing fee of 25 percent of the net film rental, after deducting all direct and co-op advertising costs off the top.

Subdistribution, as opposed to self-distribution, offered the *Cortez* group important advantages. Foremost, it provided the invaluable leverage of Embassy branch offices in securing better bookings and, what was more important, in collecting film rentals from local exhibitors. Embassy also offered easy means to acquire trailers, prints, and ad materials. However, as might be expected, most exhibitors offered GCD rental deals at much lower percentages of the gross than Embassy generally got for its mainstream product.

One of GCD's most successful subdistribution efforts occurred in Denver. Having visited the city during the course of the previous year, and building upon screenings at the Telluride and Denver film festivals, the group found strong local support for the film. Tom Bower was from the Denver area, and his numerous personal contacts were an asset for the three-week grassroots organizing campaign that GCD conducted. They were even presented with a proclamation from Mayor Federico Peña making August 31, 1983, *"The Ballad of Gregorio Cortez* Day." Mayor Peña joined Olmos and Young at the opening night ceremonies at the Vogue Theatre, where the film ran for six weeks and went on to gross $32,118. The exhibitor was paid on a sliding scale of between 60 and 70 percent.

As of December 1984, Gregorio Cortez Distribution had generated over $100,000 in box-office grosses, which translated to a gross film rental of $29,000 and net film rental of $19,500.

OTHER MARKETS

Homevideo · The homevideo rights were acquired as part of the original Embassy acquisition and were handled by its Home Entertainment division. It is reported that $350,000 has been grossed in cassette sales, with about $70,000 having been returned to Embassy.

Pay cable · To date, *Cortez* has been sold to HBO and Showtime, among other cable services. It is reported that the HBO deal was for between $50,000 and $60,000.

Nontheatrical · Embassy sold 16mm nontheatrical distribution rights to Films Incorporated, which reports that the film is performing very well in that market. Embassy underwrote the production of an accompanying study guide that was prepared by the Mazur Corporation. The film has been rented extensively for use in Hispanic Studies programs in high schools and colleges and by Hispanic community groups. Nontheatrical rentals are reported to be at $118,000, with costs for nontheatrical prints at $23,000.

Broadcast · The film was broadcast over PBS in June 1982 (prior to its theatrical release) as part of "American Playhouse." In April 1986, Olmos arranged an unprecedented offer from NBC for

$300,000 for a single primetime showing (no film has been purchased by a network following release in cable and homevideo markets). Olmos reports that the deal was declined by PBS, the broadcast rights holder, because of its plan for an encore airing of *Cortez* that summer.

Foreign · The film has been released in about twenty-five countries and has grossed about $300,000 from all markets. The film has performed well in Canada, Italy, and Germany. However, the *Cortez* group feels that its performance in foreign territories would have been strengthened had Embassy's overseas distributors utilized Olmos in personal appearance tours.

REVIEW

The Ballad of Gregorio Cortez was produced in 1981 by Moctesuma Esparza Productions and the National Council of La Raza. With principal funding from the NEH and CPB, this $1.3 million film was originally conceived as a television production. It was broadcast over PBS's "American Playhouse" in June 1982 and subsequently went into theatrical release, an unprecedented reversal of the distribution sequence.

Just prior to and following the PBS broadcast, the filmmakers, under the leadership of the lead actor, Edward James Olmos, launched a limited promotional release in San Antonio and Los Angeles. As a result of the Los Angeles run, the filmmakers were able to secure a theatrical distribution deal with Embassy Pictures. In addition to a sizeable advance ($500,000) and a commitment to market the film with specialized grassroots techniques, Embassy further agreed to hire Olmos and a group he put together as a subordinate marketing unit.

Following a successful opening run in San Francisco in the late summer of 1983, *Cortez* was rushed into release in major markets throughout the country. Whereas the run in San Francisco was accompanied by an ambitious campaign to build word-of-mouth, other markets did not have the same attention and consequent success. This led Embassy to withdraw the film from distribution; the special *Cortez* marketing group secured an independent subdistribution deal to continue to pursue theatrical release.

Robert Hoffman sums up his experience with the distribution of *Cortez* as follows:

The real investment [in the film], financial and otherwise, cannot be measured in dollars, nor justified by common sense in terms of the conventions of commercial film marketing. It resides in the realm of artistic commitment, passion, zeal, and near fanaticism. A passionate concern for the film's subject matter was the chemistry binding the *Cortez* group together. Our experience does not provide a very useful model for others, for it is rare that the necessary elements would occur: a gripping and important story, masterfully filmed, combined with the willingness of the actors and director to make great personal sacrifices of time, energy, and money in order to see that the film gets its best shot at distribution.

The *Cortez* story does, however, reveal what can be accomplished through dedication and perseverance. These qualities, which consistently informed our work on the marketing of the film, were inspired in the rest of us by the example of Edward Olmos. Without Edward's unflagging commitment, the film would never have received the attention it has garnered.

Olmos says of his experience:

If I got to do one more film like this in my lifetime, I would consider myself very lucky. Very seldom do you get this kind of feeling in a motion picture—Bob Young did a brilliant job. And not only am I proud of the product, but the process was one of the finest learning experiences of my life. I take my hat off to Esparza, Young, and Hausman for being secure enough to allow me to participate so fully in so many aspects. Finally, I believe strongly in the importance of the *Cortez* story. I know that this film's life is not over, that in fact more people will see this film in 2050 than will see *Star Wars*, because it is such an important story in American history.

COLD FEET

(June 1984)

Abstinence makes the heart grow fonder.

COLD FEET
A Reluctant Romance

vanDUSEN Films presents "COLD FEET" Starring GRIFFIN DUNNE · MARISSA CHIBAS and BLANCHE BAKER as Leslie
Music by TODD RUNDGREN   Executive Producer THERON M. vanDUSEN   Written and Directed by BRUCE vanDUSEN

PRINCIPALS	*Writer/Director*	Bruce vanDusen
	Executive Producer	Theron M. vanDusen
	Producer	Charles Wessler
	Associate Producer	Leslie Larson
	Principal cast	Griffin Dunne, Marissa Chibas, and Blanche Baker
DISTRIBUTORS	*Theatrical*	Cinecom International Films
	Homevideo	CBS/FOX, via Cinecom
	Pay cable/other	Cinecom International Films
	Foreign	Interama
THEATRICAL	*Opening date*	June 1984
	Total playdates	50
	Box-office gross	$100,000
	Gross film rental	not available
	Total distributor costs	125,000
	Advance	Minimal
	Publicity	10,000
	Prints	20,000 (10 prints)
ANCILLARY	*Homevideo*	$25,000–30,000
	Nontheatrical	5,000
	Foreign	75,000
PARTICIPANTS CONTACTED		Bruce vanDusen
		Ira Deutchman
		Sara Risher
		Charles Wessler
		Steve Seifert

FILM SYNOPSIS

Cold Feet is a romantic comedy about Tom and Marty, two successful professionals in their early thirties. Fresh from breakups with longterm partners, they meet and, cautiously, begin to date, carefully balancing their fears of being rejected with their fears of being trapped. The story centers on their courtship. Each date leads ever so much closer to the point where they can no longer remain "just friends."

DEVELOPMENT

Bruce vanDusen was, at the age of twenty-nine, a successful businessman. His television advertising production company had made over 1,000 commercials. His clients included Anheuser-Busch, Procter & Gamble, and Lever Brothers.

In 1982 he conceived and wrote the screenplay of *Cold Feet*, his first feature film. "It is," in his words, "a romantic comedy in which two people come off separate, terrible relationships; they slowly date, recoil, and find each other. It is about the shy little dance that precedes the beginning of a relationship."

As a businessman, vanDusen felt that this was the most intelligent type of film he could develop. "I wasn't interested in a *Porky's* or a horror film, so a romance was the most accessible type of movie I could make—accessible for audiences in general, and particularly for the twenty-five-to-forty age group I was targeting." In addition, it was a story he could realize within his proposed budget of $250,000. The production was self-financed, and every dollar came from vanDusen's business.

The cast featured Griffin Dunne (whose next film was to be Martin Scorsese's *After Hours*), Marissa Chibas, and Blanche Baker.

VanDusen expected a solid payoff from the application of his film-making talents to this concept. He explains:

> I made a film intended for the widest audience in order to give me the greatest range of distributors to choose from, including the studios. I didn't want a film that would lie in my basement. I expected it to be a hit on the order of *Annie Hall* or *A Man and a Woman*, and I expected to make millions.

PRODUCTION

The $250,000 budget for *Cold Feet* was split evenly between production and editing. The talent was paid at SAG rates; the technicians were paid under the National Association of Broadcast Employees and Technicians (NABET) contract.

"Everyone told me that it was impossible to create a film with high production values on my budget," says vanDusen. "I know every trick in the book from my work in commercials, and the best shortcut of all is to work with professionals."

Charles Wessler, a friend of Dunne, approached vanDusen to offer his services as associate director, a position he had filled on such films as George Lucas's *Return of the Jedi* and Wim Wenders's *Hammett*. Wessler remembers meeting vanDusen and "a wonderful group of kids who made up an efficient staff on the production of commercials, but who knew little of the specifics of putting together anything longer than sixty seconds."

Wessler quickly convinced vanDusen that he should be appointed producer. Wessler remembers vanDusen as a remarkably competent first-time director:

> Bruce has several qualities that allowed him to bring in his film on time and under budget. First, he's a trusting manager of people, which in turn inspires loyalty. Second, he was not overambitious. He quickly sensed when the script called for something that was too big to handle on his budget, and he'd change it. And third, he understood costs. He was always on the lookout for a way of getting what he wanted for less.

VanDusen shot *Cold Feet* in fifteen eight-hour days, two days short of the planned seventeen-day schedule. The director recalls:

> We knew none of the rules of feature filmmaking—how many pages you were expected to shoot in a day, for example. We averaged six-and-a-half pages each day. After filming was completed, we found out that the industry average was two pages.

By May 1983, the film was shown in roughcut to approximately thirty distribution companies, six of whom asked for a followup screening of the finished film.

DISTRIBUTION DEAL

Making the deal · VanDusen had targeted Cinecom International Films as his first-choice distributor from the beginning. "They were young, committed to American independent filmmaking, and they seemed to know how to customize a release." He had observed how Cinecom entered into a "distribution partnership" with its filmmakers, and had stuck with films like *Come Back to the Five and Dime, Jimmy Dean, Jimmy Dean*; *Starstruck*; and *Angelo, My Love*—all "very difficult movies with troubled release patterns."

Cinecom was established in August 1982 to compete with the classics divisions of the Hollywood film studios. Its principal competitors at that time were United Artists Classics, Fox Classics, Universal Classics, and Orion Classics, as well as the Samuel Goldwyn Company and Triumph Pictures. However, a bidding war for the works of established foreign directors, like François Truffaut and Eric Rohmer, forced the new distributor to look for alternative sources of product.

Robert Altman was at that time completing *Jimmy Dean*, and Cinecom saw it as an English-language work by a director as acclaimed as Truffaut, and for a similar audience. *Jimmy Dean* was released in New York in October 1982, where it was mauled by the critics. Ira Deutchman, then Cinecom's executive vice-president of marketing and distribution, recalls that "the audience in New York was far greater than we expected, given the reviews, mainly due to the attraction of its stars—Cher, Karen Black, and Sandy Dennis—and to the stature of Altman himself." In Los Angeles, rave reviews helped generate house records at the Cineplex Theater, and a run of over six months followed. *Jimmy Dean* racked up over 400 dates nationally with rentals of over $1,500,000.

Cinecom drew the following lessons from this experience:

· There was a market for American independent films.
· It was even bigger than the audience for foreign-language films.
· The marketing principles underlying American independent and foreign films were essentially compatible.
· There was less competition among distributors for these films, since the bidding war had not yet extended to American independents.

Finally, the distributor saw that it had smashed the conventional wisdom that "without New York, you've had it!" Cinecom was ready to challenge more of the so-called rules of the game.

The Cinecom releases that followed *Jimmy Dean* were *Starstruck* (October 1982), by Australian director Gillian Armstrong; *Angelo, My Love* (February 1983), directed by Robert Duvall; and *El Norte* (December 1983), directed by Greg Nava (see case study).

Angelo, My Love also demonstrated an unusual release pattern. Robert Duvall was a powerful drawing card for the press, and positive reviews set up strong expectations. The film did not live up to the expectations of its initial audiences, however, and poor word-of-mouth led to quickly waning box-office response. Cinecom responded by planning for one good week at each playdate of its national release. Rentals of $1,500,000 followed from 400 playdates.

It was in the context of these experiences that Deutchman previewed *Cold Feet* as a roughcut with a temporary soundtrack. "I enjoyed it . . . it showed positive production values . . . and was entertaining. But we couldn't commit to it. We were very concerned about how it would fare in the marketplace."

Deutchman explains his cautious assessment of *Cold Feet* in terms of the structure of today's movie audience. He distinguishes between two types of moviegoers: teens, the frequent attendees who are pursued by the studios; and adults, who don't go to movies very often, with the crucial exception of the art filmgoer. He explains:

Before Cinecom makes an acquisition, we must be satisfied that it will reach our primary audience—the art filmgoer. And we must be able to identify a secondary audience, which differs from film to film.

We had doubts about the appeal of *Cold Feet* to our primary audience. Art filmgoers expect a rough and quirky product, particularly from first-time directors. Along with the critics, they tend to give these movies the benefit of the technical doubt. However, *Cold Feet* was a low-budget movie that was shot as beautifully as a big-budget studio production. It inadvertently gave the wrong impression to the very audience that needed to support it.

Deutchman also felt that the romantic subject matter of *Cold Feet* "dealt with the concerns of the general adult audience." This factor encouraged Cinecom to think that a secondary audience might be found in the broad mass of adult TV watchers, but Deutchman was initially unsure of how to devise a campaign to reach them. Deutchman summarizes his initial assessment of *Cold Feet*: "The problems of marketing this film were easy to identify but, at that stage, we had no solutions."

By contrast, Sara Risher, head of acquisitions at New Line Cinema, pursued *Cold Feet* from the first preview. "It seemed a perfect followup to *Smithereens*, for which we promoted Susan Seidelman as a young, independent director. I planned to play up *Cold Feet* as a first director's film, made for little money, and showing lots of talent."

New Line made an offer that included an advance, with revenues split 50/50 after costs. But vanDusen felt that New Line lacked experience with this kind of movie. "The dilemma posed by New Line was that they had made their reputation on exploitation films," says vanDusen. "And after discussing their strengths and weaknesses with filmmakers who had experience with them, I felt that they would do well in New York, but lacked clout in other markets."

Terms of the deal · In a matter of weeks, a deal was struck with Cinecom. It was the then-standard Cinecom arrangement, a 50/50 percent split of net revenues for all of the U.S. and Canada, after deduction of distribution costs. There was no advance. Cinecom was the distributor for broadcast TV, pay cable, and homevideo, and these rights were "cross-collateralized." Thus, Cinecom's risk was minimized by its ability to offset advances for ancillary rights against any theatrical losses.

Deutchman explains his position on cross-collateralization:

> We weren't exactly waiting in line for this film: we were in a strong bargaining position. And we felt that in order to really get behind a movie, we had to have backside protection. This is true of the great majority of our deals, and only when we are completely sure of its success will we agree to a theatrical-rights-only deal.

All foreign market rights were retained by vanDusen. Cinecom's growing confidence in *Cold Feet* was based on several factors. First, the distributor was buoyed by the successes of *Come Back to the Five and Dime, Jimmy Dean, Jimmy Dean* and *Angelo, My Love*. After exhaustive discussions with vanDusen, Deutchman felt that he had developed a marketing strategy for *Cold Feet*. They agreed to position the film to the "yuppie" singles audience, who could be persuaded to see it by imaginative advertising, even if the reviews were poor. Second, Deutchman felt that the "slickness" issue could be minimized and, finally, he had become more confident of Cinecom's ability to reach the proposed secondary market—the general adult audience that might be attracted to the film as a romance.

Thus, Cinecom's change of heart was motivated partly by the perception that *Cold Feet* offered an opportunity for "a challenging experiment." As Deutchman says: "We think of ourselves as experimenters, as distributors who challenge the old formula of what works and what doesn't. There was little downside risk, so we took the challenge."

New Line's Risher was "crushed, even outraged" to learn that vanDusen had closed a deal with Cinecom. Says vanDusen, "In hindsight, I would have done better to take their upfront offer."

MARKETING CAMPAIGN

Strategy · The final version of *Cold Feet* was a "major disappointment" to Cinecom. The soundtrack of the roughcut had sparkled with popular music, including songs by the Beatles. However, vanDusen was unable to afford rights to some of this music. He invited Cinecom to share in the purchase of the rights, but the distributor declined for the same reason that it declined to make an advance: the film was considered too risky. Deutchman recalls a figure of "over $100,000" for purchase of the rights to the original soundtrack. The decision on the selection of substitute music was left to vanDusen. Deutchman says:

> The substitute soundtrack weakened the film considerably. The original soundtrack offered an ironical counterpoint to the romance. It took the edge off the sweetness of the movie. The substitute underlined the romance, lessening its sophistication. It played totally differently to us.

Nevertheless, Cinecom agreed to go ahead with the film as Bruce vanDusen presented it, using the marketing strategy they had developed together. The challenge or experiment involved creating an entirely new channel of distribution for *Cold Feet*. Deutchman explains:

> Our primary market remained the art-film audience, though we were losing faith in the positive critical response to the film. Therefore, our secondary market segment loomed larger in our planning. This was defined as the nonmoviegoing audience of singles, particularly women. We wanted to reach them with an unusual "commercial" movie on the theme of falling in love. We planned an ad and publicity campaign that was skewed to radio, because these people listen to radio more than they read the film reviews in the *New York Times*. And we planned to open in more than one venue, in the neighborhoods where this audience lives, rather than in an art-house cinema in midtown Manhattan.

Promotion and publicity · Cinecom attempted to negotiate a promotional ticket giveaway with two leading New York radio stations. The distributor pitched the love story of *Cold Feet* to WPIX, which then had an "all lovesongs" format, and WYNY, which aired a soft-rock format. The stations previewed the film and passed on Cinecom's promotional concept, citing the absence of a big-name star or director. Nevertheless, Cinecom prepared its radio spots with these two stations in mind.

Cinecom committed to an ambitious campaign. It budgeted $35,000 for advertising alone for the preopening period and the first week.

Publicist Steve Seifert pitched *Cold Feet* to Janet Maslin, the *New York Times* film critic and columnist. She obliged with a preopening column that explored the theme of Cinecom's targeting the film at the "gap in the middle" between the ready-made audience for art films and teenage movies. Blanche Baker was available for publicity, and several reporters took up the angle that she was the daughter of Carol Baker. According to Ira Deutchman, Griffin Dunne was not happy with *Cold Feet*, and declined to make himself available for publicity.

The extensive use of advertisements in the "personal" columns of the *Village Voice* and *New York* magazine also aroused interest in the release. Preview screenings were well attended.

Trailer and ad · A trailer was cut by a freelance editor at a cost of $5,000. With planned simultaneous openings in cinemas owned by the Cinema Five, Guild, and RKO chains, Cinecom knew that the trailer would be cross-plugged throughout the New York area. Radio advertisements were edited at the same time as the trailers.

THEATRICAL RELEASE

Strategy · Cinecom planned to release *Cold Feet* simultaneously in five metropolitan New York theaters. Deutchman intended to schedule the film's national rollout based on its performance in New York. However, even if *Cold Feet* received poor reviews in New York, Cinecom intended to proceed in other major markets, believing that New York was not the nation.

Opening run · *Cold Feet* opened simultaneously in five New York–area cinemas on Memorial Day weekend 1984. The two Manhattan locations were the 72nd Street Cinema, in the heart of the Upper East Side singles area, and the Embassy on Broadway at West 72nd Street. These were not traditional first-run cinemas, although *Das Boot* and John Sayles's *Lianna* had opened successfully at the Embassy. The other locations were the Manhasset Triplex in Long Island, the Bellevue in Upper Montclair, New Jersey, and the UA Bronxville in Westchester.

The only other film opening that weekend was Steven Spielberg's blockbuster *Indiana Jones and the Temple of Doom*, a "plus" says Deutchman, "since it should have been easier to position *Cold Feet* as an alternate to the teenage drama."

The opening reviews were poor. Vincent Canby slammed *Cold Feet* in the *New York Times*:

> The filmmaker refused to recognize the humor of the cant Tom and Marty talk, and since there's not a truly satiric moment in the film, *Cold Feet* appears to be as numbingly self-absorbed as they are. Because the film doesn't place them in any kind of larger context, one gets the impression that they are the entire world, which makes *Cold Feet* more truly depressing than any comedy can be and survive.

On vanDusen's background in television commercials, Canby adds:

> This background is all too apparent in the film's slick style, including overlapping dialogue so insistent that at times you think the soundtrack is out of sync.

Daily News critic Harry Haum gave it two stars, concluding that "the film is a bit too thoughtful, cautious, and distant for its own good—like its characters." Gannett critic William Wolf, summing up the prevailing response, gives vanDusen

> credit for the technical achievement of putting together a decent-looking movie with competent characters. But his characters are bland and their sparring so trivial that one may not care much what happens to them.

The *Village Voice*'s David Edelstein was the most complimentary, describing the film as

> an appealing fantasy which zeroes in on the giddy period between first kiss and lovemaking, and the longer they take to consummate their relationship—the more "shy" and "proper" the lovers are—the giddier and happier the audience feels.

Commenting on the reviews, Ira Deutchman admits that opening wider than usual for an art film might have been a miscalculation: "The heavy advertising campaign and simultaneous openings built up a very large expectation in the press and among moviegoers. We promised too much." He particularly points to the *New York Times* review:

Canby treated this movie as if it were a big-budget release. He went after it. Usually a director's first film is given a briefer review. I can only guess that the Janet Maslin preopening piece and publicity motivated Canby to treat this as a major offering.

Cinecom responded by adjusting its newspaper advertisements to feature quotes from Judith Crist, *Newsday*, and the *Daily News*. In the second week, the *Village Voice* quotes headed the advertisement. However, Deutchman felt that the "overwhelmingly" negative reviews were killing *Cold Feet*. Grosses in the five New York–area theaters in the first week were $25,534; in the second week they slipped to $18,887. At the Embassy, first-week grosses were $6,989, and $4,844 in the second week. *Cold Feet* was then withdrawn from all five theaters.

Deutchman feels that these grosses, disheartening as they were, reflect a partial success for the breakout strategy: "They were a great deal higher than you would expect from a specialty film receiving reviews like these."

Advertising costs were $38,443 in the first week; $25,000 was spent on print and the balance on radio. In the second week $4,896 was spent, all on print ads.

VanDusen was involved throughout in the planning of the release strategy. He remembers taking issue with his partners on several points. First, he strongly advocated a winter opening, arguing that since the story was set in winter, audiences were most likely to identify with it during the colder months. He favored the last three weeks of March, a very quiet period for new releases, which would have given *Cold Feet* more time to find its audience. VanDusen argues that he might have been vindicated the following January when his film opened in Toronto to rave reviews. (Cinecom hoped that these reviews would generate favorable box-office response, but, according to Deutchman, "business in Toronto was still poor.")

Second, vanDusen felt that the impact of the poor reviews could have been minimized if Cinecom had featured quotes from *Box Office*, which called the film "the sleeper of the year" and "the *Annie Hall* of 1985." Deutchman counters that audiences don't read trade papers like *Box Office*, and emphasizes that the thumbs-down from the *New York Times* and the *Daily News* were insurmountable obstacles to the development of strong word-of-mouth.

National playoff · Cinecom was not devastated by the New York opening; after all, *Jimmy Dean* proved that failure in New York was not the end of the story. The distributor prepared for San Francisco, where *Cold Feet* was to open in a single cinema. All mention of vanDusen's profession as a producer/director of commercials was stricken from the publicity, and preopening feature articles were not pursued in order to avoid setting up false expectations.

The response by audiences at preview screenings at the Ghirardelli Cinema (held before the New York opening) had been excellent; in fact, it was so good that the exhibitor had offered a guarantee in order to secure the film. But when the movie opened, a *San Francisco Chronicle* second-string critic, Gerald Nachman, went for the jugular, calling the film "mushy" and "cute," with a "bleating" soundtrack: "[*Cold Feet*] takes all the clichés and tries to rearrange them into something new . . . it's not a bad movie, just one that's been made 500 times." The film lasted one week at the Ghirardelli, grossing only $2,466. Advertising costs were $9,552.

Portland was next. A new print-only campaign was developed at the suggestion of Roger Paulsen, a local exhibitor. It used the theme: "Finally! A summer movie for people over twenty-five!" *Cold Feet* opened at the Fifth Avenue Cinema to a rave review and ran for eight weeks before moving to the Clinton Theater, where it stayed for another two weeks, before breaking out to other locations in the Portland area. According to Deutchman, "this was seen as a sign of life in the film, even though the Portland numbers were hardly impressive."

Dallas and Houston followed in June. Four-week runs in both cities followed excellent reviews. The Texas print campaign reflected the original artwork developed for New York and San Francisco, rather than the Portland version. However, the modest grosses were far from the level required for *Cold Feet* to repeat the *Secaucus Seven* (see case study) success by building up more playdates regionally before rolling back into New York. The Dallas grosses were $3,585; $4,375; $3,166; and $2,558.

A flurry of playdates followed, but none showed the promise of Portland or Dallas. They included San Jose, Cincinnati, Louisville, Columbus, and Miami. At this point, *Cold Feet* was sold to cable and Cinecom stopped promoting its theatrical release. The following January, after an excellent response at the Los Angeles International Film Exposition (Filmex), it opened in Toronto to rave reviews in *Maclean's* and in the local media, and ran for six weeks. *Cold Feet* was sub-distributed in Canada by Northstar.

OTHER MARKETS

Homevideo · Homevideo rights were purchased by CBS/Fox, for an advance in the $25,000–$30,000 range. A remarkable 4,000 units were sold in the first quarter of homevideo release, and *Cold Feet* is now in overages. The strength of this performance can be gathered from a comparison with *Carmen, Das Boot,* and *Fannie and Alexander,* the only foreign titles that have sold in excess of 5,000 units. Ira Deutchman suggests that this indicates that *Cold Feet* succeeded in homevideo as a "B" or "C" commercial romance rather than as a specialty film.

Pay cable · Domestic cable sales are handled by Cinecom. The Movie Channel, Bravo, and Home Box Office have purchased *Cold Feet*. Deutchman feels that given the film's weak theatrical run, its sale to all the pay services is "a remarkable achievement."

Nontheatrical · No activity.

Broadcast · No activity.

Foreign · Foreign theatrical release of a film with no stars and an unknown director was difficult enough, but given its poor American run the odds against it were enormous. VanDusen reports no foreign territory sales to date.

Foreign television rights were assigned to Interama, a New York and Paris agency managed by Nicole Jouve. Television sales were made throughout Europe, and in Venezuela and Brazil. Interama also closed a number of foreign homevideo deals. VanDusen estimates that his earnings from foreign homevideo advances and television sales are "approximately $75,000."

REVIEW

Cold Feet was Bruce vanDusen's first feature and he expected to transform the abilities that had brought him success as a producer/ director for commercials into greater success as a film director. Offers from New Line Cinema and Cinecom International followed the standard specialty film pattern—a 50/50 percent split after costs. However, vanDusen passed over New Line and its upfront guarantee in favor of the commitment by Cinecom to a wider New York opening than is conventional for a specialty film. Unfortunately, very negative reviews killed Cinecom's attempt to position *Cold Feet* in the space between an art film and a more commercial venture. Good performances in isolated regional markets failed to break the pattern of poor reviews established in New York.

EATING RAOUL

(October 1982)

"'EATING RAOUL' IS ONE OF THE FRESHEST, FUNNIEST COMEDIES IN YEARS.

Impudent, outrageous and murderously madcap like 'Arsenic and Old Lace.'"
—Bruce Williamson, Playboy

"A VERY FUNNY COMEDY about sex and murder... full of smiles, punctuated by marvelously unseemly guffaws."
—Vincent Canby, New York Times

"A sense of fun so different from most movie comedies as to hit us with the shock of what we've been missing."
—Roger Greenspun, Penthouse

"A KINKY, TWINKY, LAFFAPALOOZA. Succulent and spicy humor that sneaks up on your funny bone. A sexual romper room for assorted lovable fruits and nuts."
—Robert Salmaggi, WINS Radio

"A simply delicious outrageous comedy."
—Judith Crist

"A wildly funny, lunatic spoof of the sex-and-violence scene."
—Lynn Minton, McCall's Magazine

"FINGER-LICKIN' GOOD. You're apt to be convulsed with laughter. Paul Bartel and Mary Woronov are uproarious. Robert Beltran is delicious. 'EATING RAOUL' is a fabulously flavorful flick."
—Guy Flatley, Cosmopolitan

20th CENTURY-FOX INTERNATIONAL CLASSICS in association with QUARTET\FILMS INCORPORATED presents
MARY WORONOV · PAUL BARTEL and introducing ROBERT BELTRAN in EATING RAOUL
also starring ED BEGLEY JR. · BUCK HENRY · SUSAN SAIGER   Screenplay by RICHARD BLACKBURN and PAUL BARTEL
Original music by ARLON OBER   Produced by ANNE KIMMEL   Directed by PAUL BARTEL

R RESTRICTED
UNDER 17 REQUIRES ACCOMPANYING PARENT OR ADULT GUARDIAN

QFI Quartet / Films Incorporated International
© 1982 CLASSICS

STARTS FRIDAY, OCT. 1st
68th St. Playhouse
3rd Ave. at 68th St. RE4-0302

PRINCIPALS	Director	Paul Bartel
	Producer	Anne Kimmel
	Writers	Richard Blackburn and Paul Bartel
	Principal cast	Paul Bartel and Mary Woronov
DISTRIBUTORS	Theatrical	20th Century-Fox Classics and Quartet Films
	Homevideo	CBS/Fox Home Entertainment
	Pay cable	20th Century-Fox
	Nontheatrical	Films Incorporated
	Broadcast	20th Century-Fox
	Foreign	Films Around the World
THEATRICAL	Opening date	October 1, 1982
	Total playdates	275
	Box-office gross	$3,850,000
	Gross film rental (domestic including Canada)	1,593,733
	Total distributor costs (including advance)	2,007,248
ANCILLARY	Homevideo (gross)	$3,000,000
	Pay cable	1,299,014
	Nontheatrical	48,585
	Foreign	275,000
	Television	10,000
	Merchandising	473
PARTICIPANTS CONTACTED		Paul Bartel
		Anne Kimmel
		Jane Alsobrook
		Ed Schuman

FILM SYNOPSIS

A prissy, middle-class couple, Paul and Mary Bland, living in a swinging singles apartment complex, raise capital for a new restaurant by killing their sinning neighbors and lifting their wallets. After the Blands meet Raoul, their commercial operation goes into high gear, as Raoul uses the bodies to raise additional cash. Only when his amorous ways become too much do the Blands turn against their partner.

DEVELOPMENT

Genesis · In the early 1980s, Paul Bartel wrote and directed *Secret Cinema*, an eerie comedy about a fragile young woman who believes—correctly, as it turns out—that persons unknown are making a film about her private life. Since then he has directed *Naughty Nurse*, a short; *Private Parts*, a feature; several exploitation films for Roger Corman, including *Death Race 2000* and *Cannonball*; *Lust in the Dust*, starring Tab Hunter; and *Scenes from the Class Struggle in Beverly Hills*.

Eating Raoul was motivated by Bartel's desire to make a personal, eccentric film that would showcase Mary Woronov and himself as actors. The first draft of the script was written by Bartel and Richard Blackburn while the two were attending the Berlin Film Festival in February 1980; after returning to Los Angeles, they continued to rewrite the script until it was in finished form.

Financing · The film was initially self-financed, with Bartel investing his own limited resources to shoot two scenes that were

42

screened for numerous studios and potential investors. When no one responded to the material, Bartel's parents invested almost $200,000, covering the film's out-of-pocket expenses.

According to Bartel, the final costs of the production broke down as follows:

Personal	$ 95,760
Investors (Bartel's parents)	186,000
Presale (Sweden)	60,000
Deferrals	166,000
Total	$507,760

Anticipating an audience · Both Bartel and his producer, Anne Kimmel, believed that the film would find an audience, but they were not sure who it was, nor how large it would be. They recognized that the film's commercial value could only be determined after it was finished, but were confident that Paul's comic vision would find an audience.

PRODUCTION

Bartel started shooting during the spring of 1980. With free stock, equipment, and labor from friends, he organized a weekend shoot and edited a thirteen-minute sample. He showed the sample to Roger Corman, who passed on it.

Up to this time, Bartel had been writer, director, producer, and star. He then brought on Anne Kimmel as producer; she had extensive production experience but had not as yet produced a feature. She agreed to take half of her salary up front, with the other half deferred in exchange for "points." They then undertook a second weekend shoot of another scene and enlarged the sample reel. This exhausted Bartel's savings. Unable to raise any outside financing, he showed the film to his parents, who volunteered to invest the balance needed to complete the film.

Bartel's parents dispensed the investment in outlays of about $50,000. With each of these payments, Kimmel was able to organize a shoot. The entire production consisted of twenty-two days of shooting over the course of a year, including the initial weekend's work. The production was a Directors Guild of America (DGA) and SAG signatory, although special low-budget terms were struck with both guilds.

Because of the extended and intermittent production period, the filmmakers ran into numerous problems, ranging from periodic unavailability of crew and cast to the imminent demolition of the principal location.

Editing and soundtrack postproduction took several weeks; the film was completed in February 1982. Of the total budget of $507,760, approximately $350,000 was for direct production and postproduction and the balance for legal and deferred expenses.

DISTRIBUTION DEAL

Making the deal · While the film was still in postproduction, the filmmakers negotiated a Scandinavian presale for $60,000 with the help of Telluride Film Festival codirector Tom Luddy. These revenues, however, would be available only upon presentation of the completed film. During this period, the filmmakers also decided not to self-distribute, but to seek a professional distributor for the film.

While in postproduction, David Chute, film critic of the *Los Angeles Herald Examiner*, wrote a feature piece about the film. It generated a lot of interest, but no investors. (An embarrassing moment occurred when the filmmakers were invited to screen their film for the investment group Producers Service Organization. A number of other filmmakers were there showing slick, Hollywood-type sample reels. The *Eating Raoul* workprint, with poor color quality, went out of sync when the interlock broke during the screening!)

With the film still in production, Bartel and Kimmel tested it as a work-in-progress at a screening for the Los Angeles Filmex Society; it generated considerable enthusiasm. Some Paramount executives were interested, although a low-level marketing executive had already passed on it. Paramount offered a $1 million advance, pending the result of a test-marketing campaign. If the test failed, they would not take the picture. Bartel rejected the offer for two reasons. First, Paramount would not allow Bartel's involvement in designing the test.

Second, if the film tested poorly, he would lose the million-dollar deal and probably sour his chances of securing a deal elsewhere.

The filmmakers decided to premiere the film at Los Angeles's Filmex in July 1982. They were also invited to the 1982 New York Film Festival as well as to London, Edinburgh, and several other festivals. The filmmakers invited all the Los Angeles distributors to the Filmex screening; only representatives from Fox Classics came.

The 20th Century-Fox Classics division had recently been created as a separate profit center at the studio. In 1983, Fox Classics released ten films that contributed between $8 and $10 million clear in profit to the parent corporation that year. (The unit is now defunct.) The decision of "Little Fox" to acquire *Eating Raoul* was based on a number of factors, including:

- It was a popular, funny, nonexploitative film with potentially strong audience appeal.
- The entire staff liked it.
- They could afford it in terms of the advance required and projected expenses.
- *Eating Raoul* fit in well with the diversified list of titles Fox Classics planned to acquire.

While Fox was showing strong interest in the film, New York–based Quartet Films was also competing actively. According to Ed Schuman, Quartet felt that *Eating Raoul* was a quality American film, with a theme that could appeal to younger filmgoers, and strong cable and homevideo sales potential. They joined with Fox Classics to make a joint acquisition offer, in order to reduce each party's upfront expenses and to spread the risk of losses. The two companies agreed to a 50/50 percent split on all costs and revenues, and to collaborate on all important decisions. Fox Classics would generate all advertising, publicity, and promotional materials, in consultation with Quartet.

Terms of the deal · During the period between the Filmex screening and the New York Film Festival, the filmmakers and Fox Classics were negotiating a deal. When news of the Fox offer became public, Embassy, Universal, and other distributors also sought to acquire distribution rights. However attractive the other offers were, the filmmakers decided to go with Fox. Their decision was shaped by the following factors:

- They wanted a major studio logo on the film, believing that it would help both theatrical distribution and future ancillary deals.
- The filmmakers liked the personnel at Fox Classics, and particularly their early enthusiasm for the film.
- Fox offered a sizeable advance of $300,000. The filmmakers had implied that the film had cost $750,000 in order to strengthen their bargaining position and secure a sufficient advance to repay Bartel's parents and deferrals owed.
- *Eating Raoul* was to be Fox Classics's first theatrical launch. The filmmakers correctly perceived that they would receive special attention from a management eager to establish a profitable new division. This would guarantee the careful supervision so important in making a film a "hit."
- The filmmakers were guaranteed what they initially thought were excellent terms on the homevideo sales through CBS/Fox.
- The filmmakers were promised a great deal of direct input into the campaign and distribution process. While final decision-making was in Fox's hands, the distributor actively encouraged the filmmakers' participation.
- The filmmakers agreed with Fox's overall marketing, distribution, and ad campaign plans.

A major sticking point in the negotiations was Fox's insistence on recouping any possible loss from theatrical distribution from the filmmakers' share of ancillary earnings. Instead of the common 50/50 split of net revenues, Fox bargained a 55 percent share on theatrical earnings, with the provision that if there were no profits in theatrical earnings, the split would revert to 50/50. Thus, the filmmakers conceded 5 percent in theatrical earnings in exchange for Fox's agreement to deduct any losses from theatrical distribution off the top (not out of the filmmakers' share) of profits in other markets.

Under the terms of the distribution contract, Fox/Quartet made commitments to consult the filmmakers when spending rose above $200,000 on prints and ads. Ultimately, promotion and advertising costs reached $1.25 million on film rentals of $1.6 million. An advertising budget of over $1.4 million was necessary to secure the very favorable terms of cable and homevideo sales. While the film-makers remain pleased with Fox Classics's handling of the film, not everything went smoothly when some distribution and accounting functions were later taken over by the parent studio's operations.

Initially, while the film was being released through Fox Classics, the filmmakers received regular, sometimes daily, reports regarding the number of screens playing, grosses, etc. However, some three months into the film's release, the studio transferred the accounting and collections responsibilities from the Classics division to Fox Domes-tic. Reporting on grosses and other "hard" statistical information was slowed considerably after this change took place. Based on the initial performance and projections, the reported box-office grosses and collected film rentals were lower than anticipated. A subsequent audit initiated by the filmmakers—costing $6,000—ultimately uncovered about $30,000 in monies owed to them.

MARKETING CAMPAIGN

Strategy · The distributors, together with the filmmakers, sought to create an identity for the film that would move beyond that of a mere cult film. Jane Alsobrook, then director of marketing and acquisitions at Fox Classics, recalls their major concern:

> Because of its low-budget look and bizarre subject matter, there was a risk that it could be seen as a strange exploitation movie. *Eating Raoul* is too sophisticated for an exploitation audience, and if we had posi-tioned it that way, it would have failed. We wanted to position it as an unconventional comedy.

The primary audience was defined as the twenty-to-fifty age group, which could readily understand the fifties setting of the film; and sophisticated, regular patrons of art-house theaters, who are open to experimental and offbeat cinema. A secondary target audience was the younger, college-age group.

A New York opening was scheduled at the 68th Street Playhouse, which was partly owned by Quartet Films, the codistributor of the film. Quartet hired Renee Furst, a publicist associated with quality projects, to coordinate publicity for the New York opening. It was felt that her involvement would prevent any possible association with exploitation movies in the minds of the critics.

Promotion and publicity · The film's zaniness, as well as the fact that *Eating Raoul* was Fox Classics's first release, inspired an imaginative promotional effort. In addition to the traditional screenings for the press and opinion-leaders, they mixed both conventional and innovative techniques:

· Two men wearing sandwich boards advertising the film distributed fliers among lines of ticket holders at a major Los Angeles rock concert for The Who.
· Postcards and a comic book were produced and distributed by Bartel at a cost of $10,000, only partly reimbursed by Fox.
· Pins in the shape of frying pans (the murder weapon in the film) were distributed.
· Cookies with a bite missing were distributed at Filmex.
· T-shirts were worn at Cannes.
· A closed-captioned version of the film was prepared for viewing by the hearing impaired.
· A "wild postering" campaign was carried out, particularly in the Los Angeles area, and to a lesser extent in New York and other cities.
· For many months, they held midnight weekend screenings in Los Angeles and New York.
· Special theater marquees were created in New York, Los Angeles, and Seattle, and exhibitors were encouraged to come up with eye-catching artwork.
· One-year anniversary screenings were held in New York and Los Angeles. Party hats were given to the audience.

Fox Classics experimented with radio and television spots. In addition to ticket giveaways, the distributor had Bartel and Woronov prepare a funny radio spot reminiscent of an old Burns and Allen skit. Fox also ran a thirty-second TV spot in Phoenix to determine whether the film could reach a more middle-of-the-road audience. A soundtrack album merchandising deal was struck with the Varese-Saraband record label, and the record jacket used film-ad art.

Bartel and Woronov played an important role in the promotional efforts. Fox sent them to openings in both major and secondary markets, and they crowded their schedules with media interviews in every market. Quartet supervised the New York press and opinion-maker screenings set up by Furst. There were about ten press screenings scheduled in advance for the ten key critics and thirty secondary critics; usually five or so would attend a screening. Bartel and Kimmel did not attend these press screenings, but they did attend a screening for about one thousand opinion-makers.

Favorable critical reviews were a key to the film's success. Vincent Canby's *New York Times* review, published after the New York Film Festival screening, is recalled by all participants in the release of the film as the principal catalyst for its success. His extremely favorable comments generated the initial audience. He praised Bartel's earlier accomplishment as writer/director of *Secret Cinema*, describing it as "one of the eeriest, funniest comedies I've ever seen on paranoia." Canby called *Eating Raoul* "an extremely nice comedy about people who know that niceness is next to godliness and that sex is simply disgusting." He continued:

> One mustn't blunt its pleasures by calling it a laugh riot. It is full of smiles, punctuated here and there by marvelous unseemly guffaws, but most of the time it works its little wonders quietly. The comic style is purposely flat, plain, and arduous, like a piece of pop art.

Later, when Canby included *Eating Raoul* in a special list of films recommended for Thanksgiving 1982, film grosses doubled. Other favorable reviews were published by *New York* and *Time* magazines; *Playboy* listed it as one of its ten best films of 1982. Siskel and Ebert, however, gave it a mixed-to-negative review on "Sneak Previews."

Trailer and ad · Paul Bartel initially produced his own trailer. Fox, upon review, decided to produce their own in-house version at a cost of $8,000 (as opposed to the usual studio costs of $40,000 to $100,000 by an outside vendor), which did include a small section of Paul's original effort.

The artwork and ad were created with extensive input from the filmmakers. Stills could not be used as the basis for the print ad as none was acceptable. There was concern about referring to the subject of cannibalism in the print ad. Co-writer Dick Blackburn and graphic designer Jimmy Wachtel each independently proposed the image of a foot in the mouth, suggesting some of the humor and offbeat character of the film. To their satisfaction, Fox Classics worked with Wachtel and an airbrush artist to create the final product, a one-sheet that received an award from the *Hollywood Reporter* and became the print ad and image. Lobby cards and stills for the press kits were created from film-frame blowups.

THEATRICAL RELEASE

Strategy · When the filmmakers signed with Fox/Quartet, it was agreed that the film's theatrical release would follow the conventional pattern of a specialty film. It was to open in New York City shortly after the New York Film Festival, and, depending on its success, roll out to other markets thereafter. *Eating Raoul* performed far better than anticipated, achieving approximately 275 playdates in its national release.

Opening run · *Eating Raoul* opened at the 68th Street Playhouse on October 1, 1982. Quartet Films, in conjunction with Fox Classics, handled the logistics, which included placement of ads through Diener, Hauser, Bates, and Co., and coordination of the publicity efforts of Renee Furst. Total opening costs were approximately $58,000, including preopening and first-week ad costs, a promotional trip by the principals to New York, a cocktail party reception, and an opening-night dinner for forty people.

According to Jane Alsobrook, the distributors chose the 68th Street Playhouse for the following reasons:

· This Upper East Side theater is known to be especially receptive to comedies and to long, open-ended runs. *La Cage aux Folles* and *The Gods Must Be Crazy* are the most notable recent examples.

- It fulfilled our overall marketing goal of presenting the film in a quality theater.
- Quartet is part owner of the theater (although it is run under an "arm's length" agreement), an aid in cutting anticipated costs.

Box-office grosses for the first four weeks at the 68th Street Playhouse were $32,926; $32,392; $29,508; and $21,056.

The film ran in New York for a total of forty weeks, during which time it also ran downtown at the Greenwich II in mid-October. In June 1983, it was still playing at the New Yorker and Waverly theaters.

National playoff · Two weeks after its successful New York opening, the film opened in Los Angeles. Shortly thereafter, it opened in other major markets and, eventually, in the smaller secondary markets. Between eighty and one hundred prints were struck.

The film made nearly 50 percent of its total box-office gross of $3.6 million in New York. However, New York accounted for only approximately 22 percent of its net film rental of $1.5 million, due to the extremely high advertising costs. Net film rental contributions from other markets were:

City	Net Film Rental Contribution (%)
New York	22.0
Los Angeles	8.3
Seattle	8.7
San Francisco	10.9
Dallas	4.4
Jacksonville	7.4
Other	38.3

OTHER MARKETS

Homevideo · Because of its strong theatrical performance, good word-of-mouth, and critical acclaim, the film has done well in homevideo sales. Fox sold the film to CBS/Fox Home Entertainment and the filmmakers estimate homevideo revenues at $3 million. In this deal, CBS/Fox has an 80 percent share. The filmmakers received 65 percent of Fox's 20 percent—or 12 percent of the gross—which is the normal homevideo deal.

Pay cable · Because of the film's strong theatrical release and Fox's relative strength within the market, the distributor was able to secure extremely favorable cable deals totaling $1.3 million. The filmmakers received 65 percent of all cable sales, but must absorb the 1½ to 2 percent guild residuals on all sales out of their share. For Paul Bartel—director, co-writer, and one of the principal stars—this is a favorable arrangement.

Nontheatrical · Nontheatrical rentals totaled $94,000.

Broadcast · Television sales were $10,000.

Foreign · Foreign sales are being handled by Films Around the World. The terms of this agreement are a flat 15 percent commission plus expenses. To date, the film has grossed approximately $275,000 in all foreign markets. Films Around the World has received approximately 40 percent in commissions and expenses, leaving the filmmakers with a net of $165,000.

REVIEW

Eating Raoul performed far better in all markets than any of the principals anticipated. Despite its initial rejection by both studios and such major independent producers as Roger Corman, Bartel was able to finance the film through personal investments, loans, and deferrals. Because of the filmmakers' perseverance, strong performances at the New York and Los Angeles film festivals, and a number of important critical reviews, notably Vincent Canby's in the *New York Times*, *Eating Raoul* found a remarkably supportive audience throughout the major urban markets.

The joint release by 20th Century-Fox Classics and Quartet Films followed the conventional "platforming" techniques for specialty films. However, the distributors used a number of clever marketing schemes to attract favorable attention. *Eating Raoul* was successfully positioned as a quality product aimed at an audience of adult filmgoers aged twenty to forty.

Because of the strong theatrical run and favorable critical reviews, *Eating Raoul* has done very well in all ancillary markets. The strongest sale was in pay cable, for which Fox has collected more than $1.3 million to date. In homevideo, gross revenues have exceeded $3 million; foreign revenues have reached $275,000.

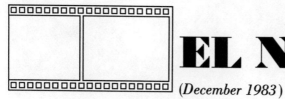

EL NORTE

(December 1983)

The magical film that reveals the world between the dream and the reality

THE NORTH

AN INDEPENDENT PRODUCTIONS FILM in association with AMERICAN PLAYHOUSE "EL NORTE"
starring ZAIDE SILVIA GUTIERREZ and DAVID VILLALPANDO   screenplay by GREGORY NAVA and
ANNA THOMAS   produced by ANNA THOMAS   directed by GREGORY NAVA

Copyright © 1983 Cinecom International Films   Cinecom INTERNATIONAL FILMS / ISLAND ALIVE

Exclusive Engagement Starts Wednesday

THE BARONET   A WALTER READE THEATRE
59th St. at 3rd Ave. • EL 5-1663

PRINCIPALS	Director	Gregory Nava
	Producer	Anna Thomas
	Writers	Gregory Nava and Anna Thomas
	Principal cast	Zaide Silvia Gutierrez and David Villalpando
	Producer's rep	Jesse Beaton
DISTRIBUTORS	Theatrical	Cinecom International Films/Island Alive
	Homevideo	CBS/Fox Home Entertainment
	Pay cable	Producers
	Nontheatrical	Cinecom International Films/Island Alive
	Broadcast	PBS/"American Playhouse"
	Foreign	Represented by Cinecom (Amir Malin) and Island Alive (Cary Brokaw)
THEATRICAL	Opening date	December 15, 1983
	Total playdates	Over 400 during first year of distribution
	Box-office gross	$5,500,000 (e)
	Gross film rental	2,200,000 (e)
	Total distributor costs	
	Guarantee*	250,000
	Advertising and publicity**	
	Prints**	
ANCILLARY	Homevideo guarantee	$140,000
	Nontheatrical	not available
	Foreign	not available
PARTICIPANTS CONTACTED		Gregory Nava
		Anna Thomas
		Jesse Beaton
		Amir Malin
		Ira Deutchman
		Cary Brokaw
		Lindsay Law
		Steve Seifert
		Irwin Young

e = Estimate based on uncorroborated data derived from *Variety*, Cinecom published materials, and other sources.

*Guarantee covers both theatrical and nontheatrical markets.

** An audit has been conducted; financial and other distribution data are not currently available.

FILM SYNOPSIS

Two young Guatemalans, brother and sister, fearing for their lives, flee their native land following the brutal murder of their father by government soldiers. The film follows their harrowing journey through Mexico and across the border to the promised land of "el Norte." Sustained during the hazardous trip by visions of the American "good life" gleaned from mail-order catalogs, they finally arrive in Los Angeles only to confront a far harsher reality.

DEVELOPMENT

Genesis · Gregory Nava developed the original concept for *El Norte* in 1979 while his wife, Anna Thomas, was completing post-production on her film *The Haunting of M.* Anna agreed enthusiastically to Greg's request that she serve as producer of the film and collaborate on the continued development of the script.

Originally conceived to be about Mexican Indians, the story was placed in Guatemala following extensive research on the experience of Guatemalan Indians. The filmmakers' goal was to make a highly dramatic epic of poetic realism that would place the native people at the center of their own story. To be true to the experience of its Mayan peasant lead characters, the story would have to be told in Mayan, Spanish, and English. Clearly, those characters could not realistically be portrayed by recognizable American actors.

From the start the filmmakers recognized that the subject matter of the film, the nonstar casting, and the multilingual approach it mandated would preclude studio interest. Its style was based on the magic realism typical of contemporary Latin American literature. The film's

58

defining characteristics, though incompatible with studio tastes, contributed to its stunning originality.

Financing · After completing the script, the filmmakers spent two years seeking financing. They applied to NEH and, in Nava's words, were "cruelly" rejected. They contacted hundreds of potential private investors and members of the Los Angeles Latino community seeking support. However, those who expressed interest would not commit funds until a major investor came forward. Greg and Anna describe the fundraising process as exhausting, demoralizing, and expensive (for instance, the travel and entertainment costs incurred in pitching investors, and the cost of forgoing paid work).

In June 1981, the filmmakers were accepted to the Sundance Institute's first summer workshop, which they hoped would increase their credibility and, therefore, their funding opportunities. They had a valuable opportunity at the Institute to work with their principal actress, Zaide Silvia Gutierrez, and they gained helpful advice on working with nonprofessional actors. (They received some bizarre advice from industry professionals at the Institute, too, including the suggestion that, in order to secure financing, Los Angeles Dodger pitcher Fernando Valenzuela should be cast in the male lead!)

By the end of 1981, the filmmakers still had not found a major investor. Utterly discouraged, they reluctantly decided that *El Norte* would never be made. They shelved the script and began work on other projects.

In early 1982, while working with IFP/West, Greg and Anna met Lindsay Law, executive producer of "American Playhouse." Having heard of the property, Law asked to read *El Norte*. The filmmakers were hesitant to resurrect a project that had caused them so much disappointment, but Law was persistent and they finally acquiesced.

A few days later, Law called Nava and Thomas, extolling the script's promise and saying he wanted to put "American Playhouse" money behind it. From this initial commitment, events moved quickly. Building on the contacts established previously, it took the filmmakers only a month of hard work to line up the necessary financing, which came from the following sources:

"American Playhouse"	$425,000
Private investors	110,000
Britain's Channel Four	45,000
Deferrals	120,000*
Total	$700,000

Production costs ultimately totaled $850,000, due to overruns resulting from difficulties with the Mexican shoot and other unforeseen expenses. The $150,000 overage was eventually covered by the theatrical advance.

PRODUCTION

Film production commenced almost immediately after financing was in place. Casting for the leads was the principal activity of the preproduction phase. It was a long, tedious process in which Nava and Thomas interviewed innumerable actors in the United States and Mexico. They were committed to Zaide Gutierrez for the female lead role. She, however, had other, potentially conflicting commitments, forcing the filmmakers to cast a backup in case she became unavailable. Gutierrez and the male lead ultimately cast, David Villalpando, were both experienced stage actors in Latin America, although they were unknown to North American filmgoers.

Production was planned as a twelve-week shoot, with a one-week break for relocation. However, the shoot turned out to be more complex than planned, entailing a fourteen-week schedule for principal photography, spread out over seventeen weeks. Shot in 35mm, the production involved almost sixty speaking parts and used over one hundred different locations in Mexico and the United States.

The filmmakers confronted serious difficulties with the Mexican shoot. Logistical problems in the remote Mayan highlands of Chiapas state in southern Mexico were compounded by terrible weather conditions. They had to work with many Mayan extras who spoke neither Spanish nor English. Making matters worse, they found themselves caught up in local hostilities, which led to many threatening inci-

* Deferrals included payments to DuArt Labs, of which a small balance remains, and Nava's and Thomas's salaries, which have been partially recouped.

dents, including armed men visiting their location site, the local mayor holding the company paymaster at gunpoint, and 300 locals with machetes confronting the crew.

Production moved to central Mexico, where the filmmakers expected an uneventful shoot. Here the worst crisis occurred. While shooting at a ruined hacienda, a group of armed men came to the set. Claiming to be government officials, they seized the Mexican production manager and demanded that all the exposed film be turned over to them. Jim Glennon, the cinematographer, scheduled to visit Los Angeles for the birth of his child, took the exposed film and fled to Mexico City Airport. A car chase ensued in which the gunmen finally caught Glennon and took the negative at gunpoint. In the confusion, Glennon escaped unharmed and made his flight to the States.

While the gunmen had been on the set, filming continued at another part of the location. When Thomas finally reached Nava with news that the film had been seized, they feared a disastrous end to their production. Over the next twenty-four hours, however, they contacted the men who had seized the film and bargained back the kidnapped production manager and film for a ransom of 1.3 million pesos ($17,000). This was an enormous expense for an already tight budget.

Like a scene from a "B" movie, the payoff took place at midnight in a Mexico City parking lot. With submachine guns drawn, the thieves counted the bundles of pesos and gave up a large metal box containing the film cans. But the filmmakers still didn't know whether the stock had been exposed; in fact, they had to wait for its processing at DuArt Labs in New York to know for sure. Fearing further danger to cast and crew, they canceled plans to finish production in Mexico.

This unbudgeted relocation to Los Angeles added several weeks to the production and put the filmmakers under enormous financial pressure. They had to build a set to match the Mexican location, recreate a Mexican bus, and fly up some of the cast to complete several scenes. This forced the filmmakers to return to their investors for additional support.

DISTRIBUTION DEAL

Making the deal · During postproduction, Nava and Thomas initially decided not to show *El Norte* in roughcut to anyone other than
their investors (including representatives of "American Playhouse"
and Channel Four). They also decided to forgo audience test-
screenings, not wanting to risk poor word-of-mouth based on an
unfinished product.

While still cutting the film in the spring of 1983, the filmmakers felt
pressured to complete a viable distribution deal well in advance of
their scheduled "Playhouse" airing. They could then negotiate more
time for a theatrical release window. They decided that a successful
screening at a major film festival would enhance interest among
distributors.

Cannes was a year away, leaving two viable options for the fall, the
Telluride Film Festival and the New York Film Festival. The filmmakers decided to approach Telluride because it featured American
independents and was well attended by distributors. Also, Telluride
was farther from the critical eye of major reviewers. Nava says,
"Telluride was the better choice. It gave the film its first opportunity to
generate heat, but at less risk than if it had been presented in a major
market."

Nava and Thomas invited Telluride Festival directors Tom Luddy
and Bill Pence to private roughcut screenings in Los Angeles. Without
music or special effects, and with Nava offering simultaneous transla-
tions at the back of the room, both festival directors reacted enthusiastically. They invited Greg and Anna to premiere *El Norte* at the
festival over the Labor Day weekend.

With only six weeks to finish their film before the festival, Nava and
Thomas worked around the clock. On the Friday before Labor Day,
Greg picked up the first print at DuArt Labs in New York and flew to
Telluride. The filmmakers saw the first finished version at the Monday
screening, and were greeted by a standing ovation. The theater was
packed for the second screening and the audience responded as
before.

Following these successful screenings, nearly every distributor at
the festival approached the filmmakers with offers. Having made poor

deals with distributors on their previous films, Nava and Thomas proceeded with caution. They decided to secure a producer's representative because they wanted the advice of an expert on distribution to guide them through the negotiations, and because they wanted someone else to be tough, to push their interests, so that they would not personally alienate the distributor, with whom they would be working closely over the following year or more. After considering numerous lawyers and reps (as producers' representatives are called), they asked Jesse Beaton to represent them.

In order to secure the most favorable distribution deal, the filmmakers initiated a vigorous self-promotion campaign. Riding the wave of Telluride, they undertook the following activities:

- They developed a set of criteria regarding the terms and conditions they hoped to secure, along with a plan of action that included extensive screenings for distribution in Los Angeles and New York.
- In New York they held distribution screenings at DuArt Labs, controlling the screenings by refusing to send out a print; if distributors were interested, they would have to come to scheduled screenings. The filmmakers tried to hold exclusive one-on-one screenings, but because of the high level of interest, some small-group sessions ensued. Strongest interest was indicated by Cinecom International, Orion Classics, United Artists Classics, and Frank Marino (then an independent).
- In Los Angeles, they held a screening for the cast and crew, to which they invited distributors who had not seen *El Norte* at Telluride or in New York. Following this screening, Island Alive and Samuel Goldwyn expressed interest.

This campaign, which took place over two weeks, helped to identify the most serious distributors and to generate additional interest in the film, thus increasing the filmmakers' bargaining power.

Thomas, Nava, and Beaton held long followup discussions with each interested distributor, discussing such issues as promotion and marketing techniques, possible release plans, other films in their release schedule, receptivity to filmmaker involvement in the distribution process, and prior track records with comparable films. Following these discussions, Jesse would obtain from each distributor its proposed terms regarding advance, splits, rights, minimum commitments for opening and release, and promotion and advertising expenditures. Within one week of negotiations, the selection came down to Cinecom, Orion Classics, and Frank Marino.

Cinecom was founded in 1982 and had, up to that time, distributed *Come Back to the Five and Dime, Jimmy Dean, Jimmy Dean; Starstruck*; and *Angelo, My Love*. Ironically, Cinecom had boycotted the 1983 Telluride Film Festival, but key personnel heard about *El Norte* from Roger Ebert, the *Chicago Sun-Times* film reviewer, while at the Toronto Film Festival.

Through Irwin Young of DuArt Labs, Cinecom's Ira Deutchman was able to reach Nava and Thomas and persuade them not to make a deal until Cinecom could see and bid on the film. The filmmakers narrowed the competing choices to two leading specialty distributors, Cinecom International and Orion Classics. For the filmmakers, the final choice was made on the basis of the following factors:

- Cinecom offered a guarantee that was $50,000 more than Orion Classics.
- Cinecom was willing to accede to the filmmakers' terms for a separation of rights, and acquire only the theatrical and nontheatrical rights.
- Cinecom needed *El Norte* to establish, in Beaton's words, a "track record"; the filmmakers believed they would work harder than the more established Orion Classics.
- Cinecom had no other film on its release schedule, whereas Orion Classics was then about to release its (ultimately successful) *Carmen*.
- The filmmakers were impressed with Cinecom's personnel, considering them some of the most knowledgeable in the field of specialty film marketing.

However, while the filmmakers were striking an in-principle agreement with Cinecom, the distributor was working out the terms of a joint venture with Island Alive. Thus, the final acquisition of *El Norte* involved two separate deals: one between Cinecom and the filmmakers, and another between Cinecom and Island Alive.

The two companies undertook the joint venture to share the risks— and potential rewards—of acquiring *El Norte*. This was the first such joint venture for both companies, and was the culmination of discussions begun prior to their mutual interest in *El Norte*. Discussions for the joint venture on *El Norte* were initiated by Island Alive, and Cinecom's Deutchman felt that "it made good business sense to split the risk between ourselves and a partner." That risk involved not only a sizeable advance, but marketing costs as well.

Island Alive, the distributor of such films as *Koyaanisqaatsi* and *Android*, was very interested in the film, and had established a good rapport with the filmmakers. After Cinecom's president, Amir Malin, had solidified the deal with Island Alive, Deutchman notified the filmmakers of his company's plans. The filmmakers agreed to the terms between the two companies as part of the contract. The agreement between Cinecom and Island Alive was essentially as follows:

- The partners were to share equally in financing the advance and marketing costs.
- Cinecom International was responsible for the logistics of the release, including bookings, shipping of prints and ads, billings, and collections.
- Principal decision-making responsibility for the marketing campaign rested with Cinecom, while Island Alive retained approval rights over those decisions.
- The partners were to split all net revenues.

Terms of the deal · Specific features of the distribution agreement between Cinecom and the producers of *El Norte* included:

- A guarantee of over $200,000.
- Acquisition of only theatrical and nontheatrical rights. (Cinecom was fearful that an early "American Playhouse" broadcast would diminish the ancillary market value.)
- A "step deal," specifying increases in the filmmakers' percentage share of revenues at higher levels of gross receipts.
- A guaranteed minimum marketing commitment.
- Input and veto power on the part of the filmmakers over artwork and theater selection in the top ten markets, and agreement that they would cut the trailer.

· A stipulation that the filmmakers would receive monthly accounting statements regarding expenditures and revenues in each market.

In order for the film to achieve its maximum potential in theatrical release, the filmmakers had to renegotiate their contract with "American Playhouse" to avoid premature television exposure. These negotiations were handled by Thomas and Malin, himself a former PBS counsel, with the full cooperation of David Davis, the executive director of "American Playhouse." Under the new contract, an extended theatrical window was secured, with an additional automatic six-month extension to be made if a box-office gross of $2 million was achieved by April 1984. These levels were easily reached in the course of the film's successful theatrical run, and the extension helped the filmmakers secure favorable terms on the homevideo sale.

MARKETING CAMPAIGN

Strategy · The overriding concern that shaped the marketing campaign for *El Norte* was, in Thomas's words, to "sell what we had." This was the filmmakers' primary goal throughout the long development and production phases, and something they insisted upon as the film was about to enter the marketplace.

According to Thomas, the most critical issue facing the filmmakers and distributors was

to find a way to communicate to the public what the film was like. We wanted to convey the universal theme and quality of the story, not letting people get confused by the political associations they might have with the subject matter.

Therefore, the filmmakers and distributors consciously attempted to depoliticize *El Norte*'s image. The filmmakers had strong beliefs regarding the crucial issues posed by the film, but they didn't want it pigeonholed as a political movie. As Deutchman pointed out, a film identified as political tends to be restricted in its audience appeal. He adds:

We had to avoid the traps so many independent films fall into. We didn't want *El Norte* to appear too ethnographic, like a documentary. That would kill it. We wanted it to play like a Hollywood film, as if [Steven] Spielberg had made a socially conscious film. We wanted people to experience it as a well-told story.

Accordingly, the selection of images, words, and review quotes for the trailer, ad, and publicity packet was intended to reinforce the film's magical and dramatic qualities. Further, in contrast to the promotional policy adopted for many social-issue independent features, the distributors limited the film's use for benefit screenings. "We didn't want the film to appear [to be] a political tool and divide the community," Beaton says. Finally, they opened the film in the East as opposed to the West, where, by traditional logic, it should have had a natural constituency (see next section).

In defining the target audiences, *El Norte* was seen by both the filmmakers and the distributors as a "crossover film." Two distinct primary audiences were identified, with the hope that success among these audiences could lead to a breakthrough to the wider mass audience. These two primary audiences were the traditional art-house patrons, or specialty filmgoers, who are generally supportive of quality American independent and foreign films; and the sizeable Latino audience that might be attracted by the film's subject matter.

Promotion and publicity · Reaching these distinct audiences involved a variety of outreach efforts specially tailored to each respective group. The two primary audiences were subdivided into the following audience segments:

- Art-house filmgoers. These viewers, normally white, middle-class adults, would be attracted by favorable press coverage and would, in turn, help extend positive word-of-mouth.
- Middle-class Hispanic adults. This group, while numerically very small, was the bilingual, opinion-leader segment of the Spanish-speaking community, and could therefore generate positive word-of-mouth in the larger Hispanic community.
- Adults within small markets oriented to more mainstream movies. These English- and Spanish-speaking audiences could be reached only through positive press and strong word-of-mouth.
- Monolingual Spanish-speaking people. These audiences located in southern California, the Southwest, and in some northern urban

settings would require a version of the film with Spanish subtitles over the English dialogue.

Outreach to the art-house audience was made through the established techniques of specialized promotion. These included extensive prescreening for press and opinion-makers, a reliance on favorable reviews, and platforming at prestigious houses. For example, in New York, about one thousand people, including the staff and readers of the *Village Voice*, saw *El Norte* in special prescreenings before its official opening.

Key to *El Norte*'s eventual overall success was the scope of positive media coverage, including newspaper and magazine feature articles as well as editorials and television reviews. The press generated a high level of awareness and name recognition, despite the fact that a few key publications such as the *Village Voice*, *New York*, and the *New Yorker* gave the film mixed reviews. But in many of the major outlets, from the *New York Times* and the *Los Angeles Times* to *Variety* and New York's *Daily News*, the critics not only reviewed the film favorably, but went further, championing it to their readers. For example:

- The *New York Times* gave it four separate write-ups, including strong reviews by Vincent Canby and Janet Maslin and two feature articles on Nava and Thomas. (Maslin called it "a small, personal, independently made film with . . . solid, sympathetic performances by unknown actors and a visual style of astonishing vibrancy. . . . [The film] must be regarded as a remarkable accomplishment.")

- Roger Ebert gave it his highest praise. Writing in the *Chicago Sun-Times*, he urged that the film be considered for a special Academy Award.

- The *Los Angeles Times* ran numerous articles and reviews.

Positive reviews also appeared in many smaller papers, such as the *San Diego Union*, the *Sacramento Bee*, *USA Today*, the *Cleveland Herald*, the *Milwaukee Sentinel*, and the *Catholic Voice*. The filmmakers made themselves available for about one hundred interviews, especially important in the smaller markets, where art films have weaker runs. According to Thomas, while Cinecom's press relations work was well handled, the press attention was not the most critical component in their success. She believes that the excellent word-of-mouth was "key to making the film work. It was the most important factor."

The same techniques, prescreenings and reliance on favorable press reviews and feature articles, were utilized in promoting the film in the Spanish-language community. The campaign was strengthened by Nava's first-hand knowledge of the Los Angeles Chicano community and Spanish-language exhibitors. Cinecom also sought the help of Hispanic community marketing consultants.

The Spanish-language campaign was different, however, in one important respect. It operated from a belief that Nava stressed from the inception: the Hispanic community, and especially its more educated, middle-class stratum, would take its cue on *El Norte* from the dominant mainstream press. While immigration is a theme common to many Spanish-language movies, they are usually action-oriented. For Spanish-language critics, exhibitors, and filmgoers to accept *El Norte*, an art film, it would require favorable reviews and strong box-office performance within the traditional art-house circuit.

Riding the film's critical success in the English-language press, *El Norte* drew strong interest from the Spanish-language press. In addition, both the filmmakers and principal cast received considerable attention through feature articles and interviews. Prescreenings held for Spanish-language community leaders produced strong emotional responses; many of those in attendance had either personally experienced the story of *El Norte* or knew others who had.

The lack of high-quality production stills was a problem. The filmmakers realized in retrospect that they did not budget adequate production funds for this need. While hundreds of rolls of photos were taken, there were not enough shots of sufficient quality to be used. Supplying production stills is, in Nava's words, "a monstrous problem." The demand was huge—many stills went to "American Playhouse," others to the magazines and festivals, and still more were needed by the theatrical distributors and their publicists. What the filmmakers hadn't anticipated at the beginning of production was that publicity outlets, particularly within the same market, usually want to have the exclusive use of an image. A large number of different shots were needed for a national publicity campaign.

Trailer and ad · The trailer was cut by Nava with input from Cinecom. In general, Cinecom does not permit a film's director to cut the trailer, but uses independent editors. In this case, however, they agreed to Nava's contractual demand that he edit the trailer, confident that he fully understood the marketing feel they sought to achieve.

The ad was designed by Tom Moody, the director of Cinecom's advertising and publicity department. The artwork was suggested by Nava's research into Mayan culture, and embodies the sensibilities of the film. The romantic imagery was intended to help mark *El Norte* as an art film, reinforcing its timeless, universal, and nonpolitical qualities.

THEATRICAL RELEASE

Strategy · The strategy for the theatrical release of *El Norte* was carefully designed. It consisted of platforming the film in individual markets so as to maximize overall exposure, and placing the film in a specially selected theater within each market to achieve maximum recognition as a quality film.

While *El Norte* performed as well as or better than expected in nearly every market, an examination of its performance in specific markets is needed to understand the effectiveness of the overall campaign.

Under the terms of the distribution deal, Cinecom committed to a theatrical release by the end of 1983. This timing was important for a number of reasons. First, there was a strong possibility that several critics who had seen the film at Telluride, in particular Roger Ebert, would include *El Norte* among their lists of the year's ten best films, which would be of great benefit to any advertising campaign. Second, and much more of a longshot, was the possibility of an Academy Award nomination in the foreign-language category. The issues, then, were in which market to open the film, and in which theater.

As part of the general plan to prevent audiences from seeing it as a political film, Nava argued that *El Norte* should open in the East, where the issue of illegal immigrants from south of the border would not dominate the reviewers' attention. As he says:

> The details of the film would get in the way of most Los Angeles reviewers and they would lose sight of the film as a film. They wouldn't be able to tell the forest for the trees. We believed that in the East,

where the issue of undocumented workers is not as emotionally charged, the film would be taken more objectively.

While most independent films open in New York in order to garner as much press attention as possible, there is an equally strong countertendency within theatrical distribution to launch a film in the market that represents its strongest natural base of support. In this instance, Cinecom agreed with Nava's reasoning and rejected a Los Angeles premiere in favor of opening simultaneously in New York and Chicago.

Opening run · The booking of the film at the Plaza Theater for the New York engagement had been set, according to Deutchman, with the signing of the distribution deal. However, the Plaza, part of the Cinema Five chain, was run on the basis of open-ended bookings, allowing films to play for as long as their performance warranted. This was desirable in the case of *El Norte*, but such a policy obviously cuts both ways. The film preceding *El Norte* was Carlos Saura's *Carmen*, which was handled by Orion Classics. Attendance for *Carmen* was building during the pre-Christmas period, so that Cinema Five was obliged, in Deutchman's words, "to renege on its agreement with Cinecom to open *El Norte* at Christmas." The issue for the distributor was whether to continue waiting for the availability of the Plaza or to move to another theater.

As these difficulties with the New York opening developed, Cinecom went ahead with its Chicago launch. The city was selected because of a number of factors, chief among them the strong support for the film, noted above, on the part of the *Sun-Times*'s Roger Ebert. He praised it on his weekly PBS-syndicated television show, "At the Movies," and he put it on his year's ten best list. Equally important, the existence of Mexican, Puerto Rican, Cuban, and other Latin American immigrant community groups in Chicago made the city an ideal market in which to test how various Hispanic as well as Anglo audiences would respond to the film. (No significant difference in response was seen among the different ethnic groups, except that the Cuban-Americans responded negatively.)

El Norte received its theatrical premiere in Chicago's Fine Arts Theater on December 15, 1983, during one of the most severe cold spells in Chicago's history. Opening date temperatures dropped to nineteen degrees below zero, and never rose above zero during the first two weeks of the run. This contributed to the low attendance patterns expected during the holiday season for all but family-attended Hollywood blockbusters. Nevertheless, *El Norte* ran for fourteen weeks at the Fine Arts and four weeks in a breakout to other theaters in the area.

Meanwhile, back in New York, at year's end Cinecom was less inclined to continue waiting for the Plaza. Given the strong opening and favorable press in Chicago, they wanted *El Norte* reviewed by the New York–based national press. The *New York Times*, for example, had already committed to run a feature article on *El Norte* in its Arts and Leisure section to appear on the Sunday before the awaited opening.

The Plaza Theater, with *Carmen* running strong, wouldn't commit to an advance date for *El Norte*, thus hampering Cinecom's ability to plan a coordinated publicity campaign. This threatened to dissipate the momentum generated in Chicago. Therefore, Cinecom began discussing alternatives with Island Alive and the filmmakers. Cinecom's Deutchman recalls that "Greg [Nava] pushed for the Baronet. It was a slightly smaller theater, but available."

The Walter Reade Baronet Theater is a prestigious first-run house on Manhattan's Third Avenue, and is the site for openings of major Hollywood films. According to Deutchman, an opening at the Baronet would aid in positioning *El Norte* with the national press. Above all, it offered a set opening date, crucial to coordinating the national press campaign. Bill Quigley, then Walter Reade's vice-president and film buyer (now with Vestron Pictures), recalls that he offered Cinecom space at the Baronet and pulled another film to make room for *El Norte*.

The 418 seats at the Baronet (compared to the Plaza's 510) limited potential box-office gross per screening. While specialty films rarely achieve full gross potential, per-screening estimates were particularly important to *El Norte*. Because of the film's long running time (140 minutes), the number of screenings per day was limited to four instead of the usual six, making every seat count. Despite this slightly smaller seating capacity, the Baronet's house "nut" was nonetheless higher than that of the Plaza, thus requiring stronger box-office performance to achieve the same financial results for the distributor and producers. In Deutchman's words, "If we didn't get high grosses, we'd be in trouble."

Another drawback to the Baronet was that, unlike other theaters in the Walter Reade chain such as the Waverly, it operated on a locked booking policy. It was available in early January for a fixed, six-week period. This meant that if *El Norte* met with its anticipated success, it would eventually have to be moved to another theater, risking temporary loss of audience and/or incurring extra advertising expenses to effect a successful move. (Deutchman recalls that although he signed a six-week booking agreement, he had "the promise of a possible holdover if the film did good business." Quigley vigorously denies this, insisting that the contract reflects the full terms of the booking, and recalls no promise to extend the run.)

Despite these concerns, the timely availability of the Baronet was clearly the decisive factor. *El Norte* opened there on January 11. The film performed well and generated strong word-of-mouth during its run (shortened, in the event, to five weeks and two days). Cinecom was able to successfully move it out to three other Manhattan theaters. In retrospect, Deutchman believes that "it was a gamble to open at the Baronet, but one well worth taking."

El Norte's box-office grosses at the Baronet during the first four weeks were $5,461 (2 days); $26,903; $28,770; and $23,508.

By the eleventh week of its New York run, *El Norte* had broken out to a total of eight theaters in Manhattan, New Jersey, and Long Island, at which point the advertising, which had consistently been placed in the *Times*, the *Post*, and *El Diario*, was expanded to include placement in suburban papers. In all, it ran eighteen weeks in the New York area.

National playoff · Building on the success in New York, the film was soon launched in other markets. On March 9, 1984, it opened in Los Angeles at the Music Hall Theater in Beverly Hills, whose 800-seat capacity allowed for adequate grosses despite a four-showings-per-day limitation.

Apart from its Los Angeles setting, *El Norte* held a special interest for those in the large Latino immigrant community with first- or second-hand knowledge of the story it told. Island Pictures's Cary

Brokaw recalls that on Sundays at the Music Hall, middle-class Anglos and poorer Latinos would often be standing in line together, creating a strange tension in the theater, as if the two groups were viewing each other through the eyes of the film. A version with Spanish subtitles over the English dialogue ran in the barrio sections of the city.

In San Francisco, Cinecom delayed the opening until March 23 to allow momentum to build from the Los Angeles opening. The distributor booked the Gateway Theater for two reasons. Its owner, Ben Myron, had personal relationships with both the Cinecom staff and the producer's rep Jesse Beaton and, more importantly, offered a very favorable deal. Negotiated by Cinecom's Malin, the deal was, according to Deutchman, "better than any offered by any other theater in the Bay Area . . . a large guarantee and very high 'floors' throughout the engagement." On April 6, *El Norte* opened in Berkeley as well, and subsequently played in Palo Alto, San Jose, Santa Clara, Fresno, Santa Rosa, and Cotati.

The film performed poorly in both Miami and Minneapolis, for quite different reasons. As the research during the Chicago run had indicated, Cuban-Americans, who make up a very large proportion of the Miami audience, were the one Hispanic immigrant group that didn't respond well to the film. This is easily understood, and could have been anticipated; the experience of the largely middle-class Cuban immigrants, the bulk of whom left early revolutionary Cuba on airline carriers and entered the U.S. with special legal status, predisposed them to be unsympathetic to this story of Indian peasants fleeing a right-wing Guatemalan regime and illegally entering the U.S. In Minneapolis, surprisingly, the film received only soft reviews. With no one championing the film in the press, it had a mediocre run.

Fearing that the film would also encounter a lukewarm press reception in Reagan's Washington, the distributor held off the opening there until April 6. However, Gary Arnold, the influential *Washington Post* critic, gave it a favorable review, to the surprise of the filmmakers and distributors. After building slowly for the first two weeks, the film ran for several months, finally moving to a smaller theater to extend its run as long as possible.

The overall release strategy worked well for *El Norte*. As Greg Nava anticipated, the West Coast reviewers did politicize the film. For example, Gary Franklin, the critic for the CBS-TV affiliate, criticized it for portraying a "flagrant disregard for our immigration laws." Yet he still praised the film, rating it an eight on a scale of ten. As anticipated, emphasizing the film's artistic and humanistic qualities helped to deflect an overt political reading.

Also as expected, the response pattern differed on the two coasts. Opening first in the East, it initially did moderately well, building steadily throughout the runs. Opening later in the West, with the benefit of the good reviews and strong runs in the East, the film played to larger audiences over more sustained periods.

In its first year of first-run theatrical release, *El Norte* had over 400 playdates.

OTHER MARKETS

El Norte's success in theatrical release strengthened its sales potential in the ancillary markets. Initial, universally expressed reservations over its presale to "American Playhouse," its theme, its use of trilingual dialogue, and its long running time turned out to be unfounded, and these factors have not in fact hampered sales to ancillary domestic markets.

Homevideo · The homevideo rights were sold to CBS/Fox for an advance of $140,000 in a deal negotiated by Cinecom's Amir Malin, acting in this instance in a noncorporate, private capacity as a producer's representative.

Pay cable · Neither the film's national broadcast on "Playhouse" during sweeps week nor the foreign-language element have dampened the enthusiasm of pay-cable programmers at HBO and Showtime, who are discussing acquisition terms.

Nontheatrical · Not available.

Broadcast · The film was shown on "American Playhouse" with very high ratings during sweeps week. In subsequent airings, the film has performed consistently well.

Foreign · The sale of rights to foreign territories was handled by Cinecom and Island Alive. Response to the film by foreign distributors has not been strong, however, perhaps because of the dubbing and subtitling problems posed by its multilingual dialogue. According to Cinecom's Malin, foreign sales were undercut by "political problems and local xenophobia." While there were strong reviews at numerous openings, the film still performed weakly. He feels that this experience was quite the opposite of the domestic release, where aggressive marketing efforts paid off with a strong run.

REVIEW

El Norte is the most successful foreign-language film to be produced and directed by American filmmakers. To date, it has grossed an estimated $5.5 million in theatrical release, has had a strong showing in the homevideo markets, and been shown as part of PBS's "American Playhouse."

Nearly everyone who read the original script during the years it took to secure financing told the filmmakers that the film could not be made. Not only was the dialogue primarily in Spanish and Mayan, but its subject was considered problematic at best. Compounding these difficulties was the script's innovative style, modeled after Latin American magic-realist literature.

Anna Thomas believes that *El Norte*'s overall success is due primarily to the favorable word-of-mouth generated in both the Anglo and Hispanic communities. She believes that despite a marketing campaign to depoliticize the film, *El Norte* did change people's minds. That influence, she says, was ultimately the most deeply felt satisfaction for her and her husband, Greg Nava, as filmmakers. Greg Nava's only regret is that with all the film's success, the filmmakers never saw any more money than the initial guarantee. He pointed out that the filmmakers did not entirely recoup their deferred salaries and had to personally pay off outstanding debts to DuArt Labs.

Ira Deutchman and Amir Malin of Cinecom are very proud of the release of *El Norte*, feeling that they avoided the potential traps of the film, allowing it to finally reach its intended Anglo and Hispanic audience, which in turn created positive word-of-mouth. It was also a landmark film for Cinecom since it achieved a very high profile for what was generally perceived as a tough sell. The success of the film was a strong factor in achieving a higher level of film acquisitions for the company.

THE GOOD FIGHT

(February 1984)

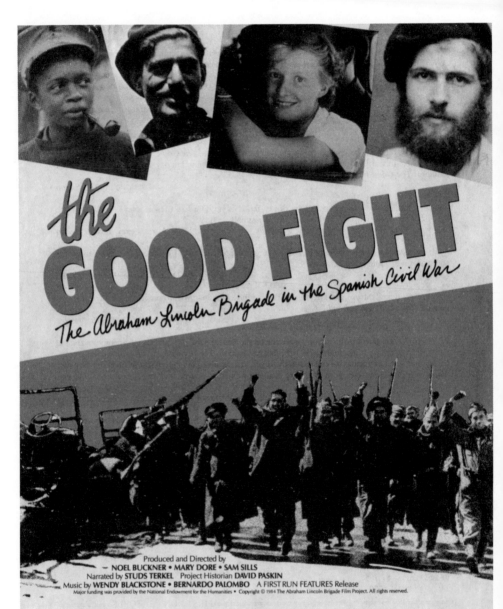

the GOOD FIGHT

The Abraham Lincoln Brigade in the Spanish Civil War

Produced and Directed by
— NOEL BUCKNER • MARY DORE • SAM SILLS
Narrated by STUDS TERKEL   Project Historian DAVID PASKIN
Music by WENDY BLACKSTONE • BERNARDO PALOMBO   A FIRST RUN FEATURES Release

Major funding was provided by the National Endowment for the Humanities • Copyright © 1984 The Abraham Lincoln Brigade Film Project. All rights reserved.

"THE GOOD FIGHT MAKES HISTORY DANCE!"

Boston Globe Editorial, February 17th, 1984

PRINCIPALS	*Producers/Directors*	Noel Buckner, Mary Dore, and Sam Sills
	Narration	Studs Terkel
	Project historian	David Paskin
DISTRIBUTORS	*Theatrical*	First Run Features
	Homevideo	Kino International
	Pay cable	First Run Features
	Nontheatrical	First Run Features
	Broadcast	Producers
	Foreign	CORI
THEATRICAL	*Opening dates*	February 17, 1984 (Boston)
		March 28, 1984 (New York)
	Total playdates	100
	Box-office gross	not available
	Total distributor costs*	$85,000
	Advance	0
	Publicity	30,000–40,000
	Prints	10,000
	Advertising	35,000
ANCILLARY	*Homevideo*	not available
	Nontheatrical	$30,000 (gross)
	Foreign	15,000 (gross)
PARTICIPANTS CONTACTED		Noel Buckner
		Mary Dore
		Sam Sills
		Janet Cole
		Karen Cooper
		Fran Spielman
		Aaron Ezekiel

* Note: The producers advanced the $30–40,000 they spent for travel and promotion. In addition, the distributor deducted $45,000 from rentals to cover its costs, particularly newspaper advertising.

FILM SYNOPSIS

The Good Fight is a feature-length documentary that chronicles the Abraham Lincoln Brigade, the 3,200 anti-fascist American volunteers who fought with the Loyalists in the Spanish Civil War. The story is told through interviews with eleven veterans of the Brigade, and integrates extensive black-and-white archival footage and still photographs.

DEVELOPMENT

Genesis · *The Good Fight* is a feature-length documentary about the experience of the Abraham Lincoln Brigade—3,200 anti-fascist American volunteers who fought Franco, Hitler, and Mussolini in the Spanish Civil War (1936–37). The Brigade was part of an outpouring of 45,000 volunteers from all over the world, including escapees from fascist Italy and Nazi Germany, who flocked to the defense of the democratically elected Spanish Republic. There were over 1,600 American casualties in this heroic but doomed campaign.

Boston filmmakers Noel Buckner and Mary Dore took the first steps in their seven-year commitment to the project in the fall of 1977. They were in New York to promote their documentary *Children of Labor*, a study of the Midwest Finnish-American community, at the New York Film Festival. Sam Sills, then an intern at the *Village Voice*, reviewed the film and sought the filmmakers for an interview. In the process, he expressed his own desire to work in documentary film.

Soon after, Sills read an account in the *New York Times* of a heroic reception given to the Lincoln Brigade veterans returning to Spain shortly after the death of General Francisco Franco. He contacted

82

Dore and Buckner in Boston with the idea of making a film on the Brigade, and met with an enthusiastic response. Says Sills:

> We had a common social perspective, and we wanted to change people's perceptions through documentary film. This was an incomparable story for us. It was a story about how people became committed to a cause, and then how their commitment fared under fire in Spain. Finally, there was a sense of immediacy to the material because the volunteers were now elderly. We needed to act then and there.

The trio agreed to move ahead with the project. Sills, as the novice who, by his own admission, "needed to earn the respect of the two pros," did much of the original spadework. With the assistance of Buckner and Dore, he wrote a proposal to the NEH for seed money and began research on the veterans. At the same time he worked at a succession of jobs to deepen his knowledge of the film business, including a stint at New Line Cinema, an apprenticeship with Deborah Shaffer on *The Wobblies* (released in 1979), and as coordinator of the 1979 Alternative Cinema Conference.

Financing • When the NEH granted $20,000 for development in late 1979, Sills and project historian David Paskin began work on a proposal for major NEH funding. In the meantime, Dore and Buckner were developing their research base, acquiring photographs and stock film footage and taping interviews with Brigade veterans.

Of this $20,000 grant, half was spent on salaries for Sills and Paskin, and the balance was used to make a 16mm pilot reel based on interviews with two veterans. Dore believes that the pilot reel, by bringing an obscure subject to life, was significant in securing further NEH support.

In December 1980, the NEH awarded the project a $225,000 grant. Since the grant was made by the Carter-appointed Endowment regime, the filmmakers feared it could be challenged in the first few months of the Reagan administration.

Anticipating an audience • Buckner recalls making a critical decision when the production grant was received:

We resolved at the very beginning to make a feature-length documentary. The subject was that big. It needed ninety minutes just to introduce the context and to tell the stories of the veterans.

However, we knew that most feature documentaries are never seen because they are tough to sell theatrically, and they're too long for classrooms. We were concerned that our egos were pushing us toward the glory associated with a theatrical release. However, the story was just too significant and too complex to do any other way!

PRODUCTION

A joint career documenting the labor movement had prepared Dore and Buckner for frugal living. *Children of Labor* had cost only $8,000. The filmmakers had equipped their own home as a production office, complete with editing and processing equipment. Buckner now comments:

> If we hadn't bought a house in a marginal neighborhood when real estate was cheap, we could never have afforded to be filmmakers. If we weren't living rent-free, we might be schoolteachers today.

Initially, the $225,000 NEH grant seemed enough to cover expenses and pay modest salaries. Salaries were set at $15,000 for one year, after which the filmmakers went on unemployment benefits. All their accommodations during their travels depended on the hospitality of friends. However, as research costs mounted, their budgetary limitations became severe. Over 130 Lincoln veterans were tracked down and interviewed on audiotape in dozens of cities in the United States and Mexico. Of this pool of interviewees, thirteen representative and articulate veterans were chosen for in-depth interviewing. Eleven appear in the film. Their personalities can be glimpsed from a *Good Fight* press release:

> Ed Balchowsky was a pianist and art student at the University of Illinois before going to Spain. He became a local legend in the Chicago area playing in bars, and still tours occasionally with folk singer Utah Phillips, who has immortalized Ed in a song.

> Ruth Davidow, a nurse in Spain, has since worked in numerous causes including the civil rights movement in Mississippi and the American

Indian occupation of Alcatraz. Ruth makes films on aging and health issues and recently retired from teaching nursing.

Evelyn Hutchins was born in Washington State to a Wobbly father and a suffragette mother. She was a children's photographer before going to Spain as an ambulance driver. After Spain, she was a dancer, union worker, and political activist until her death in 1982.

Salaria Kea O'Reilly was born to a Cherokee father and a West Indian mother in Ohio. She studied nursing in segregated hospitals in New York City before going to Spain. She returned to Ohio after her retirement from nursing with her husband Pat O'Reilly, an Irish International Brigades volunteer she married in Spain.

Milt Wolff, a Brooklyn native, friend of Ernest Hemingway, and twenty-three-year-old commander of the Abraham Lincoln Brigade, later fought with the O.S.S. in World War II. He has been a printer, short-story writer, and is still active with many organizations in the San Francisco area.

Mary Dore traveled to Spain and England, where she located treasure troves of 35mm stock film footage from the Civil War era. Most of it was offered free of royalties, but still required the expense of a reduction from 35mm to 16mm. Some footage was purchased on a deferred payment basis. About one-third of the final film is either stock footage or still photos, including some by famed *Life* photographer Robert Capa.

The filmmakers were offered encouragement, technical support, and sympathy throughout the production process. Needing someone to read a section of narration, the filmmakers sent a telegram to Colleen Dewhurst at New York's Plymouth Theater, where she was appearing in *You Can't Take It with You*. Two days later, Dewhurst replied, "I'll do whatever you want."

The editing was particularly exhausting. It went on six days a week for two years. Buckner explains the problems:

> We wanted a film that was neither simplistic trash nor the equivalent of a doctoral dissertation. It had to appeal simultaneously to viewers who lacked knowledge of the period, and to others who needed subtlety.
> We completed a roughcut, and screened it to several representative audiences including blacks, veterans, groups of workers, and our

advisors. We were stunned to find that many people didn't know what fascism was. We went back to work based on these responses.

Finally, it took time to realize that our obligation to the overall story was greater than our attraction to anecdotes that, however irresistible, nonetheless deflected the viewer from the narrative or context.

The final cost of *The Good Fight* was $245,000, divided roughly as follows:

Stock footage (royalties and processing)	20%
Salaries of coproducers	20%
Film and film processing	15%
Travel	15%
Other salaries	10%
All other	20%

Sam Sills emphasizes that this $245,000 cost of production does not take into account the enormous "in kind" contributions made by the filmmakers, including their unpaid labor for more than a year and use of their own production equipment.

DISTRIBUTION DEAL

Making the deal · The filmmakers assumed from the beginning that *The Good Fight*, like most independently produced documentaries, would not be profitable enough to interest a major distributor, particularly given its obscure subject matter.

Their marketing philosophy for *The Good Fight* recognized the difficulties of their task:

It's a hard sell: a feature documentary on a group of old Commies who went away to a war in Spain. We knew from the beginning that we would have to spend several weeks before each opening conducting a low-cost outreach campaign. This strategy involves free screenings to influential members of the film's likely constituency, such as organizations for the elderly, teachers, students, and community leaders, as well as members of labor, ethnic, political, and religious groups. It also involves exerting every effort to attract press attention, usually by working with a local publicist.

The trio discovered soon after completing the film that their need to participate personally in this intense grassroots promotion effort would narrow their options in choosing a distributor. After its screening at the 1983 IFP Film Market in New York, five distribution companies made offers: New Yorker Films, Teleculture, Cinema Guild, Kino International, and First Run Features.

Mary Dore explains how the filmmakers assessed the interested parties:

> We checked the catalogs for a good fit. Teleculture had had a hit with Fassbinder's *Berlin Alexanderplatz*, but they seemed too evasive about theatrical openings, and their proposals were lackluster. New Yorker Films had an absolutely thrilling catalog, but we knew that *The Good Fight* presented a very original marketing challenge, and they seemed unfocused about its unique theatrical problems. Cinema Guild had an excellent catalog, we liked the principal, Gary Crowdus, but he wasn't doing much in the theatrical market. Kino International is a specialist in distributing foreign classical films to the college market. We liked its principal, Donald Krim, but he lacked experience with American independents, and he had less commitment to a grassroots campaign. It seemed everyone wanted *The Good Fight* for the education market, but we lacked confidence in their theatrical proposals.

Dore recalls the strengths of First Run Features:

> We were very attracted to the principals. Fran Spielman had been in the theatrical business for fifty years, Priscilla Forance had years of experience in the educational/16mm market, and we were very comfortable with Janet Cole's experience with grassroots marketing. They loved *The Good Fight*, and they were convinced it would tie in with the controversial political films they had handled.

Buckner outlines the three alternatives they considered:

- First, we could self-distribute. The problem here was that we would take on all the risk of the release, all of the promotional expenses, and an exhausting personal schedule while we were still exhausted from producing the film.
- Second, we could successfully self-distribute in one or two major markets and then use our track record to persuade a major distributor to really commit to the film and to our involvement in the campaign.

. Third, we could go with First Run—a compromise that involved us in the release, but added their expertise.

The filmmakers had no illusions about the additional effort required by distribution through First Run. Dore saw it "as a full-time commitment to distribution over the next year of my life."

Terms of the deal · In November 1983 the coproducers chose First Run Features. Only First Run had a strong commitment to grassroots promotion and would allow the filmmakers to participate in marketing decisions. Financial considerations also played a part. All the other distributors proposed to split theatrical and nontheatrical revenues 50/50 percent after print and promotional costs.

The normal First Run theatrical deal gives the filmmakers 75 percent of net rentals, with the filmmakers required to front most of the necessary theatrical outlays, including lab and printing costs, publicity, phone, and travel. First Run normally fronted advertising costs but recouped them from gross film rentals. The filmmakers accepted these terms. A 55/45 percent split was applied to educational distribution, with the filmmakers again meeting lab and printing costs.

Sam Sills recalls his reaction to the terms of the deal:

We would have preferred a 50/50 split after distribution costs. But First Run was financially weakened from its recent commitment to *Wild Style* [see case study]. They couldn't afford another theatrical launch. Therefore we had no choice. If we wanted theatrical distribution, we had to go with First Run, on the terms that they could afford.

According to Janet Cole, then a principal at First Run, *The Good Fight* was worth competing for:

We loved the film from the first screening. It was a perfect fit for our collection, which includes *The War at Home*, *Soldier Girls*, and *Rosie the Riveter*. These titles had given us experience in grassroots audience development, and with working alongside filmmakers who were involved in the distribution of their films.

But she also knew that documentaries were bad news in the theatrical marketplace:

The truth is that documentary films, even Academy Award winners, get nowhere theatrically without the intense, exhausting on-site work that *no* distributor will ever do. Therefore, the filmmakers *must* do it if it is to happen at all. The commitment of the producers of *The Good Fight* was a critical factor in our attraction to the film. It was their determination that gave the film a chance.

MARKETING CAMPAIGN

Strategy · The coproducers intended to shift the focus of *The Good Fight* according to their target audience. For teachers and educators, it was primarily presented as a documentary of the thirties. For community groups, they emphasized that it was a portrait of a group of unusual Americans who had unapologetically taken a moral stand.

There was, however, an important factor complicating the strategy of marketing *The Good Fight* as a progressive documentary on the thirties. Independent filmmakers Julie Reichert and Jim Klein were working on their own feature documentary about American Communists in the thirties, a film called *Seeing Red*. Grants from NEH, the American Film Institute (AFI), and Ohio arts organizations covered their $350,000 production costs. *Seeing Red* was more of a background film than *The Good Fight*, but the content necessarily overlapped. It included, for example, an important section on the Spanish Civil War, and worse, Bill Bailey was a star interviewee in both films. Noel Buckner calls it a "disastrous situation." He says:

> We were locked in step together for years. It was always so clear to me that we would come out at the same time, and that we would, at best, diffuse each other's attempts to get out to a larger audience. At worst we were cutting the same small audience in half. There didn't seem to be anything that either of us could do about it.

The producers of *Seeing Red* were determined to reach a wide audience and to avoid the traps described by associate producer Aaron Ezekiel as "the documentary film ghetto or the Left film ghetto." They were particularly aware of the opportunities and pitfalls of self-distribution. In 1982, Reichert and Klein were founder-

members of New Day Films, a co-operative devoted to the nontheatrical distribution of films about social change, and Reichert was also
coauthor of *Doing It Yourself*, a book on nontheatrical self-
distribution.

After successful screenings of *Seeing Red* at Telluride and at the
New York Film Festival, it was still almost a flip of the coin whether to
self-distribute or to go with an offer from one of several interested
distributors, including New Yorker Films and Island Alive.

According to Ezekiel, the coproducers felt that their film would not
get the attention it required from a commercial distributor, and neither
would they get the support they needed for the intensive community
work that they felt was critical to the film's success. They therefore
elected to self-distribute, but retained the services of an experienced
theatrical booker to act as consultant throughout the distribution of the
film. They were also supported by several student interns.

Seeing Red opened in Los Angeles in late 1983 before *The Good
Fight* and in time to qualify for a surprise Academy Award nomination. But for the rest of their theatrical lives, the two films were in
distribution at the same time. The result, according to Buckner, was
that "whichever film opened first in a city would exhaust the media in
that market, and do better." This competitive situation was most
actively felt in media coverage. The *Village Voice*, for instance, turned
down a piece associating *The Good Fight* with the thirties because a
short time before it had run a feature on *Seeing Red* from the same
perspective.

The marketing strategy for *Seeing Red* was very similar to that for
The Good Fight. Benefits were organized for political groups in order to
build word-of-mouth, and neighborhood community groups and
senior-citizen organizations were targeted. The subject matter of the
film was somewhat depoliticized for this audience in order to position
the film as an exploration of "what it's like to live an involved life."

The producers of *Seeing Red* downplayed the competitive impact of
The Good Fight. In fact, they felt that each film would help draw media
attention to the other. They did strive, however, to avoid simultaneous
openings in the same cities.

The totally unexpected Oscar nomination was a great boost to the
morale of the distribution team of Reichert, Klein, and Ezekiel. But it
did not directly translate into additional playdates. According to

Ezekiel, "It got us some attention from exhibitors, but their first question was always, 'What was your first week's box office in New York?' "

Promotion and publicity · In the three months before the Boston opening, Dore, Buckner, and Sills held fundraising screenings for friends and supporters in New York and Boston. The screenings grossed $10,000 (at a cost of $3,000), and helped defray startup distribution costs such as prints, advertising, and the production of fliers, posters, stills, and press kits.

The campaign involved direct mail, using lists generously provided by supporters, friends, and veterans. This effort, according to the filmmakers, "merely warmed us up" for the considerably more complex and labor-intensive work of preparing for the theatrical opening.

In addition to the fundraisers, preview screenings were held for teachers, community leaders, and critics. Fliers were sent to historical journals and leaflets were distributed at many cultural and political events. Mailing lists were obtained from local progressive organizations and publications for a mass mailing of a *Good Fight* flier. Friends and relatives were recruited to help with the mailings, to saturate colleges with posters, and to wheat-paste posters all over town. While First Run and the local theater courted the mainstream press, grassroots publicist Carol Van Valkenburgh pursued as many neighborhood, ethnic, and political newspapers as possible. Considerable press curiosity was aroused by the presence of Bill Bailey, the Brigade veteran who, as a young anti-fascist, ripped the swastika flag from the German liner *Bremen* when it berthed in New York harbor.

THEATRICAL RELEASE

Strategy · The producers of *The Good Fight* and First Run Features settled on a longterm release strategy. Theatrical dates were emphasized to generate reviews and press coverage, to expand the film's potential in other theatrical markets, and to create interest in the semi- and nontheatrical markets, including cable and public television.

The filmmakers had always planned to open in Boston (Dore's and Buckner's hometown), where they had excellent contacts. Boston's sizeable college audience was also a strength, though Janet Cole recalls that despite its demographics Boston has always been a strong but unpredictable market for independent films, *except* for those made by local filmmakers.

The timing of the Boston opening was determined by two factors. First, in October 1983, Karen Cooper, director of the Film Forum in lower Manhattan, had scheduled *The Good Fight* for a two-week locked run in March 1984. The filmmakers recognized this as "a great opportunity, since Karen Cooper has such rapport with the press that her films always get reviewed." In addition, a strong run at the Film Forum can help build sufficient press and industry attention to attract a subsequent commercial run in New York and other cities.

Second, the academic community, particularly the history faculty, was a key target market. Accordingly, the theatrical opening had to be timed to the beginning of the semester, either in February or October, so that teachers could integrate the playdates into their semester schedules. With the Film Forum committed to a March opening, the producers planned a February 1984 opening in Boston.

Throughout the process of developing and implementing their release strategy, the producers turned to other independent filmmakers for advice and support. According to Mary Dore, their advice "made the difference between total reliance on First Run, and participation with them on key decisions."

Opening run · *The Good Fight* premiered on February 17, 1984, in Boston. It was booked at the Copley Place, a new nine-screen complex that, according to the *Boston Globe*, "is decorated in marble and brass; croissants and espresso are served at the refreshment stand." Other titles scheduled for the Copley opening were Fellini's *The Ship Sails On* and *Entre Nous*. First Run felt that promotional activities associated with the opening of the complex, including full-page "identity" advertisements, would give *The Good Fight* some of the special attention it required. They also believed that the multiple miniscreen nature of the complex potentially promised a longer run with the option of moving the film to a smaller screen, rather than pulling it when admissions declined.

The Boston promotional campaign emphasized that the filmmakers were from Boston, and included radio talk-shows, free ticket distribution through the local public radio station, TV appearances, the distribution of fliers at demonstrations, extensive leafleting, and courting of the small press.

The opening was greeted by very favorable press coverage, including an editorial in the *Boston Globe* recommending *The Good Fight* as a documentary that "makes history dance." The editorial praised the film as

> a reminder that brave people are the conscience of any generation. It stirs pride at what citizens who take American values seriously have done and still might do.

The film sold out its first three nights in the 140-seat theater. This was a heady weekend for the filmmakers. A feature article in the *Boston Globe* described them as "glowing in the light of sold-out business." Despite being moved to a smaller screen, the film played for two weeks as the third-best box-office performer at the nine-screen complex, doing even better than the Fellini film. Then, on March 6, it was suddenly pulled from the Copley Place.

The filmmakers were completely dismayed. Buckner remembers the time with some bitterness:

> It's my belief that we were thrown out because we lacked clout. The exhibitor took the longterm view by keeping on films, such as *The Ship Sails On*, that were doing significantly less business than we were. They didn't want to jeopardize their relationships with the major distributors.

Dore adds that their opening at the Copley Place was sponsored by the Institute for Contemporary Art (ICA). This entailed "a three-way split" between the exhibitor, the distributor, and ICA, thereby lowering the exhibitor's return below breakeven.

The Orson Welles Theater in Cambridge was available, but only after a seventeen-day wait. It was a suspenseful hiatus for the producers and First Run, who were afraid that, despite the excellent reviews and editorial coverage, the film could sink into oblivion. They carried out an "immense" leafleting campaign and ran print ads in local publications. The move over, on Friday, March 23, was a success, and *The Good Fight* ran for six full weeks at the Orson Welles.

National playoff · Concurrent with the Boston screenings, the preopening campaign was duplicated in New York, with the addition of a major fundraising screening for the local Committee for Medical Aid for El Salvador. The fundraiser was hosted by Colleen Dewhurst and Dr. Charlie Clements, who was to be the subject of Deborah Shaffer's 1986 Oscar-winning documentary, *Witness to War. The Good Fight* opened at the Film Forum on March 28, shortly after the opening of *Seeing Red*. After two weeks it moved to the smaller Bleecker Street Cinema, where it ran for six weeks. It was also booked for two weeks at the uptown New Yorker Cinema, and made the *Variety* "top fifty." Again, the press coverage was favorable, including positive reviews and features that picked up on Bill Bailey's colorful contribution to the advertising campaign. Vincent Canby recommended the film as "both sorrowful and inspiring," though his review suggests the problems raised by *Seeing Red*:

> The spirit of the old American Left remains undiminished, at least on movie screens. Already in the middle of a successful New York first run is the Oscar-nominated *Seeing Red*. Now comes another equally fine documentary, *The Good Fight*, which features the moving testimony of eleven veterans of the Lincoln Brigade.
>
> Though *The Good Fight* covers some of the same ground as *Seeing Red*, the two films should be seen as complementing each other. *Seeing Red* is the story of an era. *The Good Fight* is about that same era as it is reflected in the various American responses to what was probably the single most important event of that era, the war in Spain that, after the fact, could be recognized as the curtain-raiser for World War II.

The humor of Bill Bailey's contribution to the promotional campaign can be understood from the lead paragraph of David Hinckley's *Daily News* feature article on *The Good Fight*:

> "One way you get political," says Bill Bailey, "is when you're out on the picket line, asking for a few more dollars in your pay and some cop comes along and knocks you down and calls you a Communist. And you get up and say, 'I'm no Communist, I'm an anti-Communist,' and he says, 'I don't care what kind of Communist you are' and knocks you down again. It's an old joke, but that's one way it happens."

Buckner remembers that the New York run confirmed his sense of the marketing challenge posed by the film:

First, the importance of the preview screenings became more obvious. This was a film that people on the Left would see, and realize that it said something meaningful about themselves that they could not so powerfully express in their own words. They would not only tell their friends to go see it, they would actually buy tickets and take them along. It was, therefore, critical for us to make the exhausting efforts of an outreach campaign to capture our core audience. This was not something that our distributor could do alone.

Second, we saw that we would face enormous skepticism in each new market. In New York, they said, "Yes, it's a wonderful film, and it's doing well in Boston, *but* this is New York." And later in Seattle they'd say, "Yes, *but* that's the East Coast." No one would ever believe that it would do well because of the appeal of its subject matter.

The Boston and New York openings cost the filmmakers between $30,000 and $35,000 in distribution costs, including advertising, travel and entertainment, publicists' fees, prints, fliers, one-sheets, mailings, and screening room rentals for preview audiences. These costs were usually paid for by the filmmakers. They were partly financed by the fundraising screenings and partly by their own savings. First Run paid for some advertising costs, and later deducted them from film rentals.

The experience in Boston and New York precipitated a growing disillusion with theatrical distribution on the part of the coproducers. Buckner recalls, "We were exhausted, and yet increasingly depressed to see everyone get their pieces of the grosses and finding little left for us."

The Boston and New York openings generated excellent coverage in the national progressive press. For instance film critic Katha Pollitt, who described it as "a New Left homage to the Old Left," wrote:

Of all the movies I've seen while reviewing films for *The Nation*, *The Good Fight* is one you should be sure not to miss. Informative but not ponderous, technically skilled but not slick, heart-stirring but not maudlin, *The Good Fight* is a triumph for the school of political filmmaking that brought us *Union Maids*, *Seeing Red*, *The Atomic Cafe*, and *The Weavers: Wasn't That a Time!* [see case study].

However, *The Good Fight* did not gather momentum from favorable coverage in the mainstream national media. Reviews in *Time* and the

Wall Street Journal were negative. This, according to Sam Sills, "reinforced the crucial importance of our outreach program."

Mary Dore traveled to San Francisco to prepare for her first opening without the close support of First Run's East Coast staff. She was committed to the grassroots promotional strategy of organizing a benefit screening, but had "only a dim idea" of which community group might wish to become associated with a fundraiser of this type. Dore recalls a more fundamental problem with a preopening fundraiser:

> The theater owners simply didn't want a benefit! They saw this as a film with limited audience interest, so a benefit screening pulled tickets right out of their pockets. Mel Novikoff, of the Surf chain, was convinced that *Seeing Red*, which opened a month earlier, had eroded its audience with a benefit.

Dore remembers that Novikoff was also concerned that *The Good Fight* had been screened at the recent San Francisco Film Festival. He argued that this both eroded his audience and removed his ability to control the press. In a compromise solution, Dore organized a benefit party following the opening night screening; she describes it as a "stale nachos and dip" affair. Ronnie Gilbert, one of the original Weavers, attended, and "several thousands of dollars" were raised for the Salvadoran Medical Relief Fund.

Despite hiring a local publicist for $500 a week, Dore "had to beg" the editors of the *San Francisco Chronicle* to run a piece on *The Good Fight* in the Arts section. They obliged by reprinting a feature article from the *New York Times*. Dore felt that their tepid response "was largely based on their earlier coverage of *Seeing Red*." Other promotional activities included a direct-mail campaign to Bay Area subscribers of the *Nation* and the progressive weekly *In These Times*.

The Surf chain booked the film for an open-ended run at the Surf Theater. Based on the moderate first-week gross, they decided to pull the film after the second week, even though the grosses had picked up. *The Good Fight* moved to the Northside Cinema in Berkeley and played, according to Mary Dore, "a dim and frustrating" run of two weeks.

Dore recalls "the shocking lessons" of the Bay Area openings:

Despite their best efforts, First Run lacked the clout on the West Coast to give us decisive assistance. The responsibilities of distribution seemed to be falling more than ever on our shoulders.

The Berkeley run further confirmed the importance of a systematically organized outreach campaign, but we lacked the time, energy, and finances to coordinate such an effort in every market.

Dore summed up her personal experience as "a huge strain against overwhelming odds," and adds:

> I was completely outnumbered in a strange city, basically sleeping on the floors of people who didn't know me, frantically (and with more than a little guilt) using their telephones to ask favors of other people who didn't know me. Despite incredible generosity, it was very tough!

A Los Angeles opening was planned for early fall. Dore arrived a month before the opening to organize a series of promotional and fundraising events. These included a gala screening for Academy members and a fundraising benefit attended by over thirty Lincoln Brigade veterans and hosted by Dr. Charlie Clements with Stanley Sheinbaum. The gala raised $15,000 for Clinica Oscar Romero and El Rescate, a Los Angeles clinic for Central American refugees. Dore received $1,000 for her expenses.

Dore discovered that, as in San Francisco, it was very difficult to attract media attention. Her publicity efforts even extended to delivering a gift-wrapped cassette to a television critic who finally reviewed the film the day before it closed.

A one-week booking at the Nuart Theater was followed by a nine-day locked run at the Los Feliz, a new second-run house. On October 21, 1984, Mary Dore's one-year commitment to distribute *The Good Fight* came to an end.

Sam Sills coordinated the next opening, in Chicago, at the Biograph Cinema in January 1985. First Run had negotiated for several months with the management of the Fine Arts Theater. This was the producers' first choice due to its string of hit runs, including *Stop Making Sense*. However, after several "extremely frustrating delays and postponements following promises of firm dates for our opening," First Run switched to the slightly less prestigious Biograph, whose management committed to a January opening and an open-ended run.

The Biograph hired an established local publicist, who succeeded in placing major feature articles in both Chicago dailies. The cost of the publicist was deducted from the distributor's portion of film rentals. Sam Sills appeared on a local public television program, and *The Good Fight* was featured on Studs Terkel's radio program during opening week (Terkel was the film's narrator). Sills also organized a special preopening screening for the Hispanic community, which was attended by a standing-room-only crowd of organizers and community leaders. A similar though unsuccessful effort was organized for the South Side black community.

An opening night benefit for the Committee in Solidarity with the People of El Salvador (CISPES), hosted by Terkel, raised several thousand dollars and covered the expenses incurred by the grassroots campaign. Sills remembers the event with pride:

> The CISPES organizers were thrilled. They didn't expect the producers to roll up their sleeves or to attract Studs Terkel to one of their events. The fundraiser included a postopening reception, and a representative from the FMLN [a Salvadoran opposition group] was present. The event dramatically raised CISPES's profile in Chicago.

The opening, again preceded by an intensive campaign of mailings, leafleting, and postering, was attended by Brigade veterans from Chicago and from as far away as Wisconsin. But Sills felt that a very negative review by a second-string critic for the *Chicago Tribune* was quite damaging. He describes it as "a vicious right-wing political attack on the film," and he speculates that Siskel and Ebert's failure to review *The Good Fight* on "Sneak Previews" was "a possible consequence of their wish to avoid the political heat aroused by the *Tribune* review."

The first weekend was weak and a "mediocre" two-week run followed at the Biograph. Asked about the poor Chicago run, Sills says:

> We did a great job. We played by all the grassroots rules. We had an excellent exhibitor, and very good publicity. But no one showed up.

He offers as possible explanations: the record-breaking January cold, the absence of a Siskel and Ebert review, and the generally poor performance of documentaries in the Chicago market (*Seeing Red* also played poorly there).

However, Sills points to the CISPES benefit as a huge payoff for the producers:

Political groups desperately need events that rally their supporters and create new links with the community. *The Good Fight* created an inspiring moment for CISPES. When it happened, we realized that even though we hadn't been able to define it, this was what we had wanted to achieve all along.

There were no other open-ended runs but many one- or two-night screenings were arranged in other markets, many sponsored by universities and film societies, which occasionally offered guest-speaker fees for the filmmakers. Sills feels that the impact of *The Good Fight* on those who had little knowledge of the Lincoln Brigade or the Spanish Civil War was "particularly rewarding."

OTHER MARKETS

Homevideo · Distributed by Kino International.

Pay cable · First Run Features negotiated a sale to Bravo for $7,500 for ten screenings. Manhattan's cable channel Uptown also purchased *The Good Fight*.

Nontheatrical · First Run Features reports approximately $30,000 in income.

Broadcast · The contract with the NEH stipulated that PBS has first refusal rights. PBS required the filmmakers to raise the necessary funds for broadcast (to cover cost of feeds and the re-edit for timing, etc.), and after repeated efforts, the film was finally aired on the "POV" series during the summer of 1988.

Foreign · In Australia, the distributor Cineaction acquired the title following a screening at the 1985 Melbourne Film Festival, and opened the film in July 1986. In Israel, Histradut, a national labor organization, purchased theatrical and nontheatrical rights for

$2,500. Swedish TV rights were sold for $5,000. Broadcast and theatrical rights were sold in East Germany for $5,000. The English theatrical distributor Contemporary Films has the U.K. rights on a revenue-sharing basis. There was no advance, however, and little activity has been reported.

REVIEW

The Good Fight is a feature-length documentary about the role of a group of anti-fascist American volunteers who, as the Abraham Lincoln Brigade, fought in the Spanish Civil War.

Financed principally by two grants totaling $245,000 made by the NEH in 1980, filmmakers Mary Dore, Noel Buckner, and Sam Sills completed the project in 1983.

The producers knew from the beginning that an independently produced documentary on an obscure topic would require very special handling in distribution. In particular, they expected to work closely with their distributor to build audiences through community outreach programs.

First Run Features was chosen primarily because it demonstrated the greatest enthusiasm, experience, and competence in the theatrical distribution of a film of this type. A significant attraction was its willingness to involve the filmmakers in the distribution process. First Run offered a 75/25 percent split in favor of the filmmakers with all costs coming out of the filmmakers' share. The filmmakers' compensation for their own distribution costs was to be covered by their share.

The Good Fight opened in Boston to very favorable reviews and excellent editorial coverage, which highlighted the involvement of Brigade veterans in the promotional campaign. Openings in other cities were preceded by benefit screenings for local Central America action groups, and by preview screenings for educational and community groups. The filmmakers do not evaluate their efforts by the film's box-office results. Sills emphasizes that *The Good Fight* "helped resurrect a lost chapter of American history." Their political motives in making the film were satisfied by its extensive use for political fundraisers, and they were delighted to see audiences "recognize a part of themselves" in the stories of the veterans. According to Sills, "the film succeeded in bringing together people who took a moral stand unapologetically."

Dore, Buckner, and Sills ruefully characterize their distribution experience in terms of their own naïveté; they were shocked by how upfront expenses escalated and by the long delays encountered in receiving their portion of box-office rentals.

INTERNATIONAL ACCLAIM
Few motion pictures have ever been so honored— or so acclaimed.

Co-Winner, First Place "Best Independent Film", U.S. Film Festival
Co-Winner, Grand Prix "Golden Bear" Award, Berlin International Film Festival
New York Film Festival (American Independents)
Special Presentation, American Film Institute, Washington, D.C.
Denver International Film Festival / Baltimore International Film Festival
Seattle International Film Festival / Sydney, Australia Film Festival
Portugese International Film Festival / Community Film Association
Northwest Film Festival / Flaherty Film Festival / London Film Festival
Toronto International Film Festival /Aspen International Film Festival
Chicago Women's Film Festival / Winner, Western Heritage Award, Cowboy Hall of Fame
Special Showing, "New American Filmmakers", Directors Guild of America

"AN UNCOMMONLY BEAUTIFUL FILM! AN UNUSUALLY ACCOMPLISHED WORK!" "FILLED WITH WONDERFUL LIFE!" "A RIGOROUS AUTHENTICITY.
—Vincent Canby, N.Y. Times   —Roger Ebert, Chicago Sun-Times
CONCHATA FERRELL IS FORMIDABLE!" "HAS THE JUICE OF LIFE IN IT!
—Donald Barthelme, The New Yorker
IT IS ALSO FUNNY! WHAT A PICTURE!" "RAVISHINGLY BEAUTIFUL! A
—Michael Kernan, Washington Post
SHEER JOY TO WATCH! A REAL PLEASURE TO SEE!" "FINELY AND
—Derek Malcolm, Cosmopolitan
FEELINGLY PLAYED BY RIP TORN AND CONCHATA FERRELL!"
—David Robinson, London Times
"MASTERPIECE!" "EXCEPTIONALLY FINE!" "A SPECIAL EXPERIENCE
—Bob Ellis, Nation Review, Australia   —Rena Andrews, Denver Post
WELL WORTH SEEING!" "A VISUALLY BEAUTIFUL AND EMOTIONALLY
—Ted Mahar, The Portland Oregonian
MOVING FILM!" "STRONG, EMOTIONAL IMPACT!"
—Terry Orme, Salt Lake Tribune   —Clarke Taylor, Los Angeles Times

HEARTLAND

A Wilderness Women/Filmhaus Production "Heartland"
Starring Rip Torn · Conchata Ferrell · Lilia Skala · with Barry Primus · And Introducing Megan Folsom
Directed by Richard Pearce · Written by Beth Ferris · Executive Producer Annick Smith · Produced by Michael Hausman & Beth Ferris
Production Designer Patrizia Von Brandenstein · Costume Designer Hilary Rosenfeld · Music by Charles Gross · Edited by Bill Yahraus
Director of Photography Fred Murphy · An N E H presentation · In Color · A Levitt-Pickman release

PREMIERE
SUNDAY, AUGUST 23RD

5th Avenue & 58th Street . MU 8-2013

PRINCIPALS	*Director*	Richard Pearce
	Executive Producer	Annick Smith
	Producers	Beth Ferris and Michael Hausman
	Writer	Beth Ferris, with William Kittredge
	Principal cast	Conchata Ferrell, Rip Torn, and Megan Folsom
DISTRIBUTORS	*Distribution agent*	Jeremy Zimmer, formerly with the William Morris Agency (L. A.)
	Theatrical	Pickman Films
	Homevideo	Thorn/EMI
	Pay cable	Thorn/EMI
	Nontheatrical	Twyman Films, Inc.
	Broadcast	Wilderness Women Productions/ Pickman Films
	Foreign	Wilderness Women Productions
THEATRICAL	*Opening date*	August 23, 1981
	Total playdates	500+
	Box-office gross	$3,500,000 (e)
	Gross film rental	1,377,972 (Pickman) 70,000 (Wilderness Women)
	Total distributor costs (theatrical and nontheatrical)	541,473
	Advance	15,000 (for internegative)
	Publicity	not available
	Prints	not available
	Producer net	557*
ANCILLARY	*Homevideo*	$ 125,000
	Pay cable	63,000
	Nontheatrical	not available
	Broadcast	25,000
	Foreign	167,000
PARTICIPANTS CONTACTED		Annick Smith
		Richard Pearce
		Jerome Pickman
		Herb Hauser
		Jeremy Zimmer

e = Estimate based on uncorroborated data derived from *Variety*, other industry sources, and authors' calculations.

*Producers still owe approximately $50,000 in deferrals.

FILM SYNOPSIS

Based on the real-life experience of Elinore Stewart, Heartland *follows a recently widowed woman and her child as they relocate to the rugged wilderness of turn-of-the-century Burntfork, Wyoming. Elinore takes a job with rancher Clyde Stewart, and the film chronicles their meeting, marriage, and struggle to build a home and family amidst starving livestock, winter blizzards, and enforced isolation.*

DEVELOPMENT

Genesis · *Heartland* was originally conceived as part of "Wilderness Women," a series of films exploring the role of women in the settlement and early frontier life of the American West. The series was conceived and developed by Annick Smith (executive producer) and Beth Ferris (coproducer and writer). *Heartland* is the only film of the series yet to be produced.

Smith and Ferris developed the project because they wanted to present a true historical picture of women in the West. They felt that no serious attention had been given to the subject in films, except those depicting women as prostitutes or adjuncts to men. Smith and Ferris hoped their film would convey their deep love for the region they were from, and about which they had previously made documentaries. Their goal was to present an alternative to the cowboy stereotype so dominant in popular American mythology, in the form of a dramatic, feature-length movie. They had strong support among leading humanists and historians for this feminist approach to the American West.

The script was written by Ferris, who undertook painstaking research into Elinore Pruitt Stewart's life. Ferris conducted extensive interviews with Stewart's relatives and studied her personal diaries and two autobiographies. William Kittredge and Elizabeth Clark served as creative consultants for the first draft of the script. Clark became story editor for the final draft and Kittredge rewrote the script, adding additional scenes and dialogue.

Financing · It took three years to produce *Heartland* and secure a distribution contract for it. Film financing was divided into three distinct phases: development, scripting and production, and distribution. Each phase met with enormous uncertainty due to the nature of the public financing that underwrote production and the difficulties encountered in securing a distributor.

Smith and Ferris originally submitted a research and development proposal to the NEH in early 1977 for the "Wilderness Women" series, and received an $82,000 grant in the fall of that year. During the development phase, they brought in a number of associates to help research the proposed individual films, including Richard Pearce, an experienced director. Ferris wrote the script for *Heartland* as the pilot for the proposed series.

Pearce had been a cinematographer on the Academy Award–winning documentary *Hearts and Minds*, and had directed *The Gardener's Son* for the PBS "Visions" series. (He has subsequently gone on to direct other feature films, including the highly acclaimed *Country*, produced by its star Jessica Lange, and *No Mercy*.) Pearce recognized that the script was not a "fast-track career movie," but was drawn to its story and visual power.

With Pearce's support and the approval of the project's consultants, the producers decided to continue scripting and to make production plans for one film, *Heartland*, as the series pilot. Ferris was designated the writer. Smith and Pearce brought two other principals onto the production team: Michael Hausman as coproducer and Fred Murphy as director of photography.

With a completed script and a production team in place, Smith applied a second time to the NEH for a $600,000 production grant. The proposal was for a ninety-minute film to be shot in 16mm. In October 1978, she received a grant for the full amount requested, the largest single filmmaking grant awarded by the NEH up to that time.

While the filmmakers saw *Heartland* as an independent production, they did not originally commit themselves to a theatrical release. They sought, rather, to keep their options as open as possible. However, they did anticipate a PBS broadcast, as stipulated under terms of their NEH grant. The actors and crew worked at PBS minimums, a decision that would prove problematic when the film was being readied for theatrical release.

The film's financing breaks down as follows:

Budget	Original	$ 741,500	
	Final	1,108,000	
	Cash	807,000	
	Deferrals	122,000	
	Residuals	119,000	
	Self-distribution	60,000	(approx.)
	Total	$1,108,000	
Financing	Total funds raised	$1,007,000	
	NEH	600,000	
	Loans (20%, 2 years)	60,000	
	Deferrals	122,000	
	Foreign (TV, theatrical)	167,000	
	Unpaid bills to date	58,000	
	Total	$1,007,000	

Anticipating an audience · During the development phase, the filmmakers did not fully anticipate the marketing possibilities for *Heartland*, nor did they have any clear conception of its potential audience appeal. At that time, no clearly defined specialty film market existed; a scattering of art houses exhibiting primarily foreign films was the only alternative to Hollywood fare for American film-goers. The filmmakers recognized that *Heartland* was not going to be a money-maker; they worked on the film because they loved it and wanted to see it made. The producers were naïve about distribution, trusting that if they made a good film, an advantageous distribution deal would inevitably follow.

PRODUCTION

Preproduction began upon receipt of the NEH funding in October 1978, and ran through February 1979. The primary activities during this phase were additional research, script revision, location scouting, and budget revisions. While scouting locations, the filmmakers realized that the rugged Montana environment should figure prominently as a "character" in the film. They tested 16mm, super-16mm and 35mm stock, and found that with 16mm there would be a significant loss of picture quality in capturing the landscapes and wideshots. In addition, an investment in 35mm would provide more distribution options.

The filmmakers finally committed to shoot in 35mm. In Pearce's words, "It would be a television movie in 35mm." The filmmakers felt that casting Conchata Ferrell and Rip Torn as the leads increased the film's commercial potential. They anticipated a "negative pickup" deal after completion to cover the budget overages that shooting in 35mm entailed.

But the switch from 16mm to 35mm, while adding to the film's visual appeal and its theatrical potential, caused problems. It increased production costs and, more critically, contributed to a serious problem with the DGA.

At the time of production, the DGA did not have a low-budget waiver available, so the filmmakers simply avoided these budget parameters thinking they could work something out when the film was finished. Pearce agreed to a fee of $25,000, with an additional $25,000 deferred.

Pearce recalls that after *Heartland* went into theatrical release without guild agreements, "[the DGA] came down on us like a ton of bricks." In retrospect, he feels that had the guild been approached before production, a compromise could have been negotiated. Pearce found himself in an adversarial relationship with the guild and was forced to attend a number of disciplinary hearings. Ultimately, he and other DGA members on the crew had to be paid theatrical minimums and residuals before the film could be released. The producers had to pay Pearce an additional $30,000 and higher rates to other DGA members. Pearce canceled the deferral clause in his contract in light of the higher DGA minimums and residuals. Additional residuals to SAG actors for theatrical release totaled over $100,000.

Actual production was more difficult than anticipated. The remote locations and harsh weather hampered their work. The production team moved to their Montana location in March 1979, built sets, and had one week of rehearsals. In April, a five-week shoot began. A major uncertainty was whether they would have a spring snowstorm, necessary for several very important scenes. Just as their extensive preproduction research on weather patterns had indicated, the storm did occur. They completed shooting, with the exception of a few pickups, in May 1979.

Postproduction lasted from June through September. The filmmakers did not seek out distributors at this time but did, however, become aware of the first "American Independent Films" sidebar to the 1979 New York Film Festival. (This was the precursor to the annual American Independent Feature Film Market sponsored by the IFP.) The producer submitted a workprint and *Heartland* was accepted. They arrived at the festival with their first answer print.

DISTRIBUTION DEAL

Making the deal · *Heartland* was screened at the 1979 New York Film Festival sidebar and received a rave review from the *New York Times* film critic Vincent Canby, who described the film as "uncommonly beautiful." But it took nearly a year and a half to find a theatrical distributor.

The filmmakers undertook a comprehensive campaign to secure a distributor, anticipating that the Canby review would open many doors. First, they retained the services of Richard Pearce's agency, William Morris, to represent the film. The agency showed the film to every major distribution company in Hollywood as well as to art-house exhibitors. In Smith's words, they got "only nibbles." Most people who viewed *Heartland* liked it, but felt that it wasn't a commercial property. Ironically, it suffered from being too arty for mainstream audiences and too regional and conventionally shot for art houses.

The producers rejected self-distribution as a viable option, except in Montana and surrounding states. Based in Montana, and dealing with families and small children, they knew they couldn't mount the kind of extensive campaign that, for example, the filmmakers of *Northern Lights* had done to find their audience.

The filmmakers tried building distributor interest through festival exposure. They didn't enter Cannes because Pearce would not be eligible for a first-time director's award. Instead, they entered the Berlin Film Festival and were overjoyed when *Heartland* won the first prize, the prestigious Golden Bear. They also entered the film in the London Film Festival, and, through Irwin Young of DuArt Labs, were able to secure a European agent.

All these efforts were time-consuming and expensive. On the strength of the Berlin Film Festival showing, the filmmakers were able to make a presale to Germany for $60,000 (amounting to only $47,000 because of a weak dollar). With this sale as backup, Smith gave their Montana bank a lien on her ranch and Ferris put up additional collateral. They paid off pressing debts, including film processing fees to DuArt Labs (which had been carried interest-free for a year but had been mounting rapidly in the second year at a 20 percent rate).

With so many distributors passing on *Heartland*, the William Morris Agency was losing interest in the film. However, one of its younger agents, Jeremy Zimmer, believed in the film and stayed with it. He was able to negotiate three cable sales: Showtime ($25,000), Warner-Amex ($25,000), and Channel Z in Los Angeles ($13,000). To pick up additional short-term money, the filmmakers also launched a limited self-distribution effort during the spring of 1981 in Montana, Wyoming, Idaho, and Utah. (This was later viewed by some as premature and therefore detrimental to the film's theatrical performance elsewhere.)

During the spring of 1981, the William Morris Agency negotiated a deal with Jerome Pickman, then of Levitt-Pickman, later Pickman Films, for the distribution of *Heartland*. Jerry Pickman's interest in the film dated back to Canby's New York Film Festival review, and he initiated contact with William Morris. Pickman saw a strong parallel to *Shane*, which he had distributed as head of sales at Paramount. The producers, however, wanted a major company to distribute their film and declined to pursue his interest. In March 1980, Pickman noticed another review of the film in *Variety*, occasioned by its showing at the Berlin Film Festival, indicating that it had not as yet secured a distributor. He again contacted the William Morris Agency but felt that the asking price was still too high. Finally, another year later, Zimmer at William Morris called Pickman to inquire whether he was still interested in the film.

Pickman had been a top sales executive for over twenty-five years at companies such as Paramount, Columbia, Walter Reade, and Lorimar. He is currently in the business of distributing independent films, challenged by the difficulty of selling them but attracted to the potential financial returns. His most successful release has been *The Groove Tube*, which has returned over $11 million in rentals.

Pickman believed that *Heartland* had a limited audience, appealing to those who would appreciate its depth and beauty, but that it might falter after reaching its target group. It had no youth appeal, no action, and no name draws among its stars and director. Consequently, he offered no advance guarantee to the filmmakers.

According to Annick Smith, the filmmakers were "over a barrel" in their dealings with Pickman. After all this time, the only other distributor seriously interested in the film had less knowhow and drive. They felt that if they didn't go with Pickman, the film would die. On the positive side, they were confident that he would give the film all his attention, working hard to help it find its audience.

Terms of the deal · As noted above, Pickman provided no advance. He did, however, pay Smith $15,000 for the use of the inter-negative and the already-produced trailer Pearce had edited. This was treated as an advance, to be recouped as a distribution expense from gross receipts. He also committed to spend a minimum of $60,000 on direct advertising and publicity costs for a New York opening run.

Pickman assumed all rights for the U.S. and Canada, with the exclusion of some western states in which the filmmakers' Wilderness Women Productions had already released the film or had plans to do so. The contract included the following additional provisions:

· A theatrical distribution fee of 40 percent of gross rentals to Pickman, with his direct distribution expenses (not including overhead charges) deducted from the remaining 60 percent, and the balance going to the producers.

- A 25 percent distribution fee for network television sales and a 40 percent fee for a syndication sale, increasing to 50 percent if a subdistributor was used.
- A 35 percent fee for sales to armed forces and in-flight markets.
- A 50 percent fee for 16mm nontheatrical and repertory exhibition rentals, with no increase for the use of a subdistributor.
- A 25 percent fee, over and above any subdistributor's fee, for home-video disc and cassette sales.

However, these terms were cross-collateralized, with income from ancillary markets used to pay debts incurred in theatrical distribution.

The filmmakers retained the sales rights to all foreign territories other than Canada, and all cable sales. They also negotiated the right of approval over the ad and promotional material.

While this deal was less financially attractive than they had originally hoped, the filmmakers believed in Pickman's commitment to the film. The filmmakers believe that this commitment helped make *Heartland* as successful as it has been. Immediately upon signing, the producers sought an extension for the theatrical window from PBS, which had airing rights commencing one year after the theatrical opening, due to the conditions of the NEH grant they had received. According to Smith:

> The NEH and PBS agreed to hold off until theatrical distribution was over the hump and some cable markets had been tapped. This was done because of the large production/distribution debts still owed by the producers.

MARKETING CAMPAIGN

Strategy · Pickman, with the advice and collaboration of Smith and Ferris, enlisted the ad agency of Diener, Hauser, Bates, and Co. to help define the primary audience for the film and to create and position an ad campaign. The likely audience was identified as three-tiered:

- The "prestige" audience: the core specialty film market, which is strongly influenced by acclaim from festivals and the *New York Times*.

- The "middle-brow" audience: viewers reached by television critics like the "Today" show's Gene Shalit, who would respond to the all-American values of rugged individualism and plucky determination that the film embodies.
- The "quasi-redneck/pickup truck" audience: viewers who might be attracted to the film's story and rural setting.

Key to capturing the attention of the first, most critical market segment was an opening in a prestigious New York theater with a campaign that positioned the film as a contemporary classic, a "must-see" film.

Promotion and publicity · *Heartland* was launched at the Paris Theater in New York in August 1981. A large ad in the preceding Sunday's *Times*, together with the condensed reprint of Canby's original review, filled the house. In November, the *Times* ran another piece, a feature article in the all-important Sunday Arts and Leisure section, which was influential in attracting extensive press attention throughout the country. The strong opening performance at the Paris was followed by very favorable reviews in such national publications as the *New Yorker*. These opinion-making publications helped to bolster press interest elsewhere during the film's national rollout.

The cast and the filmmakers played an important role in generating favorable publicity. All the key players—Annick Smith, Dick Pearce, Beth Ferris, Conchata Ferrell, and Rip Torn—traveled extensively, giving interviews and making appearances in order to promote the film.

Their payoff came when critics from both the print and television press around the country designated the film as one of the year's "ten best." Such acclaim came from, among many others, Roger Ebert of the *Chicago Sun-Times*, Clarke Taylor of the *Los Angeles Times*, Joel Siegel of ABC-TV, Katie Kelly of WNBC/New York, and CBS Radio.

In order to promote word-of-mouth in addition to press attention, the distributor and producers also took further advantage of film festivals and arranged for opening-day benefit screenings for local charity groups. The filmmakers were favorably impressed with Pickman's promotional efforts.

Trailer and ad · Richard Pearce edited the trailer, working with his editor and coproducers Hausman and Smith. Three prints were initially struck, and ultimately seventy-five trailers were in circulation.

The ad highlighted the critical acclaim and festival prizes that the film had already received. Visually, it combined a production still and original artwork, and was able to suggest at once a love story and a rural environment, without specifying a time period. It featured a provocative image of the actors in winter clothing pictured against a barren and remote plains background with a railroad train in the distance.

THEATRICAL RELEASE

Strategy · Pickman's strategy was based on a "pay as you go," city-by-city approach, whereby expenditures at each stage of the release would be made on the basis of the film's performance in the previous market. He viewed *Heartland*'s distribution as a calculated risk, because the film had some obvious disadvantages: it had already been seen and reviewed in New York two years earlier, and had subsequently been poorly premiered by the filmmakers' distribution company in Salt Lake City.

On the basis of a strong New York run, Pickman planned a national rollout, cutting a wedge across portions of the country from New York and New England to San Francisco and Seattle, picking each market carefully. Instead of waiting for theater owners to call and request information on the film, he approached them aggressively, with a one-sheet, a publicity packet, and a followup call.

Pickman carefully planned the scheduling to ensure the best results. He worked with regional subdistributors to negotiate the booking deals on a sales commission basis, while he concentrated on refining the campaign elements for various markets, setting the terms for co-op ads, and monitoring spending on prints and ads.

Opening run · *Heartland* opened at the Paris Theater, the premier venue for French imports, in New York on August 23, 1981. The film was one of the few English-language films to play at the Paris, and up to that time the only American independent to have opened there. Pickman chose the Paris because of its prestigious reputation as a showcase for quality films. In addition, Ralph Donnelly, the president of RKO/Cinema Five Corporation, which books the Paris, had seen *Heartland* at Telluride and was enthusiastic about the film.

Opening costs were kept low by Hollywood standards, with between $50,000 and $60,000 spent on co-op ads, publicity, and related expenses. As noted earlier, the *Times* review was instrumental in generating sellout audiences and kept the film running for eight weeks. Box-office grosses during the first four weeks were $19,876; $38,894; $43,787; and $24,735.

Overall, the New York run was a stunning success, exceeding the expectations of almost everyone involved.

National playoff · The first-run and repertory release of *Heartland* following the New York opening encompassed over 500 playdates during a sixteen-month period. The film is still in active distribution today, being booked into repertory houses and the college film-society circuit, although recent bookings have been very slow.

The San Francisco opening followed directly after New York. The prescreenings held there for critics and film students generated positive word-of-mouth and an enthusiastic critical response, resulting in another spectacularly successful run.

Following San Francisco, the film opened in Seattle and again did very well. In Chicago, building on Roger Ebert's favorable support in the *Sun-Times* and the filmmakers' on-site publicity, it did better than expected. The film also did very well in Detroit, to everyone's surprise. The filmmakers attribute this strong showing to an appearance by Pearce and to favorable reviews.

Boston, however, was a disappointment. Given the success in New York, and Boston's reputation as a strong market for specialty films, the distributor and the producers expected a favorable performance. The mediocre run was largely attributed to the choice of theater, a large triplex downtown where mainstream commercial product was the usual fare. The distributor was unable to book *Heartland* at one of the smaller houses in the Cambridge area, which cater to the specialty audience.

Pickman lacked access to the prime specialty or art houses in some of the other highly competitive markets. As in Boston, this forced him to run the film in more commercial theaters. This was a key problem throughout the national playoff, and was an ironic contrast to what happened in New York, the most competitive specialty market. In the Minneapolis/St. Paul area, producer Smith engaged in an intense preopening publicity effort. It paid off with positive press coverage and a strong box-office showing.

Pickman held off on releasing *Heartland* in areas of moderate climate, feeling that audiences in Washington, D.C., Miami, Dallas, Atlanta, and Los Angeles would have difficulty identifying with the characters' epic struggle against the harsh, unyielding environment. In Atlanta, where the film ran as part of the showcase of American independents sponsored by the AFI and the IFP, *Heartland* performed poorly. This was also the experience throughout the Southwest, lending credence to Pickman's decision.

In Los Angeles, *Heartland* was released principally in order to qualify for nominations for awards from the DGA, WGA, and the Academy of Motion Picture Arts and Sciences (AMPAS). The audiences of film professionals responded enthusiastically. Allen Rivkin, reporting on the WGA screenings, noted that the film "was exposed to 8,000 members of the industry in twelve screenings. At each of the performances there was sustained applause—a rarity, indeed."

OTHER MARKETS

Pickman's strategy was to delay all ancillary sales until one year after *Heartland*'s theatrical opening, except for the prior sales to cable and to PBS.

Homevideo · World-wide rights were acquired by Thorn/EMI for $125,000.

Pay cable · Prior to release in the domestic theatrical market, the film was sold to Showtime ($25,000), Warner-Amex ($25,000), and Channel Z in Los Angeles ($13,500). The rights to all subsequent pay-cable sales went to Thorn/EMI as part of the homevideo deal.

Nontheatrical · *Heartland* was a favorite of the Carter White House, and was shown in embassies around the world under the auspices of the State Department and the U.S. Information Agency. Domestic theatrical subdistribution is being handled by Twyman Films of Dayton, Ohio, which reports a strong continuing demand in the institutional and repertory markets.

Broadcast · "American Playhouse" has aired the film as part of the conditions of NEH production funding. The filmmakers netted an additional $25,000 for the airing. The rights for further broadcast sales were also part of the Thorn/EMI acquisition package.

Foreign · *Heartland* has been sold extensively overseas, including sales to German and Chinese television (countries that purchase films based on a flat, per-foot rate). Many European sales were made on the basis of festival exposure prior to theatrical release. Pickman asserts that had the filmmakers been able to wait, they could have increased their revenue from these sales due to the film's strong domestic showing. The film's foreign revenues to date are: $40,000 from theatrical; $102,000 from pay cable, broadcast, and syndication television; and $25,000 from homevideo.

REVIEW

Born out of a desire to tell an important and little-known story of the role of women in the frontier West, *Heartland* took over three years to be developed and produced, and to secure commercial distribution. Funded for the most part by grants from the NEH, *Heartland* was featured in the first New York Film Festival "American Independent Films" sidebar in 1979. Even with strong critical acclaim from *New York Times* critic Vincent Canby, it took the producer nearly two years to find a commercial theatrical distributor. Pickman Films launched an imaginative and vigorous campaign that helped generate the popular attention which made it an American specialty classic.

As producer Annick Smith notes:

> *Heartland* set a pattern for the future marketing of independent films and in many ways prepared the way for industry acceptance of "small" regional films such as *Tender Mercies* and *The Trip to Bountiful*.

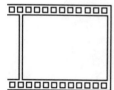# HOLLYWOOD SHUFFLE

(March 1987)

PRINCIPALS	*Director*	Robert Townsend
	Producer	Robert Townsend
	Writers	Robert Townsend and Keenen Ivory Wayans
	Principal cast	Robert Townsend, Anne-Marie Johnson, Helen Martin, Keenen Ivory Wayans, and John Witherspoon
DISTRIBUTORS	*Theatrical*	Samuel Goldwyn Company
	Homevideo	Virgin Vision
	Pay cable	not available
	Nontheatrical	not available
	Broadcast	not available
	Foreign	not available
THEATRICAL	*Opening date*	March 20, 1987
	Total playdates	not available
	Box-office gross	$5,500,000
	Gross film rental	2,750,000
	Total distributor costs	
	Guarantee	covered costs and additions
	Publicity	800,000–900,000
	Prints	95
ANCILLARY	*Homevideo*	65,000 units
		$1,000,000 gross
	Pay cable	not available
	Nontheatrical	not available
	Foreign (gross)	1,000,000
PARTICIPANTS CONTACTED		Eamonn Bowles
		Leonie de Picciotto
		Robert Townsend

FILM SYNOPSIS

This semi-autobiographical comedy pointedly satirizes Hollywood's racial stereotypes and hiring practices. The central character is a struggling young black actor, Bobby Taylor (Robert Townsend), who supports his dream of becoming a respected, serious actor by working at the Winky Dinky Dog hot dog stand.

The movie follows Taylor through a series of crafted sequences that lampoon racial clichés. It alternates scenes of his family life and work with scenes of his encounters with the Hollywood film industry and his daydreams of glory. In one sequence Taylor auditions for white producers for a role in Jive Time Jimmie's Revenge, *a black exploitation film. He doesn't get the part because he isn't "black" enough. Afterward, he dreams he's the black Superman or the first five-time Oscar winner, or else he's the superpimp—only to have the NAACP picket his successful film as an insult to his race. Another sequence depicts a white-run black acting school with classes in jive talk, how to shuffle, and the slave epic; the school's phone number is 1-800-555-COON.*

The film includes "Sneakin' into the Movies," a take-off of the Siskel-Ebert movie review show, with two black "homeboys," Speed and Tyrone, judging new releases. Having snuck into the theater, they advise audiences whether such movies as Rambro—First Youngblood, Sam Ace, Private Investigator *(which pokes fun at trendy black, gay hairstylists), and* Attack of the Zombie Pimps *are worth seeing. "There's a Bat in My House," in which a black vampire moves into the house of a white family in suburban Detroit, satirizes television sitcoms.*

All along, Taylor wishes to please his family, who give him little support. His mother tells him to give it all up and take a job with the post office. His grandmother is particularly critical of exploitative roles black actors take. His brother idealizes him, but wants to be "cool." His girlfriend puts up with his continual career setbacks. The movie ends with Taylor making a commercial for the U.S. Postal Service.

DEVELOPMENT

Genesis · Robert Townsend—producer, director, co-writer and principal lead actor—was the driving force behind *Hollywood Shuffle*. Townsend grew up in Chicago and had long pursued an acting career. He started studying at a local community theater and took improvisational theater classes at Second City. He was a member of EXBAG, the Experimental Black Actors Guild. His first role in a film was a few lines in *Cooley High*, which was being shot in Chicago. He also had a lead role in the PBS series "Another Page."

In the late 1970s he moved to New York, where he took workshops at the Negro Ensemble Company and classes with Stella Adler. Townsend made a living in New York performing stand-up comedy at the Improvisation and acting in commercials that did not use him as a stereotype rather than taking parts as a "jive-talking dude." Townsend's professional role model is Sidney Poitier, who turned down roles he felt degraded him and his race.

In 1981, Townsend moved to Los Angeles to further his acting career. He took acting classes, performed in local stand-up comedy clubs, and played numerous roles as an extra in such movies as *Mahogany* and *Parenting*. All along he carefully watched the production process.

Hollywood Shuffle took shape over the course of two and a half years, from 1984 to 1986, maturing from a series of vignettes to a full-length feature film. Initially, Townsend produced a number of self-contained shorts for use as a visual résumé to further his acting career. He recalls:

I'd just done *Streets of Fire* and *A Soldier's Story* back to back. When I came back to Los Angeles, I had all this money and my friends were saying, "What are you going to do? You going to get a Porsche? A town house?" And my agent was saying, "You should feel really lucky you did *Soldier's Story* 'cause they do one black movie a year and that's it."

I thought my life was really going to change, but it was all the same garbage. I was back auditioning for parts like a slave on "North and South," a pimp on "Hill Street Blues," an informer on "Cagney & Lacey." Then I was [supposed to be] a crack specialist on "Hard Copy."

And I'm going, "Okay, now what do I do?" I just wanted to work.

So I decided to do a short. The way Hollywood is, there's always one black in every movie so I've got all these friends who are talents, even though none of them can get work. I said, "Why don't we all get together and do a movie?"

And they said, "Who's going to direct us?"

And I said, "*I'll* direct us."

According to Townsend, the film's structure developed organically out of the production process itself, not from a prepared script. "We wrote it as we went along. First it was a short, then another short. Then we decided to add a story. 'A mother! You need a mother!' someone would say. Then it would be, 'A girlfriend! You need a girlfriend!' "

Throughout the process, Townsend worked closely with two associates—Carl Gregg, who served as line producer, equipment and location scout, and technical staff, and Keenen Ivory Wayans, who co-wrote the script and acted in the film.

Financing · Townsend spent approximately $100,000 to produce a roughcut, with financing coming exclusively from his personal risk. (The total cash outlay does not include deferrals.)

Sixty thousand dollars came from earnings from his work in films and commercials. He also had some money saved from a three-picture acting deal with Richard Pryor's defunct Indigo Productions. According to Townsend:

After I used up all the money I'd saved from my acting jobs, I still needed another $40,000. I financed the film with credit cards. Everybody now says that was so smart. But I was really desperate. I invested all my money; I was doing TV commercials; I was on the road doing stand-up comedy; I was like a junkie addicted to making a movie. I didn't think about where the money was coming from.

The first time it happened we were in the midst of a shoot and the money ran out. I was always getting [applications for] preferred Visa and MasterCard in the mail and I had a stack of them. At first I was going to tear them up, but when I opened them they said I had a preapproved credit line of $8,000 on one card, $9,000 on another and $3,000 on a third and I realized I had the money to finish the film right here. When I had no money to pay actors, I'd take them to tank up their cars with gas.

Townsend used a Saks Fifth Avenue card to cover wardrobe costs—clothes bought were given to the actors in lieu of pay. He used a Montgomery Ward card to cover catering costs. He used $40,000 of credit in all. But the worst moment came when he went to buy film stock:

> There's a place in Los Angeles that caters to film students, so I bought a T-shirt that said UCLA. I'd been out of school for years. Usually when students buy raw stock, they'll say "Give me a can of film," about one hundred feet for $200.
>
> I went into the place and the lady said, "How much film do you want?" I said, "10,000 feet." But I'm cool. So she goes in the back room and comes back with cans and cans and cans [of film] and says, "That'll be $5,000."
>
> And I say, "Okay. . . . Here, put it on my Visa."
>
> So I wait, and she takes it to the machine and it goes bdl-bdl-doop and I'm waiting and she's waiting.
>
> She looks at me and says, "Will that be all?"
>
> And I say, "Yes."

Reflecting on the precarious situation he was placed in, Townsend recalled:

> The film was held up when one new credit card got lost in the mail. The bank said it would take three weeks to send me another one. I got them to Federal Express it overnight—and I charged the Federal Express bill on the credit card.
>
> I'm just glad it all came together. My family was going through hard times in Chicago and I couldn't even tell my mother I had $100,000 invested in a film. I *didn't* tell her until we got ready to shoot the last day. I flew her out for a real small part. When I'm in the makeup chair, she's the one who says, "Here's your jacket, Mr. Taylor."

Anticipating an Audience · Initially, the film was to be a series of "show" reels for auditions; no popular audience was anticipated. However, as the vignettes were shot, Townsend decided that there was an audience for his film out there, and determined to go ahead with a feature. He felt that any good, engaging, original film—like foreign art films—could find an audience.

PRODUCTION

Robert Townsend began shooting *Hollywood Shuffle* in Los Angeles in October 1984. With a cast of friends and a student film crew, he spent approximately $20,000 in four days' work. In 1985, he shot for four days, and in 1986, another six days. It was not until 1986 that the various vignettes were put together into a feature film.

Townsend never went to film school, but he learned the basics of directing while acting in *A Soldier's Story.* He says that he spent a good deal of time watching and listening to director Norman Jewison and cinematographer Russell Boyd prepare scenes.

Townsend created his own version of the low-budget guerrilla filmmaking that characterizes many first-time films. "A lot of scenes were shot in my apartment, or outside Keenen's house." Production preparation did not stop at cost-cutting measures:

I called the [Los Angeles] airport to see when the planes were coming 'cause they flew over my house and their roar could be picked up when we shot. I couldn't afford to waste any money. They'd tell me, "We have three planes in 15 minutes," and when the last one went by, I'd tell the crew, "Let's roll!"

Preproduction planning also involved extensive rehearsals. "Technically, I walked through every shot with the cinematographer and soundperson," he recalls. From his theatrical background, he knew how important—and money-saving—rehearsals could be. "We rehearsed for three weeks [before principal photography] and we were totally prepared. Most scenes were shot in a single take."

Locations were scouted in advance, quickly invaded, and the scene shot before police knew what was happening or had a chance to check on permits. Townsend recalls:

I rented two vans with tinted windows; camera equipment in the first van, actors and wardrobe in the second. We stole locations. We drove around and drove around and just did it.

We'd literally pull up to a street light, and I'd say, "OK, cameras, that's where you're going to be, by that tree. Actors, over by the other side. OK, soon as the light changes everybody get in position. OK, it's green, let's go." And we moved like that. I'd talk to the camera operator, "How was that?" and he'd say it was great. "Everybody back in the van, and let's go," and we would pull off.

What you learn is that there are no rules.

When the police did show up, there were no real problems. Everyone was wearing a UCLA T-shirt, so the police didn't demand a permit. "We got through it," Townsend reflects, "but it took nerves, trying to sneak and do stuff in broad daylight."

In all, there were eighty-three speaking parts. Townsend recalls his experience with SAG:

I went to SAG and that was deep. Spike [Lee] had just done *She's Gotta Have It* and they asked me if I went to film school. They had penalized Spike because he knew all the rules. I told them I hadn't gone to film school and didn't know the rules. They asked me how many actors were involved—eighty-three! They asked, who directed it? me; who produced it? me; who was the first A.D.? me. So you got to gamble.

Sympathetic filmmakers often donated "short ends"—raw stock left over from their movies. Townsend observes, "When you have only one hundred feet of film, which is a minute, you're limited." This was one reason why most scenes were shot in one take. "Everything had to be planned out," Townsend points out, "and it forces you to be a little more creative."

Leveraging was the name of the game, Townsend says:

The movie was shot in fourteen days, fourteen *long* days. We couldn't get the locations a lot of times until I said I had been in *A Soldier's Story*. That hooked a lot of people into letting us use their place for free, for just a credit at the end of the film.

DISTRIBUTION DEAL

Making the deal · Making *Hollywood Shuffle* was the gamble of a lifetime for Robert Townsend. With all his personal money spent and a $40,000 debt hanging over his head, everything hinged on the film's ability to find not simply a distributor but one who would pay off his outstanding debts.

Townsend's strategy with distribution was a simple one, if a longshot. He figured that he had a month to get the film sold before his credit card bills came due. A workprint was assembled in December 1985, and he booked the Writers Guild's Hollywood screening room—charged to his credit card, of course—and invited every distributor in town to see it. The print was rough, scratched, not timed properly, and not scored. He points out:

> We didn't just invite the presidents and vice-presidents of the studios. We invited secretaries, gofers, anybody in the company. That's how the buzz started to happen. The secretaries told their bosses that they saw a film they liked. All the executives saw the film in their private screening rooms.

But Townsend knew who he wanted to handle the film:

> We wanted the film to be handled with kid gloves! I didn't want to go with a big company that would put the film in a thousand theaters and not give it time to grow. I had seen films like *Stranger Than Paradise*, *Dance with a Stranger*, *Sid and Nancy*, and I knew how Goldwyn handled films.

Keenen Ivory Wayans, Townsend's long-time friend and the film's co-writer and a principal actor, identifies another critical influence on their decision to go with Goldwyn:

> The choice was between commerciality versus critical acclaim. *Hollywood Shuffle* was very well received by the critics, which was really important in terms of establishing us in the industry as legitimate writers. If we had gone with another company the film could have wound up like a *Kentucky Fried Movie*, which is more commercial but not as legitimate.

While other distributors expressed some interest, the most enthusiastic was Samuel Goldwyn, Jr., who, Townsend said, "got the humor *and* the message of the film." His reaction contrasted sharply to the generally poor reception the film received at the roughcut screening. Other distributors saw it quite superficially as low-budget, episodic, amateurish, and thought that Townsend was a "nobody." Townsend felt that the other distributors really didn't know how to market his film. In addition, Goldwyn agreed to advance sufficient cash to pay Townsend's outstanding debts, including what he owed the actors. As he recalls:

It was one funny scene. The first thing I wanted was to make sure my friends were paid. I didn't want word going around town, "Rob did a movie and used us and we haven't seen any money." So as soon as I signed with the Samuel Goldwyn Company they said they'd send the check in the mail in three weeks and I said, "No, no, these actors have worked for two-and-a-half years and I can't come to my friends and say you've got to wait another three weeks." So, on a Sunday afternoon they had two lawyers and three accountants in the bedroom of my house and we signed. I sought Goldwyn out, and I wasn't wrong.

The roughcut ran seventy to seventy-five minutes and included nearly all of the final film's core sequences, including the black acting school, the Sam Spade, and the audition episodes. After the deal was struck, the Goldwyn Company put up the completion money for some of the continuity links, including the Los Angeles background driving scenes, the NAACP picketing scene, and some of the family scenes. Finally, editing trimmed some of the rough edges and music was laid in.

The Samuel Goldwyn Company usually makes acquisition decisions as a result of consensus discussions. However, Goldwyn is the ultimate arbiter. According to Eamonn Bowles, East Coast sales manager, "Sam will go with films he doesn't really like if he feels that arguments are persuasive enough or enough people think it's going to be a big hit."

With *Hollywood Shuffle*, Goldwyn was the most instrumental and enthusiastic for acquisition. He had been associated with other black films in the past, including *Come Back Charleston Blue* and *Cotton Comes to Harlem*, and knew there was an audience. The strong performance of *She's Gotta Have It*, which had come out of nowhere, proved this. Finally, the financial risk required of the company was not large.

Goldwyn's direct involvement went deeper than simply acquisition approval. Townsend recalls:

Sam understood the movie. He didn't take over the baby. We'd be in the editing room and talk about the cut or the pace or what additions needed to be made. Sam is a very smart man. There's a scene in the movie with Jeri-Curl. Sam doesn't know what Jeri-Curl is; he lives in

Beverly Hills—no connection whatever. But he knew; he said, "That hair thing works!" And we looked at each other and laughed.

Terms of the deal · The deal with the Goldwyn Company covered all rights for all world-wide markets. Townsend learned as much making the deal as he did making the film:

> There are a lot of ways to learn about deal-making—you can call around and ask other filmmakers what they did, you can take seminars, or you can get a good lawyer who worked on films that you like how it was handled. You seek them out, invite them to your screening, and ask them what you can get from a distributor.

MARKETING CAMPAIGN

Strategy · The marketing strategy for *Hollywood Shuffle* was shaped by a number of factors. Leonie de Picciotto, head of publicity, identified four key ones: (1) Robert Townsend himself, who was an "effective spokesman . . . a stand-up comedian who could give good interviews"; (2) it was made for $100,000; (3) it addressed distinct target audiences, including upscale black filmgoers and traditional white specialized audiences; and (4) it would generate good press and word-of-mouth through an effective use of reviews, promotion, ad campaign, and trailer. Eamonn Bowles added another factor: the film was a comedy. According to him, "Comedies are very unpredictable." Someone on the Goldwyn staff presumed that the film would be popular with audiences but not be a "critic's film." Critical support for offbeat independent films has traditionally been due to their serious or innovative artistic qualities.

The company hosted a series of recruited test-screenings to assess audience reactions. In Los Angeles, according to de Picciotto, the first test-screenings were with white audiences. The tests went very poorly. "The audiences didn't understand that the film was by a black filmmaker," she says, adding, "they saw it as a put-down on blacks." According to Bowles, "the film did badly. People walked out. People felt the movie was offensive."

At another test-screening at the Grand Lake Theater in Oakland, with a predominately black audience, *Hollywood Shuffle* was tested following a screening of *She's Gotta Have It* and it performed strongly. Townsend recalls:

> They [Goldwyn] put an ad in the local paper and people came from miles around; we packed the theater. We sat in the back and watched. When the scene with Keenen putting on the Jeri-Curl came on, the audience roared. The lawyers and accountants didn't know what was happening, but it worked.

De Picciotto points out that Townsend was on stage and set up the audience before the film went on and "no one walked out . . . they loved it!"

Within the Goldwyn Company, as with many other film distributors, recruited audience test-screenings are looked upon skeptically. While such tests are used extensively and can often provide some useful insights, many in the industry see them as artificial. Bowles warns, "If a moviegoer is not enticed by ads and reviews to pay his money, then it's not a normal viewing situation."

Nevertheless, Goldwyn utilized a number of additional screenings to grasp audience reactions, and drew important lessons from them. First and foremost, the movie had to be clearly identified as a comedy made by a black. This was the only way to avoid confusion over the delicate issues that were at the very heart of the film: a black film-maker's view of the discrimination of blacks in the Hollywood movie industry, and his view that blacks are sometimes complicit in this discrimination. Townsend had to be the centerpiece of the promotional efforts, with him in the trailer and the credit card incident as the "hook."

The filmmakers also felt that they benefited from these screenings. According to Wayans, "Seeing the film with an audience gives you a chance to see things you didn't see before. The screenings helped us make changes in the film. And these changes weren't imposed on us, it was all very collective."

The film received an "R" rating.

Promotion and publicity · The promotion and publicity campaign was shaped by the overall marketing strategy: *Hollywood Shuffle* was identified as an "audience" as distinguished from a "critic's" film. Nevertheless, according to de Picciotto, "the audience had to be convinced. The film had to be favorably positioned by critics and through interviews to get the widest possible audience." The plan was built around Townsend. He was the core of the film, as its director, producer, co-writer, and star, and he brought the same entrepreneurial spirit to marketing that he had shown in the film's making. His enthusiasm was contagious, his charisma inspiring.

While it was not written into his contract, Townsend participated in all decisions regarding trailer, one-sheet, etc:

> When it's your kid, you want to make sure that your kid has the best possible advantage. I couldn't just sit at home and say, "O.K., they're going to do it." You fight, because you're working with people who've worked on a ton of movies and, well, they get jaded. Take the ad. In one I look like Eddie Murphy, in another I look like Tom Cruise or Pee Wee Herman. I fought for my own identity. But they're doing their job and I'm doing mine. As a filmmaker, you can't give in to the fight.

Wayans adds an important insight to the heart of the "fight":

> It's the difference between the creative mind and the business mind. Once the business people come into play, they don't think "art," 'cause they're trying to sell something. They go with what they feel will sell the film.
>
> A good example is the first trailer. They took a ten-second skit in the movie and tried to build the trailer around a guy who's trying to be Eddie Murphy, . . . as if it's the whole movie. That was a big fight. The guy who was cutting the trailer said he didn't care if he tricked the audience as long as we got them into the theater. As artists, we didn't want to lie to our audience or mislead people.

Based in Los Angeles, the Goldwyn Company's in-house publicity department oversaw all aspects of the plan and worked closely with Townsend. The lead promotional concept was his use of credit cards to finance production. According to Bowles, it "seemed to fly and everyone jumped on it." Nearly every reviewer and critic picked up on this in their coverage of the film. When Townsend appeared on "The Johnny Carson Show," Carson mentioned it.

The publicity department hosted ten screenings for critics in New York. They did not anticipate the broad critical support, especially the level of enthusiasm, that the film ultimately generated. Quite unexpectedly, the film got an extremely high percentage of favorable reviews, in such major newspapers as the *Washington Post*, the *New York Times*, and the *Wall Street Journal*, as well as *Playboy* and *Time* magazines. De Picciotto offers a perceptive insight into the double-bind position likely felt by many white critics: "Here's a black filmmaker making a critical—however comical—movie about white Hollywood's racism. How could they be critical of Townsend without being perceived as racist themselves?" Bowles thinks that much of the critical support for the film was due to a kind of mild reverse racism that worked in *Hollywood Shuffle*'s favor. "Many critics missed the boat on *She's Gotta Have It* and were falling over themselves to make it up on *Hollywood Shuffle*."

One important review appeared in *Film Comment*, the magazine of the Film Society of Lincoln Center, which favorably compared Townsend to Woody Allen. The analogy to Allen is one that pleases Townsend, particularly Allen's role as a cultural interpreter:

> I used to go to Woody Allen movies and have a great time. Somebody'd say "bar mitzvah" and the audience would fall out of their seats, and I'd be sitting there saying, "What's bar mitzvah?" I think *Hollywood Shuffle*'s going to be an education. It's like a foreign film, and I love foreign films because you hear dialogue and see stuff that is unique. And that's what movies should be about.

Ironically, some of the major black press, including *Jet* and *Ebony* magazines, were initially not interested in profiling the film or Townsend. De Picciotto recalls, "Their attitude was 'Who's Townsend?' It was only *after* the film got strong critical attention from the white press that they took a real interest in it. Townsend got a *Jet* cover feature after the movie opened."

Positive reviews helped legitimize Townsend and the film. Especially important was the one by Bruce Williamson in *Playboy*, which included the following quote: "Look out Eddie Murphy, Robert Townsend has arrived!" Bowles immediately sent out copies of the review to exhibitors, so that they could place the movie in a familiar context. The favorable reviews helped exhibitors identify the film's target audience—the well-read, educated black person, like those who had come out for *She's Gotta Have It*.

Trailer and ad · The artwork for the one-sheet was developed by Goldwyn's in-house advertising department. According to de Picciotto, "We had to reshoot the stills for the ad because of the poor quality of the original ones." The artwork had to "walk a fine line" to capture the film's complex message, she says. "The audience had to know that the film was a comedy, that Townsend made it, and that it was a sophisticated film, one that they had to take seriously," she adds. All aspects of the artwork—press kit, stills, trailer, and ad— had to embody the same message, which "had to suggest quality, yet be slick . . . had to be hip, romantic, and make Townsend a star." She feels they achieved their goal.

Townsend created and executed the final trailer himself. It features him describing how he made the film using credit cards and "pleading" with viewers to come see his film, otherwise he'd be in real trouble with his creditors. Funny radio ads featuring Townsend plugging the film were created and produced by him as well.

No television ads were used, because the Goldwyn Company did not think the film would perform well enough to justify the extremely high costs of television spots. De Picciotto notes that for a television advertising buy to be effective, the ad spot has to secure between 250 and 300 rating points in order to generate viewer awareness. She adds, "You can't just run the spot once or twice. It has to be repeated enough times in each market to build awareness. A company needs to spend a few million dollars to have any noticeable effect, and you have to do it right or not do it at all." Bowles observes, "In retrospect, if we had taken TV ads, who knows what the film would have grossed. But if TV ads hadn't helped it greatly, they would have cut deeply into the profits."

The Goldwyn Company initially made fifty prints for distribution and ended up with a total of ninety-five prints. Bowles feels that more prints earlier, as many as seventy prints, could have taken greater advantage of the initial favorable response. He believes they missed a unique opportunity over the Easter weekend—particularly Easter Sunday, which is a big black-family moviegoing day—due to lack of prints. Total promotion and publicity expenditures are reported to have been approximately $1 million.

THEATRICAL RELEASE

Release strategy · The Goldwyn Company developed their release plans for *Hollywood Shuffle* based upon their own in-house assessment of the film's potential performance and the recent experience of *She's Gotta Have It*. Up to the time of the release of Spike Lee's film, late summer 1986, no other recent black independent film was available as a basis for market performance comparison. According to Bowles, the film "unleashed a significant black middle-class audience, one that had been woefully underserved and still is." Thus, how *She's Gotta Have It* performed in different cities and at specific theaters became a model for the release planning of *Hollywood Shuffle*.

Given initial caution about the film's likely performance and concern about less-than-favorable critical response, the Goldwyn Company decided upon a "modified" release, between the traditional art-film exclusive launch employed on another Goldwyn release, *Sid and Nancy*, and the more wide-scale release used with their *Mystic Pizza*. Because *Hollywood Shuffle* was a comedy, the Goldwyn Company did not think it would be limited to the "art-house" circuit. A second aspect of Goldwyn's overall release planning was to focus on those areas with the highest concentration of the moviegoing black middle class.

These two factors led the company to open the film on the East Coast, first in ten theaters in the New York area and five in Washington, D.C., then in Chicago. Following the initial launch, the film would move west to Los Angeles and other markets.

Opening run · Opening in New York at ten theaters was, in Bowles's words, "hedging our bets." Bowles, who headed the release implementation in New York, feels that the company held back from going for a wider release because Townsend was a "nobody" at that point and there were no stars in the film. He also points out that *She's Gotta Have It* opened in only one theater in Manhattan. Strong response there convinced the company to open *Hollywood Shuffle* more widely.

Prior to the New York opening, the film was previewed at a benefit for the Black Filmmaker Foundation at the Embassy II in Times Square in March 1987. The benefit turned into a major media event when Eddie Murphy and his entourage showed up and generated considerable press coverage for the opening.

The Manhattan run opened at three theaters: the Embassy in midtown, the 86th Street East on the upper East Side, and the Quad in Greenwich Village. The opening was strengthened by favorable reviews from the major press, including the *Times*, the *New York Post*, and the *Daily News*, and local television stations, including the ABC affiliate and the independent WPIX. According to Bowles, the film performed very well in Manhattan.

As part of the overall New York launch, the film opened in seven theaters in New York's outer boroughs and suburbs. Initial performance at these theaters was not as strong as in Manhattan. Three theaters—the New Jersey Bergen Mall, the Sayreville Amboy, and a theater on Long Island—dropped the film after the first week. Nevertheless, nine weeks after the opening, seven of the original ten theaters were still running *Hollywood Shuffle*. In Manhattan and in Valley Stream, Long Island, where *She's Gotta Have It* had a strong run, box-office performance climbed and the film ran for eighteen weeks. Bowles observes, "In retrospect, it wasn't a mistake to go as wide as we did. We learned a lot about what kind of theaters it performed best in."

In the New York and Washington markets, as well as throughout the country, theaters were selected in order to maximize the potential for crossover audience appeal. Thus, the Goldwyn Company sought to place the film in art theaters that were not exclusively in upscale, predominantly white areas. *Hollywood Shuffle* didn't work in unsophisticated "action house" theaters. De Picciotto observes, "The film needed to be positioned in more mainstream houses for wider audience acceptance. When we stopped treating it as a 'black' movie, it performed better. And when the publicity started to hit, black people came out for it."

According to Townsend, the film did well in New York and Washington playing to equally mixed black and white audiences:

> Everybody seems to think it's funny, but sometimes blacks and whites—even in the same audience—laugh at different things. Like

the private eye segment with the jokes about hair straighteners. White audiences will look at each other like, "What's this all about?" and black audiences will be howling, because they recognize that there are people who wouldn't be caught dead without their hair straightened.

National rollout · Given the exceptionally favorable critical reviews and strong initial performances in New York and Washington, the national rollout followed the company's release plan without problems. However, the Goldwyn Company faced a challenge: Since they didn't want to open the film with a wide release, they had to target the right markets adroitly to set the ball rolling for the national release. They had to go directly to the audience that was to give the film support and approval.

The Los Angeles launch occurred six weeks after New York; the film opened in twelve theaters. In many ways Los Angeles is a tougher market to work a film than is New York. According to de Picciotto, "You have to fight to get attention in Los Angeles." She notes that the city is a large, spread-out area and that a distributor has to target individual neighborhoods. A distributor has to place a film in a theater within ten to fifteen minutes by car from these neighborhoods in order to draw effectively. She adds an important observation: "Middle-class blacks are not as geographically clustered in Los Angeles as in the East."

Nevertheless, the Los Angeles launch was buoyed by the effect of the East Coast run and the favorable awareness it generated. Goldwyn moved to position *Hollywood Shuffle* as a more mainstream film, not limited to a specialized release. According to de Picciotto, "It fell in between a wide release and a specialty run." They placed the film in the Baldwin, a traditional black theater, as well as more art-house theaters on the West Side and in Hollywood.

In retrospect, Townsend feels that the film got very good word-of-mouth through favorable critical and promotional efforts. He voices only one complaint:

> The only thing I think was really painful was that I thought we should have opened in a lot more theaters. The Goldwyn Company was taking a more cautious position and was afraid of opening it too widely and having to bite the bullet. I think they could have also spent more money on publicity. But in the end, it's not my money.

Wayans felt that the film failed to reach the broadest possible black audience because of limitations within the Goldwyn Company. "There was a ton of money out there that went untapped," he says, "because they did not undertake a marketing strategy geared to the black audience." He feels that the company "went with a safer campaign for the 'art audience' that they understood. I found this very frustrating."

OTHER MARKETS

Due to its strong theatrical performance, *Hollywood Shuffle* has done well in homevideo. Its initial sale of 62,000 to 65,000 units (compared to, for example, *She's Gotta Have It*, which is estimated at between 20,000 and 25,000 units) made it one of the top one hundred rental videos of the year.

One interesting point about the homevideo release concerns the effective use of cover art. The theatrical art featured Townsend with his girlfriend, suggesting humor and romance. In comparison, the homevideo jacket art shows a group of people chasing Townsend, suggesting that the film is more of an action-adventure movie. According to de Picciotto, the homevideo art was predicated on the film's likely name recognition resulting from the successful theatrical release.

REVIEW

Hollywood Shuffle was born out of a combination of what Robert Townsend describes as "love and determination and a desire to want to change the images that we were seeing of blacks in Hollywood movies." He adds, identifying what many see as the film's most appealing element, "We did not want to be bitter." Reflecting on the making of *Hollywood Shuffle*, Townsend pinpoints the most critical factor in his—and other first-time filmmakers'—undertaking:

> We took a gamble. And that's the key to the whole thing, we weren't afraid. We had fun. There are eighty-three actors in *Hollywood Shuffle*. A lot of those are our friends from years gone by, from New York and

now Los Angeles. We knew it was going to work and that's why they stuck it out. It was a labor of love. What stops people is that they're afraid of failure. That's the deep shit! You've got to go for it.

Keenen Ivory Wayans adds: "What got everyone through was being naïve, not knowing any better. It's done by hook and by crook, it's the hustle! There's no right method to this madness."

Hollywood Shuffle was unquestionably a critical and box-office success that rapidly propelled Robert Townsend's career forward. A special screening of the movie was arranged by Paramount for Eddie Murphy and he was so impressed with the film that he contacted Townsend and invited him to direct his performance film, *Eddie Murphy Raw*. Shot at the Felt Forum in New York's Madison Square Garden, the film was released in September 1987, and met with both critical and commercial success.

Townsend has also been offered a leading role in a forthcoming television series (paying $20,000 per episode), which he turned down. He has hosted a number of HBO comedy specials and performed in an episode of "Amazing Stories." He continues to perform in comedy clubs.

Reflecting on *Hollywood Shuffle*, Townsend makes clear the high personal and professional standards he lives by: "[The movie] is about integrity. A lot of actors say, 'I need work, I need a job.' But you can't compromise your art, if you are truly going to be an artist. And that says it all." He advises filmmakers, "The selling of the movie is just as big a part as the shooting and everything else. It just doesn't stop."

From the Samuel Goldwyn Company's perspective, the film was also a clear success. According to Leonie de Picciotto, all Goldwyn's decisions follow from a simple rule: "Goldwyn wants everybody— including the filmmaker!—to make money. Because of this, we operate with a very conservative spending policy. We're not into billboards on Sunset Boulevard telling the movie community we've got a new release. That's a waste of money. We aim for more effective spending." Eamonn Bowles believes that Goldwyn ran a very cost-effective campaign. He estimates that while "*Hollywood Shuffle* may not have grossed as much as *She's Gotta Have It*, I'm sure we got a better net return." He attributes this to a more modest ad campaign and resisting the impulse to "blow it out" on multiple runs.

MY DINNER WITH ANDRE

(October 1981)

MY DINNER WITH ANDRE

directed by

LOUIS MALLE

produced by
GEORGE W. GEORGE
& BEVERLY KARP

written by, and starring

ANDRE GREGORY
and
WALLACE SHAWN

MY DINNER WITH ANDRE

A New Yorker Films Release © 1981
Available from Grove Press in paperback

PRINCIPALS	*Director*	Louis Malle
	Producers	George W. George and Beverly Karp
	Writers	Wallace Shawn and Andre Gregory
	Principal cast	Andre Gregory and Wallace Shawn
DISTRIBUTORS	*Theatrical*	New Yorker Films
	Homevideo	Pacific Arts Video Records
	Pay cable	ICM
	Nontheatrical	New Yorker Films
	Broadcast	George W. George
	Foreign	Presales by Louis Malle
THEATRICAL	*Opening date*	October 11, 1981
	Total playdates	550
	Box-office gross	$5,250,000 (e)
	Gross film rental	2,100,000 (e)
	Total distributor costs	
	Advance	Minimal
	Publicity	not available
	Prints	80,000 (41 prints and facilities)
	Advertising	200,000
	Misc.	100,000
ANCILLARY	*Homevideo*	$100,000 (e)
	Pay cable	300,000 (e)
	Nontheatrical	70,000 (e)
	Broadcast	Minimal
	Foreign	150,000
PARTICIPANTS CONTACTED		Louis Malle
		George W. George
		Andre Gregory
		Wallace Shawn
		Dan Talbot
		Jeff Lipsky
		Suzanne Weil
		Michael White

e = Estimate based on uncorroborated data derived from *Variety*, other industry sources, and authors' calculations.

FILM SYNOPSIS

Not having seen each other in several years, avant-garde theater director Andre Gregory and playwright Wallace Shawn meet for dinner. During the course of this meal, the enigmatic Gregory regales his less adventurous friend with a discourse on, among other things, the meaning of life, death, and spiritual rebirth.

DEVELOPMENT

Genesis · *My Dinner with Andre* was created, written, and acted by Wallace Shawn and Andre Gregory, two old friends from New York theater circles. Wally Shawn had been writing plays unsuccessfully for six years when he met theater director Andre Gregory in 1971. Gregory was the first person in the professional theater to take Shawn's work seriously. Shawn, in turn, regarded Gregory as a "phenomenally brilliant director." In 1972 Shawn wrote *Our Late Night* for Gregory's company, the Manhattan Project, which Shawn describes as "one of the most celebrated theater companies of that time." The play was performed at the Public Theater in the winter of 1975. Other plays directed by Gregory in the eight-year history of the Manhattan Project were: *Alice in Wonderland,* Samuel Beckett's *Endgame,* and Anton Chekhov's *The Seagull.* All toured the United States and won international acclaim for the company.

Shawn described the development of the script for *My Dinner with Andre* in an article in *Sight and Sound* (1982). He recalled how the pair decided to "think of something we could do together":

> After a few false starts, I came up with the idea that Andre and I could
> do a talking-heads film, based on ourselves. In December 1978 we

began meeting two or three times a week to talk on tape—talking almost at random about everything, including the subject of what sort of film ours might be and what sort of material might be included in it.

In February 1979, I sat down with the tapes and transcripts of our endless conversations and tried to see if anything was in them. Apparently there was only an endless swamp of boring and meaningless junk. But after a few months of study, of sifting through and cataloging the material, sentence by sentence, in a sort of confused and miserable way, certain themes began to emerge; somewhere inside several layers of wrapping, there were certain subjects, certain concerns. Also, two fictional characters, distinct and amusing, seemed to be vaguely visible underneath the incomprehensible surface of the actual people we were. When the idea of the dinner suddenly occurred to me, and a certain structure began to suggest itself, all the thousands of sentences which I had carefully isolated and which lay around my room in various tiny heaps seemed to leap from their places of their own accord and pour themselves like little rivulets into certain major channels. Some long, strange monologues began to appear, made up of lines and phrases culled from dozens of different meetings. Then monologue began to answer monologue, line to answer line, and the whole thing sort of flowed together into a complete story.

Suzanne Weil, another of Gregory's old friends, was involved in the project from the beginning. She was then the director of arts and humanities programming for PBS, and was urging Gregory to develop an idea for television or the cinema. He returned with two projects, one about an acting company in Poland, the other, the piece with Wally Shawn. Weil recalls her enthusiasm about a partnership between the two:

> I had met and liked Wally Shawn and had seen *Our Late Night* at the Public Theater. The idea of Andre and Wally working together was too good to be true. I asked them how much they would need to complete a screenplay. They came up with an estimate, and I authorized a development grant of $23,800 for the project.

Weil was "never in any doubt that this would be a wonderful project." She encouraged them to work toward a theatrical release, since the exposure of theatrical distribution is a benefit to any PBS screening. However, Weil recalls that the major PBS drama series "American Playhouse" and "Great Performances" were not interested.

Several months later, she authorized another grant, this time for $10,000, from a discretionary fund supported by the Mellon Foundation. The Corporation for Public Broadcasting could not be persuaded to invest in the project.

Initially, Gregory's wife, Chiquita, a documentary filmmaker, was going to serve as producer. She tried to raise money for the project but couldn't find supporters. She approached her neighbor George W. George, a successful theatrical producer, whose credits include the Tony Award–winning play *Bedroom Farce* and the film *Rich Kids*. George had known Gregory for years and had always been fascinated by his stories. However, after reading an early draft of the script he decided to pass on it.

Meanwhile, Shawn and Gregory considered the problem of finding a director for the newly finished script. Shawn recalled the thoughts guiding their discussion in his *Sight and Sound* article:

> We obviously needed one of the world's great directors—we knew that in any other hands one could only expect our script to fall totally flat— and yet we wanted to find a director who was not a complete egomaniac, because we hated to think that we ourselves would be forced out of any involvement in our own project. Finally, we wanted someone who we knew would not get nervous at the last moment and start throwing in flashbacks, strange comical diversions in the restaurant, fights in the kitchen, and things like that. By the end of the lunch, we'd decided to send our script at once to Louis Malle.
>
> Andre and I had each met Louis casually a couple of times, but we didn't really know him. We sent him the script through a mutual friend. He read it overnight and called Andre in the morning, and we all met later that day. It was obvious that the script had affected him deeply. He agreed to direct it, and Andre and I set to work learning our lines.

Malle recalls that it was "one of the most beautiful scripts I'd ever read." He was attracted to both of the characters, and to the considerable directorial challenge posed by the script. He volunteered to direct the film himself or help them find the director they wanted. Malle believes that without his involvement, the film would not have been made. For instance, Malle's commitment helped persuade George W. George to agree to produce the film.

Before George committed to the project, Malle offered the property to a dozen or so producers, including Francis Ford Coppola's Zoetrope

Studios. However, he repeatedly received the infuriating advice that "though we loved the script, it's *not* a film, and should be produced for the stage."

When Malle joined the team, he initially served as, in Gregory's words, "a literary editor. He helped us say what we wanted to say, but more economically." Malle worked with them throughout the spring of 1980. The three met almost daily to rehearse and trim the script. Gregory and Shawn sought backers while Malle negotiated distribution for his new film, *Atlantic City.*

Script revisions took place throughout the entire development and preproduction period. During an intensive month of revisions and rehearsals, Malle videotaped scene after scene in order to strengthen the material and to overcome the severe directorial challenge posed by the film's concept. Malle recalls: "I never worked so closely on a script. The experience more closely resembled theatrical rehearsals than preparation for a film." Shawn recalled this process in his *Sight and Sound* article:

> During our rehearsals, we cut about an hour from the text. Louis would propose the cuts; I would be totally shocked and incredulous; then the three of us would talk—I suppose it must have driven Louis mad, but he seemed to accept it—and somehow I would always see that he was right, that a certain passage was secretly redundant, except perhaps for a line or so, and somehow we would all figure out how to make the cut but not lose the line.

The coauthors also gave several readings to potential investors and others interested in the film, providing invaluable opportunities to refine their script.

Financing · George W. George recalls his motives in agreeing to produce the film:

> When Andre Gregory came back with the news that Louis Malle wanted to direct the project, he asked me to reconsider and produce it. He told me that two-thirds of the money was committed. I could see no problem getting the other third, particularly with Louis's involvement. But I should have checked Andre's investors. None of this money came in. I found myself committed to a $525,000 project and all we had in hand was $90,000 or so from European presales.

The principals—Gregory, George, and Shawn—formed a partnership, The Andre Company, to produce the film. They were general partners, and retained fifty percent of the equity, selling the remainder to their investors. George describes Malle's position in the company as "an employee of the general partners. He was dying to make the film, but realizing that it was an unusual project, he didn't want to share financial responsibility." While it looked like Louis Malle's involvement would make a difference in securing financing, it didn't work out that way, mainly because of the unconventional nature of the film.

Initially, George, with Gregory's help, secured a $50,000 investment from Beverly Karp, at "a stiff price." He says, "I gave her a coproducer's credit. In reality it was a 'learning experience' for Beverly Karp, since this was her first outing as a producer of a feature film." Gregory also invested $20,000 obtained from his family.

The filmmakers repeatedly felt that they were close to securing the needed investment only to have it evaporate for one reason or another. George recalls the delicate state of the production:

> I had already put up $30,000 of my own money, and was ready to take the loss. Louis Malle was worried, but I was full of assurances that we'd start on time. They were hollow words, for I was preparing to close up shop.

George recalls that "investors were totally mesmerized by Andre's presentation of the material. But then they'd sit down and think about it—a film about two men in a restaurant. Terror would sink in. Reason would conquer intuition. They'd pull out."

At that time, Gregory and Shawn were performing the piece as a play in London's Royal Court Theatre, a ten-performance engagement that Malle had urged as a necessary, final rehearsal before shooting. Margaret Ramsey, Shawn's celebrated English theatrical agent, urged theater and film producer Michael White to invest. (White's movie credits include *The Rocky Horror Picture Show*, *Stranger's Kiss*, and *Ploughman's Lunch*.) Years earlier, George and White had worked comfortably together on the London production of *Any Wednesday*. White immediately invested approximately $100,000, and George "made him a deal that he couldn't refuse. It was more like the producer's share—dollar for dollar, half on this side, half on the other." When the film was finally in production, the rest of the money fell into place. George deferred his producer's fee.

While at Cannes, Malle was able to secure two presales from European sources: Gaumont paid about $40,000 for the French market, and a German sale was made for another $50,000.

During the fundraising period, Malle shared the script with his friend Dan Talbot, the president of New Yorker Films. Talbot declined to invest in the production, but immediately offered to distribute the film.

Anticipating an audience · Shawn and Gregory did not undertake any systematic research into potential audiences, nor did they anticipate the eventual success of their film. Nonetheless, Gregory recalls a strong conviction that the film would be accessible to a potentially large, although specialized, audience. He also felt that the chemistry between himself and Wally was basically funny and, therefore, attractive to an audience. The anticipated audience, according to Gregory, was made of "doctors, nurses, businessmen, salesmen, stockbrokers, and the like." He felt that all viewers could look at the characters and their discussions of theater and see it as a metaphor, an examination of their own occupations and lives.

George W. George leaves "audience research and all that stuff" to the studios. Recalling his expectations for *Andre*, he says:

> The creator's mind is dominated by the thought that this thing that's got possession of him—in this case making the movie—must be done. There's little room left for another type of mind which coolly and analytically forecasts the composition of his future audience.
>
> I'm more like the creator than the studio executive. As a producer, I do speculate on the audience; but in the case of *Andre*, I was compelled to do what was in my heart. All I could think of was, "How will I ever get it made?" The audience was tomorrow's problem. I didn't have time to think about it.

Wally Shawn gave no thought at all to an audience:

> I just do things because I feel like doing them, and if people happen to like them, then I'm amazed. Everything I'd done previously had been unsuccessful, so I didn't particularly expect that this would be any different.

For his part, Malle anticipated an audience resembling that of a successful foreign art film. This also meant that the film would require a similar distribution strategy. It was this perception that motivated him to take the project at an early stage to Talbot's New Yorker Films.

PRODUCTION

During the preproduction period, George secured a commitment from set designer David Mitchell, whose credits include such Broadway hits as *La Cage aux Folles* and *Annie*.

Production took only three-and-a-half weeks. Only one week was needed for on-location rehearsals, an efficiency made possible by the exhaustive video and theatrical rehearsals preceding production. Two-and-a-half weeks were required for principal photography.

The film was shot in Richmond, Virginia, to avoid the large and costly crews required by the New York craft unions. The producers feared that it would have been financially impossible to make the film under those conditions. After *Andre* had completed its theatrical release, Shawn was called before the disciplinary board of SAG for appearing in a non-SAG film.

> I was found guilty of the charges. They offered to postpone consideration of my punishment for six weeks if the Andre Company would sign retroactively with the union, pay a fine for the use of nonunion extras, and pay SAG rates and residuals to actors who had small speaking parts. For instance, the head waiter, whose only line was "I'll show you to your table," was located and paid. All of this totaled about $7,000, and I was not punished any further.

Malle engaged his French editor, Suzanne Baron, whom he describes as "one of the greatest editors in Europe." She worked under great pressure to complete the picture in six weeks. Malle describes it as one of the most difficult editing jobs he can remember. George recalls his relief that "a cutter who spoke little English could do such a wonderful job on such a wordy film."

DISTRIBUTION DEAL

Making the deal · *Andre* premiered at the 1980 Telluride Film Festival to overwhelming praise; Gregory recalls a five-minute standing ovation and Shawn recalls "our enormous delight as Andre and I found ourselves interviewed extensively and quoted in the media." Kevin Thomas, writing in the *Los Angeles Times*, called it "the festival dazzler." Roger Ebert's *Chicago Sun-Times* review was even more glowing:

> A tour de force named *My Dinner with Andre* was the surprise hit of this year's Telluride festival, receiving a tumultuous standing ovation and inspiring countless impassioned discussions. And my guess is that *My Dinner with Andre* will come down out of the mountains and become one of the most talked about serious films of the year.

Andre was shown a month later at the New York Film Festival, to an enthusiastic reception. Andre and Shawn participated in a panel discussion after the screening, and again they were pursued for interviews. In its coverage of the festival, the *New York Times* gave it a positive but not a rave review.

Besides Talbot's personal relationship with Malle, other factors contributed to New Yorker Films's acquisition of *Andre*. These included:

- No money up front was demanded.
- It was a low-risk film for which marketing costs could be contained in the $50,000–100,000 range.
- New Yorker Films would also acquire nontheatrical/16mm rights, which it foresaw as a very lucrative market.

Jeff Lipsky, who handled the actual marketing and sales for New Yorker Films, recalls his reaction to *Andre*:

> It was bursting with ideas and comedy and pathos. The concept was different. It was audacious and challenging. What these two guys do in this film is what everyone in America does. They don't go out and shoot up stores; they sit down and talk. Maybe some of it went over [some people's] heads or seemed preposterous but it was clear that no one was perfect. It had elements of human frailty and imperfection.

Dan Talbot recalls Lipsky's early response quite differently:

> He hated the film. He wouldn't talk to me for about two weeks after he saw it. Yet it's a tribute to his brilliant abilities as a sales manager that

he didn't allow his dislike of the film to interfere with a magnificent job of selling it around the country.

Talbot himself loved the film from the first screening.

Terms of the deal · New Yorker Films is an independent distributor with a low level of capitalization. Because of tight operating margins, the company cannot invest heavily in any film it acquires. Up to the time of *Andre*, it had a limit of about $25,000 per film for acquisition costs. As with other independent distributors, each acquisition, in Lipsky's words, "had to sink or swim on its own."

Key features of the deal were:

· A New York opening at a New Yorker Films theater soon after the New York Film Festival, followed by a rollout to art houses in other major markets across the country.
· A "take it as it goes" approach, whereby continuing promotion expenditures would be assessed on the basis of box-office performance.

The filmmakers accepted Talbot's offer because they had no other viable distribution options.

Even though the film had been received well at festivals and by the press, they were disheartened by the generally poor response demonstrated by distributors. George W. George recalls that there were individuals at Universal and United Artists who were very interested in *Andre*, but felt that "a film like this is such a freak to the studios that they wouldn't know how to handle it."

Of the New Yorker Films deal, George says: "It was a tough deal. They took a lot. But I had no experience with the distribution of a film like this, and deferred to Louis Malle. And this was the best we could get."

During the summer and fall of 1980, New Yorker Films prepared for the film's theatrical release.

MARKETING CAMPAIGN

Strategy · New Yorker Films's initially modest expectations for *My Dinner with Andre* shaped its marketing strategy. Surprisingly, when the film unexpectedly took off, the company did not fundamentally change the way it handled the film.

The initial strategy called for building off *Andre*'s success at the Telluride and New York film festivals with a limited release to art houses in the major markets. This was to be supported by a few press screenings and a modest print ad campaign. Further decisions would await the film's performance.

The campaign was targeted to the art-house film community, to people who followed the work of an acclaimed director like Malle, and to people who might be familiar with Gregory's and Shawn's work in the theater.

The film ultimately acquired a kind of cult status, stimulated by what the distributor sees as an impressive and spontaneous word-of-mouth following. After the film took off, the distributor maintained a modest marketing and promotional presence in each market in order to further promote the sense that each viewer could discover the movie, a tactic intended to heighten the sense of selectivity the film had achieved.

Promotion and publicity · Promotion hinged on personal appearances by Gregory and Shawn, who had never really thought about the marketing aspect of distribution, nor that they would be called upon to sell the film through extensive promotional activities. They traveled a great deal, both to major markets and to the "fly-over" cities usually bypassed during the promotion of specialized films. Because of the very literate nature of the film, Gregory and Shawn found a great deal of receptivity to *Andre* among local editors, feature writers, and film reviewers. As Jeff Lipsky recalls:

> The success of every specialized film depends on the promotional involvement of the filmmakers. Wally and Andre were relentless in their efforts. And, as they are also unusually personable, and therefore appealing to feature writers and critics, their efforts made an enormous contribution to the success of the film.

One of the more innovative promotional devices planned was a series of radio ads that featured personal endorsements by Roy Scheider, Ann Beattie, and others. According to the distributor, these spots helped to generate further word-of-mouth.

Trailer and ad · The $4,000 trailer was cut by a local editor employed by George W. George, and the continuity was written by Lipsky. Because of the low-budget nature of the production, no money was put aside for later advertising and promotional requirements. However, photographer Diana Michener's excellent production stills were available. There was no unit publicist assigned to the film during production.

THEATRICAL RELEASE

Strategy · As originally planned, *Andre* was expected to have a very limited theatrical run. The New York opening was planned to take place shortly after a screening at the film festival, thereby building on the prestige of that festival to generate interest. The distributor planned to then assess its performance on a day-to-day basis, in order to decide on how long to keep it running and in what other cities to open it. Publicity was handled in-house to control costs.

Opening run · *My Dinner with Andre* opened at the Lincoln Plaza Cinema on October 11, 1981. The reviews were positive, although usually qualified, like that in *Newsday* which advised readers that this was a film for "the discerning filmgoer." Vincent Canby's crucial review in the *New York Times* was tepid. He wrote:

> It must be added, however, that not all the talk is so fascinating that one's interest doesn't flag. It might be better if it were a conversation heard at the next table, one on which one could tune in and out at will.

Shawn recalls opening day:

> Andre and I were enormously excited by *Andre*'s fantastic reception at Telluride and at the New York Film Festival, but here was the real test! We wandered around outside the Lincoln Plaza to see if anyone was going in. They weren't! It was a big disappointment. It looked as if *My Dinner with Andre* would go on the scrapheap of history. We stood on the pavement shocked, and helpless!

The box-office grosses for the first three weeks were $4,525, $8,037, and $5,237. The house nut was $5,700, in addition to which the distributor incurred co-op ad costs.

As the downward slide continued, *Andre* was losing money. By the end of week six, Talbot prepared to replace the film with something more suitable for the holiday season. A "last ten days" notice was pasted onto print ads. However, at a momentous meeting held in Talbot's office, Talbot was joined by Lipsky, José Lopez, Sr. (New Yorker Films's vice-president), Gregory, Shawn, and George to decide on the fate of the film. In Gregory's words, he "groveled and begged" Talbot to keep *Andre* running for a few more weeks; he even volunteered to advance his own money to pay for bigger ads. He argued that the reactions at the festivals proved that people who saw the film loved it. Therefore, if *Andre* could only hang on long enough, word-of-mouth would start to work for it. Talbot refused Gregory's offer of money, but agreed to continue the run. A powerful argument in its favor was the national box-office potential promised by coverage in *Newsweek*, *Rolling Stone*, and *Vogue*. Shawn suggests that perhaps it was Talbot's fondness for the film that "persuaded him to suppress his better business judgment" and keep the film on. Lipsky recalls that "an exhibitor's decision to pull a film is almost always irreversible."

George W. George recalls how he prepared to reconcile himself to the failure of a high-risk venture, but one of which he was enormously proud.

Then, to everyone's surprise, *Andre* gained a sudden new lease on life. There are differing opinions on why this happened. According to many of the participants, a review by Siskel and Ebert on their PBS show, "Sneak Previews," helped fuel favorable word-of-mouth, leading to mounting box-office grosses. In that program, Siskel and Ebert reviewed *Andre* along with *Reds* and two other studio films, and found it to be the superior film. Later, they listed *Andre* as one of the year's "ten best." In George W. George's view, the Siskel and Ebert review was "*the* critical factor in the film's success":

It wasn't just that they reviewed it positively, they reviewed it against a film that had been overwhelmed with publicity all season long. When the reviewers recommended *Andre* as "the one you must see," it created a tremendous sense of expectation that such an unknown could be favorably compared to *Reds*. The effect of this review was as fantastic and direct as a rave from theater critic Frank Rich in the *New York Times* for a New York theatrical opening.

Louis Malle takes a different view, arguing that the most important factor was the film's own capacity to generate positive word-of-mouth. The director explains:

> The nature of this film was a great handicap to word-of-mouth. When someone says, "I saw a great film last weekend," and his companion asks, "What's it about?", the reply, "About two guys sitting in a restaurant," is not going to make anyone rush out and see it. It takes four or five positive comments before word-of-mouth becomes so forceful that it overcomes resistance to the subject matter. That process took five or so weeks in New York.

Malle points out that throughout November and December public interest was further stimulated by a series of favorable reviews and feature pieces appearing in the local press.

Wallace Shawn believes that the rave on "Sneak Previews" was decisive. He argues that word-of-mouth requires a critical mass of viewers to see a film, and that box office was below that threshold in the first weeks. According to Shawn, the Siskel and Ebert review "put those mouths into the cinema so that the good word could be spread."

All these factors contributed to a record-breaking fifty-four-week run at the Lincoln Plaza. Jeff Lipsky disclosed the gross advertising costs incurred in maintaining that record run (though he cautions that New York advertising rates are about twice as costly today): for weeks one through sixteen, $39,000; for weeks seventeen through twenty, $8,000; and for weeks twenty-one through fifty-two, $28,000.

Average costs of only $430 per week in the latter weeks consisted of very small ads in the *New York Times* and the *Village Voice*, though every five or six weeks, New Yorker Films would place a larger ad "as a reminder," for a cost of approximately $3,000.

National playoff · The New York experience was duplicated throughout the country. Shawn and Gregory traveled extensively over five months or so, to reach such markets as Los Angeles, Chicago, Philadelphia, San Francisco, Boston, and Toronto. They recall this period as a wonderful experience.

In Los Angeles, *Andre* opened at the Westland Twin Theater in March 1981. A local publicist was retained, at a cost of approximately $7,000. During the early part of the run, it performed poorly. However, there was a sense that it was catching on. Michael White, on a visit to Hollywood, found that people were hosting "Andre Dinners." In order to attend, you had to have seen the film and be able to sustain a conversation for the evening. To White, this indicated the emergence of a cultlike following for the film. Following the Siskel and Ebert review, word-of-mouth spread and grosses more than doubled and held. The film ran for forty weeks.

Lipsky has retained a revealing record of gross rentals at the Westland Twin, together with Los Angeles advertising costs during the first four months of *Andre*'s "dream run":

Week	Box-Office Gross	Gross Film Rental	Advertising Costs
1	$ 5,762	$ 1,441	$2,250
2	7,124	2,812	750
3	6,977	2,679	650
4	9,641	5,077	650
5	8,921	4,429	650
6	11,382	6,644	650
7	10,210	5,409	650
8	14,257	8,781	650
9	16,763	11,217	650
10	16,586	11,327	800
11	17,845	12,460	710
12	15,008	9,907	3,500
13	17,707	12,332	650
14	16,515	11,263	650
15	17,513	11,802	2,900

Lipsky does not recall the reason for the jump in advertising costs in weeks twelve and fifteen. Total grosses in Los Angeles were nearly $200,000 during these fifteen weeks, yet costs, including the publicist and travel, were under $30,000.

Shawn recalls "lots of excitement" in Los Angeles over "the thought that such a strange movie, with so much talking, would be so successful. It was as if it promised a future that could be different."

In San Francisco, the film opened in November 1981 at the Gateway Theater. Mixed reviews contributed to a disastrous start. Ben Myron, the owner of the Gateway, threatened to pull it for a Woody Allen festival. Only pleading telephone calls from Lipsky and Gregory convinced him to give the film a couple of extra weeks to catch on. At that moment, the Siskel and Ebert review was broadcast and grosses jumped 300 percent and kept climbing for about ten weeks. The Gateway run totaled twenty weeks. Lipsky indicates the first five-week ad costs were $7,500, a higher figure than Los Angeles due to the relative costs of advertising space.

In Chicago, grosses at the Sandburg Theater again demonstrated the dramatic influence of the "Sneak Previews" review. Performances during the first four weeks were as follows:

Week	Box-Office Gross	Gross Film Rental	Advertising Costs
1	$12,385	$ 7,425	$3,100
2	8,409	4,204	2,000
3	18,073	8,616	4,000
4	23,366	13,379	1,800

In Boston, the film opened at the Nickelodeon Theater in December and played poorly. Following the same pattern as in the other cities, performance improved considerably with box-office grosses jumping from $10,655 in week one to $19,307 in week three. *Andre* ran at the Nickelodeon for twenty-six weeks. According to Lipsky, Boston first-week ad costs were $3,500, the highest in the country outside of New York.

The performance in the major markets was duplicated in many smaller markets across the country. The pattern in Houston is typical:

Week	Gross Film Rental	Advertising Costs
1	$1,856	$1,200
2	688	400
3	1,045	242
4	2,559	650

After having opened in November and closed after only three weeks in Denver and Phoenix, the film reopened in the same theaters in February 1982 and ran for an additional six weeks. Lipsky describes this as "unprecedented." It also performed well in Texas, Oregon, and

Washington, where no one expected it to find a significant audience. In all, forty-one prints were struck and the total number of playdates during the course of the film's eighteen-month theatrical run was over 550. Lipsky indicates that the total distribution costs for *Andre* were approximately $400,000. This breaks down as $80,000 for prints, $200,000 for advertising, $15,000 for printing (of one-sheet, etc.), and $100,000 for miscellaneous expenses.

OTHER MARKETS

Homevideo · Homevideo rights were assigned to Pacific Arts Video Records, whose only other successful product at that time had been *Elephant Parts*, a cult film that George felt had been handled brilliantly. George was attracted to the firm "because I liked the guy and I always go with people I like." In addition, he feared that *Andre* would be lost in the "packaged goods" world of the major homevideo distributors. George was offered a sizeable advance "in the $25,000 range," and royalties of 15 percent, which have earned nearly $100,000 to date.

Pay cable · These rights were handled by ICM, in "a highly segmented fashion." According to George, revenues to date are "in the several hundreds of thousands."

Nontheatrical · New Yorker Films received film rentals of between $50,000 and $70,000 in the first year, which were on a par with any title in the company's catalog. There was only a "twenty or so percent" decline in the following year, according to Lipsky. It is still performing well.

Broadcast · George is currently negotiating with PBS.

Foreign · *Andre* performed well in art houses in the English-speaking markets of Canada, the U.K., and Australia. Two versions were released in France, subtitled and dubbed. Despite a positive critical response, poor box-office performance reflected the inability of either version to capture the subtlety of the dialogue. A dubbed version did not perform well in Germany. Openings were also recorded in Holland and Spain.

Other · George W. George is investigating audiocassette distribution of *Andre*.

REVIEW

Andre is a specialty film that succeeded despite the minimum amount of predetermination of its future audience. It is an example of a concept that drove its creators and its producer to complete a work because of the power of the idea, rather than of any supposed fit between the idea and an audience. Yet, in a general sense, its expected audience was the art-film moviegoer, particularly one who would be attracted to a work directed by Louis Malle.

The success of *Andre* invites a consideration of the relationship between the great influence of the major critics and the functioning of word-of-mouth. Most of the principals agree that without the accolade from Siskel and Ebert, *My Dinner with Andre* would have failed to attract enough of an audience at its New York opening run to allow word-of-mouth to develop.

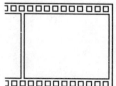

OLD ENOUGH

(August 1984)

A FILM THAT WILL HOLD, ENTERTAIN AND MOVE AN AUDIENCE."
—William Wolf, Gannett News Service

"A FASCINATING FILM...
IT'S AN INDEPENDENT PRODUCTION ALL THE WAY, AND A MOST
POLISHED EXAMPLE OF THE BREED."
—David Sterritt, Christian Science Monitor

**"THE FILM HAS AN ESPECIALLY CLEAR UNDERSTANDING OF THE
POWER PLAYS THAT GO ON BETWEEN GIRLS OF THEIR AGE.
MISS HARVEST IS A BEAUTY. MISS SILVER IS A YOUNG
DIRECTOR WHO WORKS WITH A LOT OF ASSURANCE...
SUPERB CINEMATOGRAPHY."**
—Janet Maslin, New York Times

"'OLD ENOUGH' HAS
REAL MAGIC."
—Bruce Handy, Vogue

"'OLD ENOUGH' IS A
FRESH LOOK AT
ADOLESCENCE BUT
ITS CHARM IS ADULT-
SIZED."
—Stephen Schaefer, US Magazine

"A FIRST-RATE
WORK."
—Caroline Miller, Newsday

"AN IMPRESSIVE
DEBUT FOR WRITER-
DIRECTOR MARISA
SILVER."
—Jim Calio, People Magazine

"'OLD ENOUGH' IS
GOOD ENOUGH, AND
THEN SOME."
—New York Post

"★★★
REMARKABLY
POLISHED...A
LIKEABLY BUOYANT
COMEDY."
—Kathleen Carroll, N.Y.
Daily News

"'OLD ENOUGH'
CAPTURES THE
FLAVOR OF BEING
YOUNG, RICH OR
POOR, IN NEW
YORK."
—Judith Crist, WOR-TV

OLD ENOUGH

Silverfilm Productions Inc. presents
SARAH BOYD RAINBOW HARVEST NEILL BARRY in OLD ENOUGH
Starring DANNY AIELLO FRAN BRILL Co-starring ROXANNE HART SUSAN KINGSLEY
Production Designer JEFFREY TOWNSEND Director of Photography MICHAEL BALLHAUS
Color by Du-Art Produced by DINA SILVER Written and Directed by MARISA SILVER

PG PARENTAL GUIDANCE SUGGESTED
SOME MATERIAL MAY NOT BE SUITABLE FOR CHILDREN

1984 Orion Classics An ORION CLASSICS Release

Because we weren't willing to relinquish those roles, it made sense to make the film independently.

Marisa submitted her script and a sample reel to the Sundance Institute and was accepted to its June Filmmakers' Lab in 1982. During the month at Sundance, Marisa had the opportunity to refine the script, working with actors and directing selected scenes on videotape.

Financing · Building upon contacts made at Sundance and the enthusiasm generated, the filmmakers went to Hollywood to see if any of the studios or commercial film companies would be interested in the project. While they were treated forthrightly, they were universally turned down. As Dina Silver recalls:

It was hard for studio heads to believe that a small story like *Old Enough*, which could be made for a song, could be financially worthwhile. It couldn't be profitable at the level they required.

Undaunted, the filmmakers viewed their trip in terms of their need to "leave no stone unturned" in the search for financing.

With Hollywood's doors closed, the Silvers returned to New York and planned their production effort and strategy for raising financing. They made a commitment to spend a full year attempting to raise the $750,000 originally budgeted. If, after the year, they hadn't secured financing, they would reassess their plans. Their first decision was to divide the labor: Marisa began the search for a director of photography, a cast, and a production designer, while Dina focused on the fundraising process.

The director sent cinematographer Michael Ballhaus the script. After reading it, he agreed to serve as director of photography. Ballhaus had shot films the previous year for John Sayles and Margarethe von Trotta, and was the cinematographer for nine Rainer Werner Fassbinder films, a track record that increased the film's appeal to investors. Marisa also initiated preliminary casting, interviewing scores of young girls from New York City.

Dina set up a limited partnership, the Around the Block Company. She also put together a publicity packet that included biographies of the principals, a script synopsis, the Sundance acceptance letter, the NEA grant award notification, a description of the company and its overall intentions, a discussion of the film's marketing possibilities, and the production budget. She also initiated discussions with Film Gallery, which she wanted to serve as cogeneral partner of the limited partnership along with the Silvers' newly formed production company, Silverfilm Productions, Inc. Upon its joining the venture, Film Gallery's corporate bio was included in the publicity packet.

Film Gallery was founded in 1977 to license rights of completed films in ancillary markets, particularly pay cable and homevideo. By 1983, company principals Mark Balsam and James Dudelson, formerly Wall Street investment brokers, had decided to acquire films at the production stage. As Balsam explains, Film Gallery could make better acquisition deals at the "front end" (i.e., the script stage) as opposed to the "back end," when the film was completed. Film Gallery could in this way generate more money in distribution fees on ancillary markets, as well as participate as an equity investor in its overall returns.

With *Old Enough*, Film Gallery struck such a deal, investing in the production in return for an equity position on revenues from all markets as well as securing a distribution fee for both the domestic pay-cable and homevideo markets. According to Balsam:

> The timing [of the *Old Enough* deal] was very propitious for us. First, as coproducers, we picked up an equity position in the underlying negative. We felt that the [film] business was growing to a point that with the proliferation of all ancillary markets, especially homevideo, the ownership of negatives—even partial ownership—was very important. Second, I liked the film: it was attractive as far as the cast was concerned; I liked the relationship of the two protagonists; and I'd seen Marisa's work in the past and felt she was becoming a very talented director.

Film Gallery and Silverfilm put together the partnership agreement as a step deal, with three contingent budgets based on the level of investment secured. The film cost $635,000, of which $460,000 was raised through the limited partnership. The balance was deferred; this included partial DuArt Lab costs, partial crew, director, and producer fees, and completion bond. Film Gallery committed a fixed amount of the overall budget, and Silverfilm sought to raise its portion by selling units to limited partners.

Under the terms of the partnership agreement, "first money" would go toward payment of the deferred costs. After all deferments were paid and distribution fees taken off the top, the limited partners would recoup their investment through a dollar-for-dollar share of revenues with the general partners.

Dina Silver undertook the task of finding investors. She talked to everyone she knew and anyone else she could find, and was very candid with people about the risks involved. "I wanted desperately to pay their monies back, but there were no guarantees," she says. "I made this clear to all our investors." She initially provided the promotional packet and script to prospective investors and followed this up with a formal offering plan. She also added the legal opinion she had commissioned on the tax advantages of a partnership, which, in New York, is limited to only thirty-five people. She wanted to make potential investors feel that their money was in competent hands. The final investor group included doctors, dentists, and accountants. She says:

> I made an effort in each meeting with a [prospective] investor to get someone else's name; otherwise, you come to a dead end quickly. Raising money is not magic but elbow grease. If you can talk to enough people, and you've got something saleable, eventually you find the money.

Her strategy in strengthening investor confidence included a discussion of Film Gallery's distribution experience and the potential financial returns from ancillary markets. Most of the investors she courted were unaware of how important these markets are as a means of recovering investments in feature film production. Film financing was completed with a $50,000 investment in the limited partnership by the Sundance Institute.

Anticipating an audience • The filmmakers originally conceived *Old Enough* for an adult art-house audience. They saw some potential crossover to the youth market if, as Dina said, "we could figure out how to get kids into those theaters." Because the film does not fit the formula for mass-market youth films like *Pretty in Pink*, for example, the filmmakers hoped it might become the first art film for kids.

PRODUCTION

While some preproduction activities took place during the development phase, official preproduction took eight weeks and focused on extensive preparations that would keep shooting costs down. The director worked with cinematographer Ballhaus and production designer Jeffrey Townsend, story-boarding every scene and talking it through in great detail. She also worked with the actors before going to the locations so that everything was thoroughly planned before a shot was taken.

During this phase, the filmmakers also negotiated their guild and union agreements. Because they approached the unions early, and explained their low-budget production and youth orientation, they were able to negotiate sympathetic deals. The agreements included: a SAG low-budget contract, a NABET deal permitting a mixed NABET and nonunion crew, and provisions for only one teamster on the production payroll. As Marisa Silver was not in the DGA, a guild agreement was not required for production.

Production began on July 18, 1983, and *Old Enough* was shot in 35mm with principal photography taking thirty-one days. Production was divided into two teams. The producer worked with production manager Michael Nozik and auditor Barbara Lucey to oversee the finances, keeping strict control over expenditures and budgetary allocations. This tight budgetary control permitted the creative team—Marisa Silver, Ballhaus, and Townsend—to keep the production running smoothly and costs down.

According to the producer: "There was never a time when you got to the set and you'd see Marisa thinking about what she wanted to do. She had thought it through and knew the location." No days of location shooting were lost, and, as Dina Silver happily states, "The film came in under budget."

The film was edited by Mark Burns, in his debut assignment as a feature editor, over a four-month period. No editing was done during the shoot; it was an extra expense they could not afford. Lab work was done by DuArt, under a partial deferment agreement.

DISTRIBUTION DEAL

Making the deal · Dina Silver approached many distributors during the development phase and sought to develop preliminary word-of-mouth recognition among this all-important community. When *Old Enough* was finally completed, she met with Nathaniel Kwit, former head of United Artists Classics (the first studio classics division). He advised Dina on what to look for in a distributor. Based on this advice, she made up a list of companies that she wanted to pursue for distribution.

At the top of the list was Orion Classics, a company that had expressed an early interest. Her reasons for selecting Orion Classics had much to do with its staff: they were experienced and smart, they spent less money to get a film out than other companies, they had had a lot of success with foreign art films, and they were looking for their first American film to release. She screened the film for them first, and they expressed strong interest in acquiring it.

During the winter of 1983–84, while negotiations with Orion Classics were going on, the filmmakers continued showing the film to other distributors. They premiered *Old Enough* at the U.S. Film Festival in Park City, Utah, in January 1984, where it won the grand prize. The filmmakers selected the U.S. Film Festival for the premiere because the timing was right: they had just completed the film and wanted to stimulate more visibility during the selling period. As Dina Silver recalls:

> Premiering at Park City was a huge gamble. We had an offer from Orion Classics, but felt that it was not substantial enough. We took a risk. If the film hadn't done well, we would have jeopardized our offer. But the risk was outweighed by the opportunity to show the film to all the distributors there. We knew that a strong favorable response would also have the effect of putting pressure on Orion to better their terms.

The film's strong showing did, in fact, strengthen Orion Classics's belief in the film.

Orion Classics's offer turned out to be the most attractive one, and the deal was concluded in February. Orion decided to acquire the film because of several factors. Most important, the three principals who run the company—Michael Barker, Tom Bernard, and Donna Gigliotti—liked the film. Furthermore, they thought the story of two sisters collaborating on their first film provided a promising promotional angle and, finally, that the film had other strong, marketable elements: the interest of its subject and its New York setting; the fine supporting cast of Danny Aiello and Susan Kingsley; and the work of a world-class cinematographer. However, Orion Classics had one serious reservation going into the deal: the ancillary rights had been secured by Film Gallery as part of the partnership agreement.

Terms of the deal · In acquiring *Old Enough* for theatrical distribution, Orion Classics made a commitment to the filmmakers that it would back the film even if it did not perform well. In turn, Orion expected the filmmakers to be committed to the marketing process, to be available for promotional appearances, and to consult on the campaign. While the film was not successful in its theatrical run, both parties fulfilled their commitments.

The filmmakers sought a deal that would include a guaranteed theatrical release in ten major markets, a minimum dollar commitment for prints and advertising, the acceptance of their partnership agreement with Film Gallery for domestic ancillary markets, and the retention of rights to all European markets.

While Orion Classics was quite willing to accommodate all the filmmakers' stipulations regarding the domestic theatrical release, they were very unhappy with the prospect of being cut out of all revenues from the ancillary markets. According to Tom Bernard, "We were the ones at risk in putting up money to develop an ad campaign and promotional momentum that would be used in the other markets, so we strongly felt we should participate in the ancillary sales revenues." Dina Silver appreciated Orion's concerns:

> Orion was not thrilled with the presale arrangements, because videocassette and cable markets can provide important downside protection for an investment in theatrical distribution. But we were also at risk in having to repay our investors. What was important for us was that the monies [from sales in these markets] come directly into the partnership rather than being [cross-collateralized] by Orion against other markets. So, we cut Orion in for a small percentage of those markets, and paid them directly.

Other features of the deal included a sizeable advance (between $100,000 and $200,000) and a nine-month theatrical window. While the filmmakers had the right to meet and discuss the trailer, ad, and other features of the campaign, Orion had full and final authority over marketing decisions.

MARKETING CAMPAIGN

Strategy · While working out the details of their agreement, the filmmakers and distributor held numerous meetings to develop the broad outlines of the marketing campaign. The initial objectives were to build prerelease interest in the film and to identify the nature of its potential audience.

While festival runs are not covered under distribution deals, they are an important means of building word-of-mouth prior to opening. Orion Classics worked with the filmmakers in showing the film at the Houston, Seattle, and Cannes festivals. Their publicist, Renee Furst, arranged a well-attended press luncheon at Cannes, where the film received a standing ovation.

After considerable research and discussion, the film was targeted first to the youth audience and secondarily to the adult art-house audience. This mixed strategy reflected an underlying difference between the filmmakers and their theatrical distributors. The Silvers hoped that *Old Enough* would cross over to reach younger people, as did *Breaking Away.* The distributors were less optimistic, looking initially to the older, art-house audience (who might be encouraged to bring their children) as the strongest market.

The distributors ultimately decided to adopt the youth-market strategy because of three compelling factors:

· The favorable response at Cannes, where many critics and film industry representatives expressed the opinion that teenagers would take to it.

· The successful test-marketing of the film among young people in Seattle, where the producer's local rep, Jeff Dowd, served as publicist. (The film had also received favorable press when it played at the Seattle Film Festival.)

• The favorable test-marketing in New York at the 72nd Street Embassy, where upwards of 1,000 young people saw the film. Analysis of the audience's evaluation cards indicated that boys liked it as much as girls, and that these young Manhattanites responded favorably to the film's New York feel.

The campaign strategy was finally determined during May–June 1984, and plans were set in motion for theatrical openings to coincide with the new school year. Unfortunately, this strategy failed—the youth audience simply did not come out for the film. Film Gallery's Balsam said, "We made a mistake. It's hard to sell an art film as a youth-oriented film, and we weren't able to do so."

Promotion and publicity · *Old Enough* garnered considerable press attention through reviews and feature articles. Publicity was handled by Lois Smith and Peggy Siegal, with coordination by Sally Fisher. According to Marisa Silver, who met regularly with the publicists, they did a "tremendous job [in generating] a lot of national publicity for a small film."

In New York, *Old Enough* was the subject of four *New York Times* pieces (including a mixed review by Janet Maslin, a special promo by Lawrence Van Gelder's "At the Movies" column, a special Style feature on the Silver family, and a prominent mention in a news piece covering Cannes); two reviews in the *Daily News*; single reviews in the *New York Post*, the *Village Voice*, *New York* magazine, *Women's Wear Daily*, and *Newsday*; as well as television reviews on the local NBC, ABC, and Metromedia affiliates. There were also reviews in such general-audience magazines as *Seventeen* and *Playboy*, and a three-page spread in *People*; and reviews in other leading newspapers such as the *Chicago Sun-Times* and the *Chicago Tribune*, the *Los Angeles Times* and *L.A. Weekly*, the Seattle *Post-Intelligencer*, the *Boston Globe*, and the *Christian Science Monitor*.

From the earliest review in *Ms.* magazine, at the time of the film's premiere at the U.S. Film Festival, *Old Enough* was plagued by mixed notices. Orion's Bernard explains why strong critical endorsement is so important for a film like this:

People felt so ambivalent about the film that it needed the reviewer's stamp-of-approval to make it the "number three choice"—i.e., after the new Hollywood release and the one you've missed, next you should see *Old Enough.*

Conversely, however, Dina Silver found that there was no noticeable correlation between good reviews in a given market and box-office performance. She doesn't think the reviews were a critical factor in the film's performance:

> It was surprising to me that even in markets where the reviews were extremely favorable, people did not go out to see the film. The conclusion I draw from this is that the youth audience was not interested in a delicate film about young people, and that the adult art market, contrarily, would prefer to view films about adults when given the chance. *Old Enough* fell between the cracks of these segments of the theatrical audience.

Trailer and ad · The distributor worked with the director in cutting the trailer. According to Marisa Silver, the trailer was carefully constructed so as to avoid overstating or misstating the film in a way that would create false expectations.

The ad concept was developed by Orion's Barker and Bernard, and executed by its agency, Diener, Hauser, Bates, and Co. While the filmmakers had taken stills during production, they were not used for the ad. New stills were shot. (When the film was shown at Cannes, the original stills were used. These more "arty" shots were considered more appropriate for this festival.)

Orion Classics, respecting its commitment to give the film their best shot, developed a series of radio ads that were placed on both youth-oriented and more mainstream stations. These radio spots had no noticeable effect on audience turnout. The filmmakers faulted Orion for not putting television spots on MTV and other youth-oriented music-video shows. (A breakdown of trailer and ad costs is found in the "National playoff" section.)

THEATRICAL RELEASE

Strategy · Orion Classics presells its films to most of the major markets before they open. With *Old Enough*, Orion Classics had contractually "locked" the top fifteen markets with guaranteed playdates. As of June 1985, the film had played in eighty markets and, during the course of its eighteen-month theatrical run, was expected to have a total of 250 playdates in the United States and Canada.

Concerned about mixed reviews, Orion Classics decided to open the film in Seattle. Orion had opened other films here, such as *Another Country*, a move that had led to positive trade awareness prior to moving the film into New York.

As the film began its theatrical life, the distributor had to revise the original marketing plan aimed at the youth market. Orion found that many people liked the film, though not enough to recommend it to others. In Bernard's words, the filmmakers "did too good a job," meaning that in terms of visual style the film was too much like a Hollywood film, and not distinct, eccentric, or offbeat enough to attract a committed or cult following.

Opening run · The film opened at Seattle's Varsity Theater in August 1984 to mixed reviews. The opening date was selected to precede the opening of school in order to capitalize on word-of-mouth if the picture caught on. Prior to the opening, Jeff Dowd, the local producer's rep, and Nancy Locke, the local publicity consultant, held screenings for kids, printed and distributed fliers, and ran radio spots targeted to the teen and adult art audiences. The filmmakers went to Seattle to help generate publicity. Randy Finley's Seven Gables theater organization, which included the Varsity, handled the local promotional efforts, while overall coordination was handled through Orion's New York office.

The film's first-week performance, a gross of $10,000, pleased the distributor. During the second week, however, grosses fell by one-third, and third-week grosses dropped by another half. The distributor concluded that the film was not benefiting from good word-of-mouth, and they were on the phone daily with the local publicist trying to pump it up. During the Labor Day weekend, more money was spent on bigger newspaper ads with additional favorable quotes, but with no apparent box-office impact. Nonetheless, the film ran for a total of fourteen weeks (including two weeks at the Ridgemont Theater) and, while grosses were not high enough to make a profit, the film broke even.

National playoff · Faced with the poor showing in Seattle, Orion could have pulled the film after a three-week run in the city or not opened in New York. Orion did, however, have contractual obligations for a fixed number of national openings, as well as a large financial exposure in terms of the advance and previously incurred marketing costs that they had to try to recoup. More important, according to Bernard, "We bought the film, we believed in the film, and we wanted to make it work." Orion stuck with it.

Usually in specialty film marketing, the New York run is key to generating momentum for a national rollout. Although extensive preview screenings were organized and the film received considerable press attention in New York, the film, in Bernard's words, "didn't turn the numbers." Opening at the 72nd Street Embassy, the film lasted for six weeks. Box-office grosses during the first four weeks were $16,538; $13,497; $10,327; and $7,238. To keep it alive, Orion moved *Old Enough* downtown for one week at the Film Forum 2 and then to the St. Mark's Theater.

According to Bernard, "We didn't make money in New York," but not due to lack of effort or expense. The distributor spent between $60,000 and $75,000 on the New York run. In addition to the usual newspaper ads, fliers were placed in Embassy and New Yorker theaters around the city (the help of the latter chain was secured through the cooperation of owner Dan Talbot). The film's trailer was cross-plugged in other Embassy houses, and fliers were distributed to people waiting to purchase half-price Broadway show tickets at the Times Square TKTS booth and to audiences attending the Cinemas I and II.

In the face of the poor showings in Seattle and New York, the distributors pressed on. Even though the film received three-and-a-half stars from critic Roger Ebert, the film performed, according to Orion, only "fairly well" in Chicago. In Los Angeles, *Old Enough* played for two disappointing weeks at the Cineplex. Most disappointing and surprising to both the filmmakers and the distributor was the film's poor four-week engagement at Boston's Nickelodeon Theater, where a stronger showing had been anticipated.

A partial breakdown of expenses incurred by Orion Classics for the release of *Old Enough* follows:

Advertising	$ 24,400
Trailer (cut and edit)	
Ad creation	
One-sheet	
Ad-slick	
Radio spot (creation and packaging)	
Blowups (for theater lobbies)	
Print costs	14,700
16 35mm prints	
50 trailers	
Co-op ad costs	109,000
Miscellaneous	14,700
Publicity (in Seattle, N.Y., and L.A.)	
Shipping	
Promo tours	
Mailings	
Exhibitor "blind bid" screenings	

OTHER MARKETS

Film Gallery served as distributor to the homevideo and pay-cable markets. The general partners of *Old Enough* followed the usual conventions of film release scheduling: first, the theatrical release period, or window, followed by homevideo, pay cable, foreign sales, nontheatrical, and broadcast.

Homevideo · The film was licensed to Media Home Entertainment and was made available as of March 1, 1985.

Pay cable · The pay-cable window became available as of October 1, 1985. To date, sales have been made to Home Box Office and Showtime, on terms that Film Gallery's Mark Balsam described as "a fair deal, given the film's limited performance and audience appeal." Balsam noted that the film's selling features are the quality of its production values and Film Gallery's prior relations with the cable networks.

Nontheatrical • No deal had been made as of March 1986.

Broadcast • No deal had been made as of March 1986.

Foreign • Immediately following the film's strong showing at Cannes, the Around the Block Company (the company that had been formed as a joint venture between Silverfilm Productions and Film Gallery) unsuccessfully attempted to make foreign sales directly. They found that they didn't know the market or buyers well enough to properly place the film, and that the strength of the U.S. dollar hindered sales. Nonetheless, *Old Enough* was sold to the United Kingdom and to Quebec in Canada. They have subsequently assigned foreign subdistribution rights to Skouras Pictures. Skouras has sold the film to ten different foreign markets for theatrical, homevideo, and television play, providing additional revenues for the partnership.

REVIEW

Distribution is a risky business, even for successful distributors. Looking back on Orion Classics's experience distributing *Old Enough*, Michael Barker sees it as "a film we wished had done better." He views the film's poor performance philosophically. In the context of the many successes that Orion has had, Barker says, "We'll just continue to keep our eyes open for the next good film that we can get behind." For Orion Classics, this was an instance in which they liked the film and believed it could find an audience, but for all their effort and expense, none showed up.

The Silver sisters assess their experience quite differently:

From our perspective, the making of *Old Enough* was a tremendous success. The process was satisfying on an emotional level, in that it gave Marisa a chance to direct her first feature and Dina the opportunity to produce her first film, and it has also proved to be positive financially as well.

Old Enough is a good example of a film that was a successful financial venture *despite* its poor theatrical performance. Because we were able to make the film on a shoestring, because we negotiated a favorable deal with Orion Classics with respect to their marketing of the film, because Film Gallery was able to make profitable sales to the pay-cable and homevideo markets, and because Skouras Pictures is successfully handling the foreign sales, from our perspective and that of our investors, *Old Enough* has been a financial success.

In terms of its performance in theatrical release, Orion did a good job. The film just didn't click. We'll never know the reason why—and that's the beauty and the agony of filmmaking. Particularly with respect to independent films, it's very difficult to predict performance. These are films that don't follow formulae; each one is unique.

Meanwhile, we're on to other films, and look forward to the next one reaching the silver screen.

Film Gallery's Balsam was pleased with the partnership arrangement and enjoyed working with the Silvers. Like everyone involved, he was disappointed with *Old Enough*'s poor theatrical performance and believes that it was in no way due to any fault of Orion Classics, but rather to the vicissitudes of the marketplace.

RETURN OF THE SECAUCUS SEVEN

(Fall 1980)

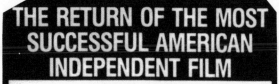

PRINCIPALS	*Director*	John Sayles
	Producers	William Aydelott and Jeffrey Nelson
	Writer	John Sayles
	Principal cast	Maggie Renzi, Mark Arnott, Gordon Clapp, and Adam LeFevre
DISTRIBUTORS	*Theatrical*	Original: Specialty Films; subdistributor: Libra Films
		Present: Cinecom International
	Homevideo	RCA/Columbia
	Pay cable	Cinecom International
	Nontheatrical	Cinecom International
	Broadcast	Cinecom International
	Foreign	International Film Exchange
THEATRICAL	*Opening date*	October 8, 1980
	Total playdates	not available
	Box-office gross	$2,000,000 (e)
	Gross film rental	800,000 (e)
	Total distributor costs	
	Advance*	25,000
	Publicity	not available
	Prints	not available
ANCILLARY	*Nontheatrical***	$ 25,000
	Foreign**	65,000
	Homevideo/Pay TV**	100,000
	Broadcast	275,000
PARTICIPANTS CONTACTED		John Sayles
		Maggie Renzi
		Jeffrey Nelson
		Randy Finley
		Ben Barenholtz
		Sam Kitt
		Joy Pereths
		Mel Novikoff

e = Estimate based on uncorroborated data derived from *Variety,* other industry sources, and authors' calculations.

* Advance does not include deduction for blowup costs of $18,000.

** Revenue to filmmaker's production company.

(Note: Advertising art on previous page is from a rerelease of the film. Original art was unavailable.)

FILM SYNOPSIS

Seven former antiwar activists of the 1960s, humorously self-dubbed the "Secaucus Seven" for the turnpike exit at which they were stopped by police en route to a demonstration in Washington, D.C., come together for their tenth annual reunion at a summer home in New Hampshire. During a weekend of gossiping, flirting, basketball, and barbecues, they struggle to confront the choices each must make to retain their principles in the "real" world.

DEVELOPMENT

Genesis · *Return of the Secaucus Seven* was John Sayles's first film; he wrote, directed, and edited it. He primarily conceived of the film as an audition piece: "I wanted to direct, and the only way you get to direct in Hollywood is to have a film to show."

Prior to making *Secaucus Seven*, Sayles's career consisted entirely of writing. His published works include two novels, *Pride of the Bimbos* and the National Book Award nominee *Union Dues*, and one short-story collection, *The Anarchists' Convention*. He had also worked for Roger Corman, rewriting *Piranha*, the successful horror send-up. Since *Secaucus Seven*, Sayles has gone on to direct *Baby, It's You, Lianna, The Brother from Another Planet, Matewan*, and *Eight Men Out*.

Sayles began working on the story for *Secaucus Seven* during the fall of 1977 and completed the screenplay in March 1978. The project grew out of his experience working with Jeffrey Nelson at the Eastern Slope Playhouse in New Hampshire, a summer stock theater Nelson had worked for for the previous eight years. As 1978 would be his last season, the film was to be made, in Nelson's words, to "culminate and memorialize our work together." The story took shape, Sayles explains, in the context of a set of financial and practical considerations:

> I knew how much money I had and then started to make certain decisions. I also had in mind many of the actors, people I knew from having worked in summer stock as an actor and director.

Financing · *Secaucus Seven* had a total production budget of $125,000. Of this, Sayles paid the direct production costs of $60,000 with personal funds, and he deferred payment of the balance.

From three screenwriting jobs and the sale of *The Anarchists' Convention*, Sayles had saved $40,000, which was used to pay for stock, crew, talent, and location expenses. Further screenwriting work brought in another $20,000, which he invested in editing and processing costs.

The actors' wage package was set on the basis of SAG rates, but during the four weeks of shooting they received only their usual summerstock wages of eighty dollars per week, plus room and board. The balance owed to the actors was to be paid with first monies earned. The actors were offered a choice of taking points in lieu of the SAG fees. Those who did so are still making money. The crew was paid on the basis of NABET rates at the time of production.

The film has grossed a reported $2 million in theatrical release, of which the filmmakers have earned a net revenue of $195,000. Earnings in all other markets during the 1980–85 period have returned to the filmmakers an additional $230,000.

Anticipating an audience · The film was originally intended as an audition piece, and Sayles neither anticipated a theatrical release, nor defined an audience. But at festival screenings and in the minds of potential distributors, the primary audience quickly became identified as the "sixties generation," like the people depicted in the film.

PRODUCTION

Sayles, Maggie Renzi, and Nelson began preliminary discussions about the film in the fall of 1977. Sayles completed the script in March of 1978; production began in September.

Shot in 16mm, principal photography was completed in five weeks. Budget limitations dictated the production more than any other single factor, says Sayles:

> Because of the budgetary limits, I decided to make the film at a ski lodge [in New Hampshire], which was cheap to rent out-of-season. We were able to use it as our set, as well as lodging for the crew and actors.
>
> We didn't have money for any artwork, so we had to use to the maximum what locations we had. That's why so many scenes take place in the lodge and in a local bar nearby. We shot different conversations from different angles.

Many reviewers have assumed that the apparent spontaneity of the dialogue between the characters reflects an improvisational working style. According to Nelson, however, the film was "completely scripted. The improvisational tone achieved is the result of John's approach as a director, and of the actors, including John, having worked together for years in summer stock."

After completing principal photography, Sayles and Renzi moved to Santa Barbara, rented an editing table, and installed it in their home. Sayles taught himself how to edit and began cutting the film.

DISTRIBUTION DEAL

Making the deal · As noted previously, *Return of the Secaucus Seven* was not originally envisioned for theatrical release. But during editing Sayles screened a version for representatives of Filmex, the Los Angeles festival, who liked what they saw. The film was screened at the 1979 Filmex, where its popular reception sparked the interest of distributors.

Secaucus Seven was invited to the New Directors/New Films series sponsored by the Museum of Modern Art and the Film Society of Lincoln Center in April 1980. The film received a mixed review from *New York Times* critic Vincent Canby, who wrote: "[This] comedy of manners . . . is about as sweet and engaging a movie as anyone could make about unexceptional lives grown stale as we watch them." He concluded with a less-than-enthusiastic appraisal:

[The film] is an honest, fully realized movie. My reservations have more to do with the dimness of the characters and their lives. Fiction— including film fiction—demands much more than mere authenticity.

Nonetheless, a number of distributors, including United Artists Classics, Libra Films, and Specialty Films, were keenly interested in acquiring it. According to Ben Barenholtz, at that time head of Libra (later part of the Almi Group):

> After we began negotiating, I got a call from John and he said that he had decided to give the film to UA Classics unless I could convince him otherwise. I invited him over and spent an hour explaining the dynamics of the classics divisions of the majors. I pointed out that the deal might be great and personal relations really fine, but someone at the studio might wake up on the wrong side of the bed one morning and there might not be a classics division. This was a convincing argument.

The company saw *Secaucus Seven* as, in the words of former Libra distributor Sam Kitt, "a nice little film that deserved a shot—it had a good chance." And Barenholtz adds:

> I wanted it for a combination of factors. You see it, you like it, you see potential audience interest, [and] assess possible critical reaction. There's no formula. Timing is also important. If *Secaucus Seven* came out now, it would probably not be a success.

After many long discussions, Sayles finally decided to go with another small, independent company, the Seattle-based Specialty Films, headed by Randy Finley.

Terms of the deal · At the time he took on *Secaucus Seven*, Finley owned a twenty-three-screen exhibition chain with theaters in Seattle, Tacoma, and Portland. Principally consisting of art houses, the chain showed films made by independent U.S., European, and Australian filmmakers, along with selected films from the major studios. In the 1970s, Finley began a distribution company to ensure his theaters a steady stream of product. The first film he acquired was a providential one, *The King of Hearts*.

Finley first heard of *Secaucus Seven* from Bob Laemmle and Jeff Dowd when it was shown at Filmex and subsequently saw it at a screening for the Seattle Film Festival. Finley was enthusiastic and actively courted the filmmakers. According to Renzi, "Randy had a vision, and that's why we went with him; Randy was a gambler, and that's why we stayed." She notes:

> Specialty had an idea about handling the picture that was different from anybody else's. They understood that the picture was unusual and needed a kind of special handling, which meant what they called "grassroots organizing."
> Their plan was simple. They would find people who had done political organizing in a certain city we were going to, send in one of their distributors, and work with these local people as their contacts. They would know what the newspapers were, where the mailing lists were, and who the group was we were targeting.
> Specialty Films was a team, with Randy, Jeff Dowd, and Bob Bogue. Jeff and Bob were political activists; they knew how to reach people.

More specifically, the filmmakers decided to go with Specialty Films for four reasons: Finley's willingness to pick up the 35mm blowup costs; Finley's enthusiasm for the film, and the trust he inspired in the filmmakers; the innovative marketing plan he offered; and his promise to include Barenholtz's Libra Films as part of the deal to handle the New York opening and East Coast distribution.

Finley offered terms and got an in-principle agreement from Sayles before he discussed it with Barenholtz. The subsidiary arrangement, however, would contribute to some of the distribution problems that developed later. Nelson felt, in retrospect, that this split between distributors was the only major problem in the overall handling of the film: "Everything could have been managed much more effectively had there been a single distributor who was making all the decisions. Sometimes it felt like there were two different films being handled in two different ways."

The key features of the deal offered by Finley included:

· The producers received a $25,000 advance, which turned out to be a $7,000 advance after deducting the $18,000 blowup costs from 16mm to 35mm.

· For theatrical release there was a 50/50 percent split on all net revenues less direct distribution costs.

· For nontheatrical release there was a net revenue split of 65/35 percent in the producers' favor.

- All other ancillary rights were to be sublicensed by Specialty to distributors specializing in those markets.

- Specialty agreed to open the film in ten to fifteen cities over a six- to eight-month period, including a New York opening to occur by a specified date.

When the filmmakers signed with Specialty, Finley warned them that he might be late with payments. This was due, he said, to the lack of leverage independent distributors had in collecting from exhibitors. (The majors tend to be paid promptly because they represent the principal source of product supply.) However, he guaranteed that his reporting and payments would be accurate, an assurance that Nelson confirms Finley lived up to.

During the course of the release, Finley asked the filmmakers if they wanted to reinvest their profits back into the film. As Renzi says:

Randy asked us if we wanted to hold off getting profits and invest more in the film's advertising. Our decision was yes because our goal with this film—as well as with *Lianna* and *The Brother from Another Planet*—was to have as many people see it as possible.

MARKETING CAMPAIGN

Strategy · The marketing of *Secaucus Seven* was shaped by the relationship between the two distribution companies. Libra served as a subcontractor with responsibility for the New York opening and distribution east of the Mississippi. Specialty took responsibility for the rest of the country and Canada, and also determined overall policy and spending levels.

The question of spending levels contributed to some problems. According to Ben Barenholtz, "I would constantly fight with Randy [Finley] trying to keep spending down, and he would always push for more spending." Finley confirms this, insisting that the differences between them stem from a fundamental difference in approach: "Ben is a film salesman; I am a promoter."

According to Nelson, the filmmakers wanted but never got a "planned marketing approach." They wanted a "coherent, confirmed plan," with real communications between Randy, Ben, and themselves. He complains that they "never got together for anything but quick meetings, [and] never had a real meeting among all the parties to decide how the film should be handled."

The distributors saw the film's hook as its appeal to the sixties generation, a target group that just happened to include many film critics. The distributors counted on them for reviews and feature pieces upon which they could build the campaign. According to Sam Kitt, who worked on the film while at Libra,

> [This film reflected] the lives of many critics then. As college radicals ten years earlier, they perfectly identified with the characters on screen. And there was a huge moviegoing audience of that generation. So it all just clicked.

To cultivate this anticipated support from the critics, the distributors held numerous screenings for media people and behind-the-scenes conversations with editors, feature writers, and others.

Promotion and publicity · Specialty did not budget for outside publicists, choosing to undertake the promotional work in-house. However, in some markets, such as Chicago and Washington, D.C., Specialty committed a substantial amount of money to advertising and word-of-mouth promotional activities. (This is discussed in more detail in the following section.)

John Sayles, as the only "name" associated with the film, became the center of much of the publicity activities. The plan was to take advantage of his success as a fiction writer, highlighting the fact that *Secaucus Seven* was his first film. Renzi recalls:

> John joined in and did a lot of work on the grueling tour. We spoke at many coffeehouses and other places where we thought we could reach the target audience. Except for possibly the self-distribution efforts of *Northern Lights*, nothing like this had been done before with unknown filmmakers.

The publicity campaign for *Secaucus Seven* profited fortuitously from a Hollywood calamity. As the film began to build strong word-of-mouth on the West Coast, Michael Cimino's *Heaven's Gate* opened to a critical and commercial disaster. When speaking with reviewers, feature writers, and editors, Specialty and Libra made a point of comparing Sayles's $60,000 independent film, with a fine script and believable characters, to the $44 million studio fiasco. This proved to be a successful news hook. Many commentators picked up on this angle as a sympathetic way to praise the film and sell it to their readers.

Secaucus Seven was listed among the year-end's "ten best" by many prominent magazine, newspaper, and TV critics, including the critics for *Time*, the *New York Times*, and the *Los Angeles Times*, and Roger Ebert of "Sneak Previews." Later versions of the advertising kit included this information, thus contributing to its popularity throughout the country.

Trailer and ad · Because of budgetary constraints, no trailer was cut. Development of the ad concept was hindered by the lack of production stills. Three different ads were eventually developed, but the principals were not happy with the results. The first image used was a photographic collage of shots cut from frames from the print, and was considered amateurish by many. The distributors also tried a line drawing, and finally used a staged photo of the cast sitting on a rock.

Finley created the original collage-based campaign in Seattle, but Libra found the material unsuitable for the New York opening. However, according to Kitt, the ad was not a key variable in the film's performance. He points out that the "bad ads were used in engagements that worked, and the final ad which everyone agreed to was used in engagements that didn't work."

THEATRICAL RELEASE

Strategy · The codistributors had different expectations for the film's initial theatrical performance, with Barenholtz more modest in his estimates than Finley. Barenholtz's caution did not reflect a lack of enthusiasm for the film, but rather a more conservative financial approach. As he has said, "There is no direct connection between money spent and grosses." Finley was much more willing to pump money into the film and give it time to prove itself, especially in the Northwest. In addition, there was a significant difference of opinion between the distributors as to whether the film should open in New York or Seattle. Barenholtz, who favored the New York premiere, ultimately won the argument.

The release strategy involved a New York premiere, to be followed within six to eight weeks by staggered openings over a ten-day period in Seattle, Los Angeles, and San Francisco. This schedule was planned in order to maximize regional visibility and impact, and would determine the film's release in other markets throughout the country.

Opening run · The budget set by Specialty for the New York opening of *Return of the Secaucus Seven* was approximately $20,000. The film opened at the 57th Street Playhouse in the fall of 1980. The theater was not Libra's first choice, but was selected to meet an opening-date deadline in the contract between Sayles and Specialty.

Barenholtz felt that the producers did the film a disservice by contractually stipulating an opening date, thus hampering Libra's ability to place the film in a more suitable house. The 57th Street Playhouse was chosen because all the better art houses were booked through the end of the year. It had a number of drawbacks, particularly the fact that it had been closed for renovation over a recent period and lacked visibility with the filmgoers. In addition, its seating capacity (620) and house nut were too large for a limited-audience art film.

Advance press from the premiere showing in the New Directors/ New Films series helped draw the aficionado audience in the first two weeks, but this couldn't sustain the film. Box-office grosses for the first four weeks were $11,247; $16,453; $8,138; and $4,534.

But even while pulling the film, Libra Films believed that it should return later for a second run in New York, at the "right" theater. Barenholtz recalls:

> By the third week it was down further, and we folded after the fourth week, to the dismay of some people. After it closed, we let the publicity catch up. I spoke to Aljean Harmetz [a *New York Times* entertainment feature writer], who liked the film and wanted to do a piece, but I told her to hold it until I built another date.

National playoff · Finley, disappointed by the film's New York opening, felt all the more committed to creating greater success for it in the West. In Seattle, according to Kitt, Finley "put his entire exhibition company behind the film, and he spent for opening week almost as much as we spent in New York."

Finley's campaign included extensive prescreenings for select groups of influential local people. (According to Finley, 1,500 to 2,000 viewers represent the critical mass needed to generate word-of-mouth following for a film.) In addition, he held numerous press screenings, produced and aired radio promos, and utilized such novel approaches as putting the film title in Day-Glo orange stickers on popcorn containers at his other theaters. He also featured it in the "Wall of the Week," displaying over 200 photos from the film on the walls and ceiling in the lobby of the multiplex theater where it ran. Finley's efforts not only paid off in terms of box-office results, but generated momentum for its move across the country. In Seattle, *Secaucus Seven* grossed $260,000.

However, the run that immediately followed, at the Surf Theater in San Francisco, was surprisingly disappointing to all the principals, who thought it would be a "natural" there. Kitt attributed the poor showing to bad reviews:

> The [San Francisco] reviewers didn't like the film and didn't like Sayles. They didn't hit it off with him; they panned the film and they panned John. There's one key reviewer in San Francisco, Judy Stone [of the *San Francisco Chronicle*], and if she doesn't like you, you're dead, and if she likes you, you've got a shot. She didn't like the film.

A second possible cause for the film's poor San Francisco run is offered by Finley. He felt that Mel Novikoff, owner of the Surf and other theaters, didn't support the film. According to Finley, Novikoff didn't follow through with the ad campaign, didn't use radio spots as Finley suggested, and pulled the film after two weeks. Finley contends that Novikoff "didn't let the film build." He also feels that part of the reason for the film's poor showing was that Novikoff did not personally handle its release, but turned it over to a subordinate.

Novikoff shares Kitt's opinion of the power a local critic can exert on audience acceptance. He feels that, in 1980, this power was a symptom of the city's underlying provinciality. But Novikoff warns that different styles of distribution are appropriate to different markets:

> When Finley says that I didn't personally get behind the film, he is really talking about the difference in *style* between his own special

firebrand type of promotion on his own turf, and that employed by exhibitors in other areas. Finley is without question a master promoter, especially when he has his own investment to protect. But his highly personalized, somewhat flamboyant, Wild West approach to promotion that seems to work in his home territory—which he felt should be emulated here—does not travel that well to a somewhat more sophisticated, if also more jaded, San Francisco.

The Los Angeles run was handled by Bob Laemmle and is reported to have been successful. In Portland, Finley handled marketing himself and booked one of his own theaters. *Secaucus Seven* grossed $140,000.

In Boston, the film received strong popular and critical support. It was identified as a New England production and was embraced by the target audience. But more important, according to Renzi, was the choice of the right theater, the Orson Welles. The campaign was further strengthened when the filmmakers went to Boston and did extensive media interviews and other promotional work.

In Washington, D.C., Finley mounted a major campaign, despite the original agreement that Libra was to handle eastern markets. He modeled it after his successful effort in Seattle, and he sent in an experienced film marketer, Bob Bogue, who implemented a grassroots campaign. Working with the cooperation of the exhibitor, Ted Pedas of the Circle Theater Chain, Bogue put up posters, ran radio promos, put stickers on theater popcorn boxes, distributed bumper stickers, held numerous prescreenings, and brought Sayles in to do many press interviews. The campaign was boosted when the influential *Washington Post* film critic Gary Arnold reviewed the film favorably. In Kitt's estimation the promotional campaign "worked like gangbusters. [It was] terrific!" The film reportedly grossed $400,000.

Finley was disappointed by Libra's campaign in Chicago, feeling that they were "dragging their feet." He decided to undertake his own heavy advertising push there in an effort to duplicate his success in Seattle and Washington, D.C. According to Kitt, Libra "felt a little chagrined because the original concept had been to not spend much money. We had gotten the short end of the stick." The campaign, however, was not successful, resembling San Francisco more than Seattle. With the exception of the *Sun-Times*'s Roger Ebert (who named it one of the year's "ten best"), the critics offered a mixed response. Larry Edwards, owner of the Biograph Theater, pulled the film after two weeks, even though, in Finley's words, "it was doing $14,000 per week and was followed by a bomb." In retrospect, Finley regretted his moves in Chicago, realizing that he had overextended himself by mounting so many expensive, energy-demanding openings in so short a time.

At the beginning of 1980, Libra brought *Secaucus Seven* back to New York for a second run. This decision was due to the strong showings in Seattle, Boston, and Los Angeles, and the good press, including the numerous citings as one of 1980's ten best films. As Barenholtz notes, "I had always intended to reopen it in a small theater, with lower costs." He booked it into the Quad, a small Greenwich Village four-plex known for art films, where it ran for twenty-two weeks from the beginning of January 1981. Libra initially four-walled the theater and spent $10,000 to reopen. Barenholtz pulled Kitt off other Libra assignments and committed him to the full-time publicity and promotion of *Secaucus Seven*. *New York Times* writer Harmetz wrote her promised piece, which ran on the day the film reopened. The *Village Voice*, which had not previously run a review of the film, printed a glowing review by Andrew Sarris. According to Kitt, Libra "pushed it as 'the film everyone had missed.' [It] made money from day one!"

Building on the national publicity and the successful reopening in Manhattan, Libra opened the film in smaller theaters on Long Island, and in Westchester and New Jersey. According to Kitt, "Our success was due to the film itself, combined with persistence on our part when it did not initially perform successfully."

OTHER MARKETS

Homevideo · A licensing agreement was set up with RCA/Columbia. The filmmakers have yet to receive any overage beyond the initial guarantee.

Pay cable · Pay-cable rights, which had been held by Sayles's production company, Salsipuedes Productions, were assigned in 1985 to Cinecom International, as part of an agreement to finance *Matewan*, a film Sayles had long been trying to get funded. Prior to that time, the filmmakers had made a few sales to small, locally based pay services.

According to the producer, homevideo and pay-cable revenues to the filmmakers have totaled approximately $100,000 as of July 1986.

Nontheatrical · Specialty originally sold the nontheatrical rights to Cinema Five. According to Nelson, the film performed extremely well in college and repertory release. Subsequently, Cinema Five, as well as Libra Films, was bought by Almi Pictures, which handled all nontheatrical markets. According to Renzi, *Secaucus Seven* was one of Almi's strongest nontheatrical titles. When Almi's nontheatrical rights expired in 1986, they reverted to Cinecom for ten years, according to the 1985 pact covering all of Sayles's prior work. Nontheatrical revenues to the filmmakers have totaled approximately $25,000.

Broadcast · Almi also handled broadcast rights, and made sales to PBS and to approximately fifty independent commercial stations, resulting in between $50,000 and $60,000 in fees to the filmmakers, paid on a quarterly basis over a five- to six-year period. The filmmakers expect additional syndication sales as the independent broadcast market expands.

Foreign · The film was originally represented by Affinity Enterprises, which secured foreign cable, TV, and theatrical sales netting the filmmakers approximately $65,000. Foreign rights are still being represented by Joy Pereths, the founder of Affinity Enterprises, who joined the staff of the International Film Exchange following that company's acquisition of Affinity.

REVIEW

Return of the Secaucus Seven, written and edited by John Sayles, was also his first directorial effort. He made the film primarily as an audition piece to increase his chances of getting directing work in Hollywood, not with a public release in mind.

This 16mm film was self-financed, with Sayles advancing $60,000 to cover production and editing; the film's total budget came to

$125,000, the difference being covered by deferrals. The film was first screened at the 1979 Los Angeles Filmex festival, where it received a standing ovation and where a number of distributors, including Specialty Films, UA Classics, and Libra Films, made overtures to Sayles. The film was later screened at the New Directors/ New Films series in New York, but received a lukewarm review from the *New York Times*.

By all accounts, the making and marketing of *Secaucus Seven* was a successful venture. Not only did it launch John Sayles's directorial career, but it helped create an innovative marketing approach for independent films.

According to Maggie Renzi, *Secaucus Seven* was "a trailblazer in terms of how it was marketed," and demonstrated that a grassroots approach to promotion and outreach could work. As Renzi points out, a distributor "could send a filmmaker around the country and people would want to talk to him."

Even the major difficulties resulting from different distributors located at each end of the continent were overcome. As Nelson admits, he was "surprised and delighted by how well things worked out on the two separate tracks."

Ben Barenholtz, long involved with specialty film exhibition in New York, points to what was then a unique accomplishment: "It is the only specialized film that bombed in its original engagement and returned to a smash second run." Kitt believes that much of the problem with the first New York run could have been avoided had Specialty given Libra greater financial support. "Libra was given bows and arrows to take the fort," says Kitt, "while they [Specialty] came in with guns and tanks." The fact that *Secaucus Seven* has become a contemporary independent classic, according to Kitt, confirms his belief.

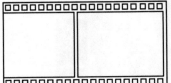

STAND AND DELIVER

(March 1988)

A New Troublemaker
Hit Garfield High...
He was tough.
He was wild.
He was willing to fight.

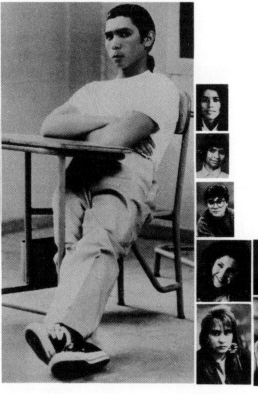

He was the new math teacher.

At a tough school
one teacher
and one class
proved to America
they could
Stand and Deliver...

EDWARD JAMES OLMOS · LOU DIAMOND PHILLIPS

Stand and Deliver

A true story about a modern miracle.

WARNER BROS. Presents
An AMERICAN PLAYHOUSE THEATRICAL Film A MENENDEZ / MUSCA & OLMOS Production
"STAND AND DELIVER" EDWARD JAMES OLMOS · LOU DIAMOND PHILLIPS · ROSANA DE SOTO
ANDY GARCIA   Music by CRAIG SAFAN Executive Producer LINDSAY LAW
Written by RAMON MENENDEZ & TOM MUSCA Produced by TOM MUSCA Directed by RAMON MENENDEZ

THEATRE

PRINCIPALS	*Director*	Ramon Menendez
	Producer	Tom Musca
	Executive Producer	Lindsay Law
	Writers	Ramon Menendez and Tom Musca
	Principal cast	Edward James Olmos, Lou Diamond Phillips, Rosanna DeSoto, Andy Garcia
DISTRIBUTORS	*Theatrical*	Warner Bros. (all markets except PBS)
	Homevideo	
	Pay cable	
	Nontheatrical	
	Broadcast	PBS/"American Playhouse"
	Foreign	
THEATRICAL	*Opening date*	March 11, 1988
	Total playdates	2,741
	Box-office gross	$14,104,200*
	Gross film rental	6,229,000
	Total distributor costs	
	Guarantee	3,500,000 (all markets)**
	Marketing	6,500,000
	Prints	822,465
ANCILLARY	*Homevideo*	
	Pay cable	$ 500,000
	Nontheatrical (gross)	92,460
	Broadcast (PBS)	500,000
	Foreign (gross)	2,900,000
PARTICIPANTS CONTACTED		Ramon Menendez
		Tom Musca
		Edward James Olmos
		Robert Hoffman
		D. Barry Reardon
		Larry Bershon

* As of October 30, 1989.
** Theatrical guarantee only.

FILM SYNOPSIS

Stand and Deliver *is the story of an extraordinary man, Jaime Escalante, a high school mathematics teacher who inspires his East Los Angeles barrio students to overcome their low sense of self-esteem and rise to remarkable heights of academic achievement.*

Escalante (Edward James Olmos), a Bolivian-born computer technician, quits a high-paying job at an electronics firm to teach at Garfield High School. On his first day, he is confronted with a class of surly kids. The students share a similar, defeatist attitude with the school's administration—a low sense of expectation: they will amount to very little and thus should not be challenged by education.

Escalante disarms the students' sullenness with a mixture of wit, mockery ("Tough guys don't do math; tough guys fry chicken for a living"), sincere respect, compassion, and, most important, humor. The school administration sees math as simply basic skills training: the students are expected to count change and balance their checkbooks. Not surprisingly, Escalante encounters administrative hostility when he announces that he will offer a preparatory class for the calculus Advanced Placement exam.

The film profiles a representative mixture of student types and the different ways Escalante has to reach out and motivate each one of them. The toughest student is Angel (Lou Diamond Phillips), a cholo, or bad boy, who wears a hair net and zoot suit–type baggy pants. However, Escalante's encouragement of his students is only half the film's story.

The class's scores on the Advanced Placement exam are questioned by the Educational Testing Service (ETS), which suspects the students of cheating because many made the same mistakes with a couple of particularly tricky questions. Escalante accuses an ETS representative (Andy Garcia) of racism for challenging the students' scores. The students, forced to choose between accepting failure or taking the test again, accept the challenge and triumphantly pass the retest without question.

DEVELOPMENT

Genesis · The original idea for *Stand and Deliver* emerged on August 11, 1983, when Ramon Menendez, a recent graduate of the UCLA film school and an American Film Institute fellow, noticed a front-page article in the *Los Angeles Times* that profiled Garfield High School math teacher Jaime Escalante and how his Advanced Placement calculus class had passed a second exam after being initially accused by the Educational Testing Service (ETS) of cheating. Inspired, Menendez and his friend and fellow UCLA graduate Tom Musca met regularly with Escalante for the next six months, seeking to get the rights to his story.

Throughout this period, however, Escalante resisted. According to Menendez, "Mr. Escalante was too busy teaching and he didn't want a film made about his life—he wasn't interested." Musca adds: "Jaime is a man who didn't watch movies. He's a very dedicated math teacher who, literally, puts in fourteen-hour days." Finally, in early 1984, Escalante agreed to a one-dollar option. Musca amusingly recalls that at the time the option wasn't a legal document because neither he nor Menendez had the dollar to pay Escalante.

Nevertheless, they established a deep friendship with Escalante. While they contractually agreed to pay him $10,000 for the rights to the story of his life, the filmmakers eventually gave him a $185,000 bonus and profit participation points when they finally sold the film to Warner Bros.

Menendez and Musca wrote a twelve-page story treatment and then spent the next eight months seeking development support to write the script. The filmmakers initially thought they could pitch their concept as a made-for-TV movie, but they were quickly dismissed by NBC. Menendez recalls, "They said things like 'Sorry, we already have a story about a teacher' and 'Who would watch if ABC programmed a James Bond picture against it?' " He also took the project to several production companies, who were very lukewarm about the project. "In a period of 'high-concept' movies, it didn't make for a good pitch," he explains. "Latino kids take a math test . . . twice!"

They eventually submitted their treatment to "American Playhouse" and, in October 1984, were awarded a $12,000 scripting grant.

During November and December, Menendez and Musca sat in on Escalante's classes and, over the Christmas vacation, interviewed twelve of the fourteen students who had been accused of cheating. They wrote the first draft of the script, originally titled *Walking on Water*, during the first five months of 1985. However, they had a difficult time getting Escalante to read the script. Initially, he simply didn't understand what they were going to do. "He thought we were going to walk around his class for an afternoon with a video camera," Musca says. They submitted the script to "American Playhouse" in the summer of 1985 and a second, revised script was approved in October. "Playhouse's" commitment of $500,000 was made in December 1985, conditional upon the filmmakers' raising the balance of the $1 million–plus budget.

In early June 1986, Musca met (through a mutual acquaintance) Bob Hoffman, the producer's representative for *The Ballad of Gregorio Cortez* (see case study). Intrigued by Musca's presentation of the story, Hoffman suggested that Edward Olmos play the lead role. He also suggested that they pursue a theatrical—as opposed to a made-for-television movie—release and a marketing campaign based upon the *Cortez* model. Since mid-1984 Hoffman had been looking for another project for Olmos in which they could continue to develop the outreach conducted with *Cortez*. Two weeks after the initial meeting, the *Los Angeles Times Magazine* published an extended profile of Edward Olmos. The cover story confirmed for Musca what Hoffman had pitched regarding the *Cortez* approach.

Financing · The total budget for *Stand and Deliver* was $1.37 million. Financing sources were:

"American Playhouse"	
script development	$ 12,000
production (TV rights)	500,000
ARCO (Atlantic-Richfield Corporation)	350,000
National Science Foundation	172,000
Ford Foundation	50,000
Corporation for Public Broadcasting	175,000
Other Sources	
Pepsi (product placement)	37,500
Anheuser-Busch (product placement)	12,000

As producer, Musca took principal responsibility for securing financing, and it took him approximately one year to raise the balance. The "American Playhouse" commitment, he felt, increased his chances immeasurably: "Once you've got a commitment, you've got distribution." However, he was concerned about additional presales and the ultimate impact such deals would have on any eventual theatrical sale.

Because of the film's subject matter, Musca felt he would find support from foundations. He put together an impressive forty-page bound proposal. As he recalls, "I made the error of a blanket mailing to 250 foundations without finding out which were predisposed to give money to a film project."

To his chagrin, the only initial support he got was a grant from the National Science Foundation (NSF); the other foundations simply passed on it or didn't respond. The NSF is mandated to use popular media, most often educational television, to advance understanding and appreciation for the sciences. In addition, it plays the role of "first money" supporter to help seed a project, with a relatively modest 5 to 10 percent contribution. The film spoke directly to the NSF's concerns for mathematics and math instruction among minority cultures.

Musca's big break came when he convinced ARCO's director of creative services, Larry Bershon, to support the project. While the ARCO Foundation had supported Escalante's summer teaching programs, the corporation had never contributed to a movie project. Bershon was a supporter of the project from the first and worked closely with Musca to build the necessary credibility and push the film through. He points out that ARCO has a long and distinguished history of PBS support, particularly in providing the seed money for "American Playhouse" during its first three years. ARCO has also funded such major series as "The Adams Chronicles," "Cosmos," "The Brain," and "In Performance at Wolftrap." According to Bershon, "The film rang a lot of bells." He identifies five critical factors about the film:

> First, we knew and have worked with Jaime since 1983. Second, the film had a Los Angeles focus [where the company is headquartered]. Equally important, it had an Hispanic focus! Lod Cook, ARCO's chairman, has been a major supporter of Hispanic education and other causes, so this was invaluable. Fourth, "American Playhouse's" com-

mitment was critical. Finally, Tom got the active support of KCET [a Los Angeles PBS affiliate], which strengthened the local focus.

A wrinkle in the deal with ARCO arose, ironically, from the film's very success. Its evolution from a made-for-television to a theatrical movie and a major studio release affected the PBS scheduling. "We would have to wait another year for the TV broadcast," Bershon points out. "I was afraid that our management would lose excitement about the project and I would have difficulty getting promotional and advertising support—which, for us, is as important as production support." Bershon admits that he "got heat" over the theatrical deal. Musca recalls:

> ARCO was supportive of the PBS broadcast, but were initially concerned that a theatrical deal would delay the television broadcast. When we reassured them that they would get involved [with the release] they got excited and got very involved with Warner on promotions.

With backing from "Playhouse," NSF and ARCO, the filmmakers knew they could move to the production phase. Musca says, "Once we had $350,000 from ARCO, it was enough for me to say, 'Let's sail.' I knew if I got out of production alive, I could raise the money to finish the film."

Postproduction support was provided by a grant from the Ford Foundation. Ford representatives reviewed the script, budget, and other print materials, assessed the other financing, and visited the set, which clinched their interest. They were most impressed by the depth of community support that the film had received.

Anticipating an audience · From its beginning, Musca believed that the film would attract a strong Latino audience. He knew that *La Bamba* and *The Milagro Bean Field War* were in production, and felt that the Latino community would respond favorably to a motivational film. He was less sure as to how successfully the film could reach a more mainstream American audience.

PRODUCTION

Through Hoffman, the filmmakers approached Olmos in July 1986. He enthusiastically agreed not only to star as Escalante, but to contribute his considerable industry knowledge and contacts to help the project along. Olmos was one of the principals of the popular NBC television series "Miami Vice" and has been a lead actor in such films as *Zoot Suit*, *The Ballad of Gregorio Cortez*, and *Triumph of the Spirit*. In addition, the filmmakers were fortunate to attract other local actors, including Lou Diamond Phillips and Andy Garcia, neither of whom had yet become celebrities. Phillips later starred as Richie Valens in *La Bamba*, and Garcia appeared in the very successful *The Untouchables*.

For Olmos, the opportunity to perform in *Stand and Deliver* was a dream come true. "This was a film that I could passionately get behind and understand," he says. "Initially, however, I went into it with tremendous reservation," he recalls. "This was the last thing I needed in my career—to get involved with a first-time producer and director and co-writers. But the values and ideals of the film won me over." Musca and Menendez opened up the film production to Olmos for his comments and active participation; he became associate producer. Having nine months to prepare for the performance gave Olmos a rare chance to fully develop the role. "I knew for nearly a year that I was going to do the part. That's a gift given only to people like [Dustin] Hoffman, [Robert] De Niro, and Meryl Streep. Actors like myself usually get two weeks' notice." Perhaps equally important, the film was a source of cultural pride, not simply focusing on the Los Angeles Hispanic community but on celebrating its strength in overcoming institutional racism.

To prepare for his performance, Olmos spent many hours viewing videotapes of Escalante's classroom teaching techniques. As Olmos recalls, "[Escalante] is one of the most stylized men I've ever come across. He's one of the greatest calculated entertainers." Olmos also taped thirty hours of conversations with Escalante in order to master his patterns of speech and thought. Olmos adds, "I asked him intimate questions about his house and his life . . . and we joked a lot."

During the last month before principal photography began, Olmos spent eighteen hours a day with Escalante to capture fully the teacher's personality so he could do justice to the role. "I felt," Olmos insists, "that we were trying to document this man's life in a way that would allow him to hold his head up high." At one point Olmos forced Escalante to kick him out of his house so that he could see how the teacher would do it. Also, instead of simply using padded clothing, Olmos gained forty-one pounds, to capture Escalante's body type and movement. "The body moves differently when there's real weight," he says, "even doing simple things like tying one's shoes."

Olmos's invitation to Escalante to be on the set during shooting at first caused great tension. The reason was that Menendez had previously had a bad experience with that sort of thing. Menendez had served as assistant director to Oliver Stone in *Salvador*, and in that film actor James Woods played a character based on the reporter Richard Boyle. Boyle, with Stone's backing, insisted on being on the set. This proved very difficult for Woods. Menendez didn't want this to happen to his film, and was concerned about the delays that might occur if Escalante insisted upon literal accuracy of events. "Facts are not necessarily art," Menendez points out, "and films are a metaphor for reality—they are not reality." However, Olmos was adamant about Escalante's participation, threatening to quit if it wasn't agreed to. According to Menendez, "Escalante didn't come often and when he did it was a good thing. He was very helpful during some difficult scenes when mathematical formulas had to be presented."

Five schools in Los Angeles were used to give Garfield High School its look over the two-year period of the story. The production got full cooperation from the Los Angeles Unified School District and, most important, from Garfield's principal, Henry Gradillas. *Stand and Deliver* was embraced by the Los Angeles Hispanic community.

The film received some very valuable press coverage during the production phase. Two pieces of particular importance appeared on the day the film was wrapped: a *Los Angeles Daily News* cover story that was syndicated across the country and a *Washington Post* story about Escalante and the success of his teaching program.

There were no deferrals involved in the production. Musca does not believe in deferrals and feels the deferral model has been abused; he feels that the Los Angeles film community has been burned by the numerous first-film deferral packages that proliferated during the 1980s. In addition, he feels that the producer must provide written contracts to participants, particularly those who are friends, to avoid confusion at the end. He stresses that this is especially important if the film secures studio distribution in order to guarantee credits. With *Stand and Deliver*, the cast was paid scale.

Film production commenced in April 1987 and principal photography lasted thirty-two days, with one week for second-unit photography. The film was produced through Eastside Productions.

DISTRIBUTION DEAL

Making the deal · *Stand and Deliver* was edited by Nancy Richardson. When the film's principals saw the first roughcut, they knew they had a winner—a film rather than a television movie. According to Hoffman:

> We went to great lengths to correctly position the production, as a theatrical film and not a PBS/KCET show. This is not to denigrate PBS, but this is a difficult reality of "Playhouse"-type projects. The imprimatur of a public-television-only production would limit the theatrical sales potential.

During production, the film principals made an important decision: they would wait until the film was completely finished before screening it for distributors. They decided to screen it only to a paying audience, to clearly demonstrate the film's "playability." However, given that Olmos and Phillips were in the film, the filmmakers received innumerable calls from distributors to screen the film in roughcut, which they refused to do. Nevertheless, the filmmakers, through Olmos, showed a roughcut to director Robert Young (*The Ballad of Gregorio Cortez*, *Dominic and Eugene*), who helped spread favorable word-of-mouth in Hollywood. Thus, in Musca's words, by the time the filmmakers finally screened *Stand and Deliver* publicly, "every studio in town wanted to see it."

During postproduction, the producers determined when they would have a working timed print, and based on this date, Hoffman secured a featured spot at the Mill Valley Film Festival. This festival was selected because it had provided a very favorable reception for *The Ballad of Gregorio Cortez* in 1983. The festival directors work with independent filmmakers who receive the same treatment as established directors and producers. The audience is also extremely film "literate." In addition, local critics and newspapers respect a filmmaker's wish to withhold reviews.

The filmmakers will never forget the drama of the film's first screening. In Los Angeles, Musca picked up the first answer print at noon, took a 1 P.M. flight to San Francisco, and screened the film at 7 P.M. that night. The screening won a standing ovation and sent distributor's representatives running for telephones. That night Universal, Miramax, and Skouras made tentative distribution offers. (Warner Bros. president of distribution, Barry Reardon, heard about the film through a friend who called him the next day, and he had the acquisition department schedule a screening at the Warner lot for the following week.) When the film was shown again the next afternoon, it gained an equally enthusiastic response from the 400 people in attendance. In Olmos's words, "it became an event."

Musca had entered the IFP Independent Film Market, which took place a few days later. The "buzz" generated at Mill Valley followed them to New York. Ironically, on the morning of the screening, the *New York Times* ran a piece by Aljean Harmetz describing the difficulties facing specialty distributors trying to hold theaters.

The single Market screening was a spectacular success. A 157-seat theater was filled to capacity and there were over a hundred people outside who couldn't get into the screening. More important, no one walked out during the screening, as often happens at commercial screenings. Olmos points out, "Distributors usually walk in and out, staying for twenty to thirty minutes. It's a constant flow of people, which drives the filmmakers crazy. It's intimidating. You don't know what you've got."

Returning to Los Angeles the following week, the filmmakers were wined and dined by most of the major and all of the specialty distribution companies. During the whirlwind of the first three days, there were many humorous situations. The filmmakers had struck only one print of the four reels. Twice, this one print was being screened simultaneously at two different studios, and two reels at a time had to be trucked back and forth across Burbank. The film was screened at Disney, Paramount, Fox, Universal, Skouras, and, lastly, Warner Bros.

According to Menendez, "We didn't want a bidding war. We wanted somebody who would believe in the film. Jeffrey Katzenberg, the chairman of Disney, told us it put Hollywood to shame. But his marketing staff said they didn't know how to sell it. Universal wanted it, but we didn't want to be at the same studio that had [Robert Redford's] *Milagro* [*Bean Field War*]." (*Milagro*, a film with an Hispanic theme, opened in New York on the same day as *Stand and Deliver*.)

According to those in attendance at the Warner screening, Barry Reardon came out with tears in his eyes. Sharing his feelings with the filmmakers, Reardon compared the film to *Chariots of Fire* and declared, "I loved it . . . it moved me very much."

The filmmakers thought Warners was a company that had adroitly embraced specialty films based upon a true story—such as *Chariots of Fire*, *The Mission*, *The Killing Fields*, and *Local Hero*. Warners had also recently distributed *'Round Midnight* and *True Stories*, two "art" films. In addition, whereas other studios that screened the film saw it as hard to market, Reardon saw it as a "marketing challenge . . . one we'd like to take on." Reardon contacted Terry Semel, Warner Bros. president and CEO, and said he'd seen a magnificent film and wanted to buy it. Semel said, "If you like it that much, go ahead." He invited the filmmakers back the following day at 4 P.M. to negotiate a deal.

Terms of the deal · The following day the filmmakers met with Warner Bros. executives in an extended evening meeting in which the deal was cut. Reardon felt that *Stand and Deliver* was an important film for Warners to distribute, had "great upside potential," and should be distributed by Warners even if it did not make money. He stressed how much he liked it and that, if Warners handled it, it could be a hit. "We really believed in the picture, believed in it 100 percent," he recalls, "and would go the extra mile to make it a success. It was our honesty and integrity that finally swung the deal." Jokingly, he also told the filmmakers, "We're not going to leave here tonight until we have a deal. What do you want for dinner?" At about 10 P.M. that night, the filmmakers agreed to terms with Warner Bros.

The filmmakers didn't bring an attorney to the meeting, but had met before the scheduled meeting and worked out the basic parameters of the terms they wanted. The deal was for front-end rights, with all the back-end, ancillary market terms to be negotiated later by the respective lawyers. As Olmos warns, "A filmmaker really shouldn't negotiate the back end unless he knows what he's doing."

The basic front-end terms were straightforward: Warner paid $3.5

million for world-wide rights to all markets, plus $500,000 for pay cable, except broadcast public television, and awarded the film-makers steps based upon gross theatrical performance. While it took from the end of October 1987 through January 1988 to put together a final, signed contract, the in-principle agreement served as the basis to go forward with distribution.

Negotiations were complicated by the "American Playhouse" initial broadcast window. PBS had a preemptive showing after the theatrical release, which was a problem for Warners because of its first-window television agreement with Home Box Office. Warners wanted to honor that agreement before the PBS airing. Nevertheless, they eventually worked out these aspects. As a result, $1 million was taken off the upfront advance and, because it was a gross deal, placed on the back end.

According to Hoffman, "There was a great deal of 'trust' involved in the negotiations—outside the nearly 100 pages of contract." He points out that Reardon agreed to bring on a special team to work within the Latino and educational community. Led by Hoffman, it included Danny Haro, field representative from the *Cortez* gang; Luis Reyes, special Latino publicist; and Kirk Whisler, Latino print expert. Hoffman recalls:

> The grass-roots team was welcomed by Robbie Friedman's [then vice-president of marketing] marketing department, especially Charlotte Gee [vice president of publicity], who oversaw the effort. They listened to our ideas and acted on most of them. That's not to say we didn't make some mistakes. But Warners deserves all the credit for honoring the intent of our sales agreement and the spirit of the project.

MARKETING CAMPAIGN

Strategy · One of the critical differences distinguishing a Hollywood studio from an independent specialty distributor is the scale and thoroughness of planning and preparation in the marketing campaign. Although a relatively small film in terms of conventional Warner or Hollywood releases (as measured by both acquisition investment and marketing financial commitment), *Stand and Deliver* was handled like other prized Warner properties: it was going to be a box-office winner.

Warner Bros. assessed and positioned *Stand and Deliver* on its own merits. If things went favorably, they felt, it could duplicate the success of the recently released *La Bamba*. Extensive audience testing was designed to evaluate the strongest selling features and other marketing factors. Among the key factors that occupied the Warner staff were: defining the marketing "hook" (in this case, the teacher and students, or barrio kids, overcoming the system), positioning the film effectively for the various audiences to whom it would appeal (Hispanic vs. Anglo, adult vs. youth), positioning the release (West Coast vs. East, large markets vs. small), and meeting both critical and performance objectives.

Promotion and publicity · The Warner Bros. promotional and publicity campaign underwent careful preparation before it was implemented. A series of prerelease screenings tested the market for the film. The first two test-screenings took place during November and December 1987 in Sherman Oaks, California, and Seattle, Washington. In the Los Angeles area, audiences were more familiar with Latino issues and the film's lead actors were more well known. The screening went over very well and the results showed strong teenage interest in the film. In Seattle, the screening brought together a very different audience, including many very esoteric filmgoers. Nevertheless, the results showed strong adult interest and were assessed as more nationally projectable.

These screenings were intended to provide insight into a variety of concerns, including whether cuts were necessary, and audience response to the film's original title, *Walking on Water*. Warners was particularly concerned about the title, especially in terms of how the film would play in the Midwest and during an Easter time release. As part of its overall strategy for a youth-oriented film, Warners felt that the movie needed a song included in the film that could be made into a hit single. They optioned a song entitled "Stand and Deliver," sung by the group Mr. Mister, and it was incorporated at the film's end.

The filmmakers had long been unhappy with the title *Walking on Water*, feeling that it was at once religiously suggestive and tended to weaken an already soft film. They even had a list on the wall in their production office asking for new title suggestions and had about eighty alternatives, but none seemed just right.

The test-screenings showed that the film dragged in several spots and the filmmakers cut approximately four minutes. They also showed that the ending left people somewhat dissatisfied. Both Musca and Menendez, who attended the screenings, believe that the screenings were "extremely helpful" and that the cuts helped the film's pacing and made it more appealing to a larger audience. They feel that nothing in the film was compromised by the cuts. Menendez says he will use audience test-screenings with his next pictures.

Tom Musca remembers when he and Menendez had to make a final decision as to the film's title. One evening at about 5 P.M. they took a long walk around the Warners lot, struggling over their decision. Finally, he recalls that their decision came down to a simple choice: "Can you see a teenage guy asking a girl for a Friday night date to go see *Walking on Water*?"

Once all the film's elements were finalized, campaign implementation was rigorously planned. According to Reardon, this was one of the most extensively publicized and prescreened efforts Warner Bros. had undertaken in a very long time. The campaign included the following elements as part of a coordinated undertaking to generate maximum visibility for the film:

1. Nearly 220 screenings in all markets were held, designed to target specific critical audiences, such as:

   • English- and Hispanic-language print, television, and radio.

   • Opinion-leaders, ranging from key congressmen and members of the Department of Education, to New York Governor Mario Cuomo, members of his Hispanic Task Force, and his educational staff, to a USC class taught by Charles Champlin.

   • Hispanic organizations across the country, including the League of United Latin American Citizens (LULAC) in Chicago, the National Association of Hispanic Publications in Las Vegas, and the California Chicano News Media Association in San Diego, among others.

   • High school and junior college students and teachers, including 1,500 East Los Angeles students, 300 media educators specializing in film, the California Association of Bi-Lingual Educators, and 300 university deans at the twenty-fifth Annual Engineering Deans Institute convention.

- Numerous benefit screenings, such as for the Garfield High School Alumni Association and the United Farm Workers.

- Film festivals.

- Sneak previews promoted with radio station–sponsored ticket giveaways.

2. There were extensive interviews with leading television, radio, and print media critics and with feature editors and reporters in all markets. Major responsibility for these interviews fell to the film's principals, most notably Edward Olmos and Jaime Escalante as well as Lou Diamond Phillips, Andy Garcia, and occasionally the producer and director.

3. Many of the principals participated in promotional tour visits. Olmos undertook an extensive tour that covered Washington, D.C., San Francisco, Chicago, Dallas (where he joined Phillips for a benefit), Boston, Philadelphia, Atlanta, Denver, Toronto, Detroit, Minneapolis, St. Louis, and other cities. Because Olmos was then based in Miami due to his role in "Miami Vice," he also undertook extensive outreach to the major media in Florida. Perhaps the greatest media response came on April 26, 1988, when Escalante attended a White House luncheon, hosted by President Ronald Reagan, to honor outstanding educators. A photo of Escalante and Reagan with a mention of *Stand and Deliver* was featured in the *Los Angeles Times*, New York's *Daily News*, and many other papers.

4. Special educational support materials and activities took advantage of the film's content:

- A study guide written and distributed by *Fast Times* student magazine was distributed to 35,500 math and social studies classes, reported by Warners to have reached 1.1 million students. It was sponsored by Pepsi.

- The script was serialized in three Scholastic magazines: *Scope*, reaching 3 million high school students; *Action*, reaching a half-million 12–15-year-olds; and *U.S. Express*, for English-as-a-second-language junior high students.

- Warner Bros. had cast members visit junior and senior high schools to screen film clips and talk to assemblies, drama classes, and math and social science classes. In New York, cast member Lydia Nicole visited thirty schools. In Los Angeles, a group of actors led by Danny Villareal mounted a similar campaign.

- Press conferences for high school and college student journalists were held in Los Angeles and New York. In Los Angeles, thirty student editors attended an interview with Olmos, Garcia, Villareal, and Will Gotay.

5. Electronic media support materials were prepared for both Spanish- and English-language television. These included videotaped interviews with Olmos, Phillips, Rosanna DeSoto, and Ramon Menendez. The interviews, together with Spanish-language-dubbed film excerpts, were provided to the two Spanish-language television networks, Telemundo and Univision. In addition, Warners produced a promotional film of Escalante teaching a class at Garfield High School.
6. A music video was produced for the single, "Stand and Deliver." It was prepared with RCA and featured the group Mr. Mister. It was shown on MTV and other outlets.
7. A special community outreach team composed of Bob Hoffman, Danny Haro, and Luis Reyes visited cities with a major Hispanic community and mobilized support for the film. The team's activity was coordinated with Olmos's visits so that he could attend meetings of local Hispanic groups, talk to Hispanic media, and generally ensure that this support base was enthusiastic.

These coordinated activities were extremely beneficial. They contributed to the extensive and favorable media quotes that came from national, New York, Los Angeles, and regional critics. Many of these preceded the opening and were the result of the earlier screenings. National magazine coverage included *Newsweek, Glamour, Self*, and *Penthouse. USA Today* and the *Los Angeles Daily News* ran favorable reviews. There were also numerous television reviews, including the nationally syndicated Siskel and Ebert show, New York WWOR's Pat Collins, and the Los Angeles critics Gary Franklin (KABC), Steve Kmetko (KCBS), and David Sheehan (KNBC).

In addition to reviews, the film became an editorial or news story for both television and print media. The CBS Network show "West 57th Street" ran a segment on Garfield High School and the film. The Los Angeles CBS affiliate, KCBS, produced a half-hour special, "Shoot for Success," about Escalante and the film, which included interviews with Olmos, Phillips, Garcia, Menendez, and Musca. A number of television services, including Desde Hollywood (Univision) and HBO, ran coverage of the film's premiere. On the print side the biggest coup was the color cover story about the film that ran in the VISTA Sunday section of the *Los Angeles Herald-Examiner* and in 160 other major metropolitan newspapers in cities with significant Hispanic populations. These proved invaluable in helping to position the film and generate initial favorable word-of-mouth.

Trailer and ad · Both the filmmakers and Warners were dissatisfied with the print ad and the trailer. The artwork for the ad was developed by the Warner publicity department and strongly featured Phillips, to draw in younger people. However, the filmmakers and Warners were both far more pleased with the revised artwork featured on the European release materials.

THEATRICAL RELEASE

Strategy · Warner Bros.' overall release plan for *Stand and Deliver* was developed by Barry Reardon. In a January 1988 memo prepared for Terry Semel, Warner president and CEO, Reardon spelled out the strategy succinctly:

> The plan that I have developed for *Walking on Water* is based on the assumption that the publicity and advertising people will have sufficient time to do the necessary screenings and other radio promotions, etc., that they plan to do.
>
> I have thought a great deal of where and when we should open the picture. I ended up with a Los Angeles opening, on a platform run of approximately thirteen theaters. I didn't want to open exclusive because of the heavy ethnic appeal. On the other hand, I did not want to go too wide so as to dissipate the opening. I plan to expand two weeks later to a full multiple in Los Angeles on the presumption that the picture would be "working," and that word-of-mouth has spread. I also plan to open my Spanish dubbed prints day-and-date with the original opening.
>
> After Los Angeles, I thought that the best areas to work into would be those where there was an ethnic appeal. These areas would play limited multiple in the major cities and exclusive in the lesser markets. As you can see, I was moving in the areas where weather would not be a factor in the early part of the plan.
>
> The final phase of the plan would be to play the northern and

Midwest markets, except New York and Chicago, somewhere in mid- to late April. Canada would obviously be at the end of the cycle.

Reardon opted *not* to go with a New York opening, which, in his words, "happens on 99 percent of all movies that are released in America." He felt that opening in Los Angeles would play into one of the film's strengths. In an accompanying list, he specified the roll-out moving through three distinct phases or waves or breaks (see Table 1).

TABLE 1
Stand and Deliver Release Sequences

Date	City
3/11/88	Los Angeles (platform run; 12 runs)
3/18/88	New York
4/1/88	San Diego, Dallas, Houston, San Antonio, Oklahoma City, San Francisco, Miami, Jacksonville, and Chicago; it would reach a total of an additional 225 runs—197 English and 28 Spanish-dubbed—and bring the total to 252 theaters
4/15/88	Memphis, New Orleans, Boston, Philadelphia, Washington, D.C., Indianapolis, Cleveland, Cincinnati, Charlotte, Atlanta, Kansas City, St. Louis, Denver, Salt Lake City, Seattle, Portland, Detroit, and Minneapolis; it would reach an additional 413 English-language theaters, and bring the total openings to 665

Source: Warner Bros. memos (2/1/88)

One of the more problematic aspects of the launch involved the effective targeting of the primary audience. According to Reardon, when he first saw the film he felt it would appeal primarily to a somewhat older audience—over eighteen years of age. The research screenings, however, showed strong interest among younger people. He felt that the film could bridge both groups, but here the research seems belied by the marketplace, as Reardon points out: "We were never quite successful in crossing over to young people. Every time we screened the movie for young people—and we had screenings all over the place—they loved it. But they never gravitated to the movie in a big way." As Musca noted, "Kids didn't tell their friends."

Opening run · *Stand and Deliver* opened in Los Angeles over the March 11–12, 1988, weekend at thirty theaters and grossed $411,884, running in twenty-six hardtops and four drive-ins. Following the break, Warners prepared a new trailer and a new one-sheet, which were shipped to appropriate theaters.

Two "exit surveys" were conducted "in order to learn who had been attracted to the movie, how they had learned about it, and how they liked it." The surveys were conducted in Burbank and Orange County among 1,891 movie attendees. Among the key findings were:

- Attendees came from all age groups, with slightly more women than men present; 40 percent were Hispanic.
- Television commercials were the most frequently mentioned source of awareness (68 percent), "which usually occurs when movies aimed at a broad base of moviegoers open." However, "newspaper ads were reported at a below-average level."
- The film was "incredibly well received by nearly everyone at both theaters." There were no important differences in reaction on *any* measure: age, sex, ethnic group, or location.

These results revealed strong, favorable audience response to the movie. However, as a Warner executive astutely noted in the conclusion to the survey,

> The tougher test will be when the movie moves out from its protective home base and has to charm moviegoers who have no ties to the place or to the ethnic group portrayed in the movie. So far, the sneaks in New York suggest that there is a very good chance that the movie will work there.

National rollout · In anticipation of the New York launch, Warners held sneak previews on March 12 at about thirty screens in New York City, Long Island, New Jersey, and Connecticut. Reactions were judged to be very favorable, including applause and cheering at the end.

Exit surveys were conducted at two theaters, in Manhattan (Plaza

Theater) and Brooklyn (Kings Plaza 3). A total of 402 attendees completed response cards. Among the key findings were:

- Manhattan attendees were older (69 percent to 53 percent) and slightly less female (51 percent to 53 percent). However, the big difference was in terms of the ethnic/racial composition—Manhattan was overwhelmingly white (66 percent white to 13 percent Hispanic); Brooklyn was more mixed (45 percent black, 42 percent white but only 6 percent Hispanic).

- The preview was advertised only through newspapers, and this affected audience demographics: "newspaper advertising tends to pull an older audience." However, whereas 72 percent in Manhattan came to see the preview in response to the ad, only 44 percent did so in Brooklyn.

- The film was very enthusiastically received at both screenings—79 percent found it "excellent" or "very good," and 60 percent said they would "definitely" recommend the film—and these responses were nearly the same for the two samples. Particularly impressive was the strongly favorable response by young males under twenty-five—85 percent found it "excellent" or "very good," and 70 percent said they would "definitely recommend" the film.

At the time of the New York launch, Warners conducted exit polls at the same two theaters. A total of 1,089 moviegoers filled out exit cards. Among the key findings were:

- Again, Manhattan attendees were older and predominately white; in Brooklyn, the majority was under twenty-five and more racially mixed. However, relatively few Hispanics attended—18 percent in Manhattan and 16 percent in Brooklyn.

- Television commercials were the most frequently mentioned source of awareness (69 percent), but there was a noticeable difference of influence between Brooklyn (77 percent) and Manhattan (59 percent) attendees. This pattern was reversed with regard to print-based information, newspaper ads, and reviews.

- The film was again very enthusiastically received at both screenings—86 percent found it "excellent" or "very good," and 70 percent said they would "definitely" recommend the film—with higher recommendations in Manhattan. However, in these screenings, females (both under and over twenty-five) responded more positively in terms of their willingness to "definitely recommend" the film.

Based upon these exit polls, Warners concluded:

These results seem to answer the question of how well *Stand and Deliver* can *satisfy* audiences outside of its home base in Los Angeles. These New York moviegoers liked the picture as much as any audience. They should spread very positive word-of-mouth for the movie, which should help to attract further audiences in the coming weeks.

Stand and Deliver's performance was carefully measured against the very successful *La Bamba*. While both naturally appealed to Hispanics, they are qualitatively different movies. *La Bamba* has more exploitable elements (it is a romantic musical celebrating the tragic death of rock-and-roll icon Richie Valens). *Stand and Deliver* is a harder sell, with its focus on an obscure calculus teacher in a Los Angeles ghetto school. Nevertheless, during its first week in New York it grossed $342,000—61 percent of what *La Bamba* had grossed when it was released during the previous July. (And *Stand and Deliver* was opened at fewer theaters.)

On April 9, Warners held sneak previews of *Stand and Deliver* at theaters in the United States and Canada. The film was paired with another film, most often a popular release like *Fatal Attraction*, *Good Morning Vietnam*, *Moonstruck*, or *Police Academy*. Entertainment Data, a Los Angeles market research company, conducted a survey of audience responses at 121 theaters. Forty-one percent of the audience found the movie either "excellent" or "very good," another 40 percent found the film "good," and only 15 percent found it "fair."

By April 20, *Stand and Deliver* had grossed over $4 million in five critical markets—Los Angeles, New York, San Francisco, Texas, and Miami. Warners had expended nearly $190,000 for media placements costs—44 percent for television, 32 percent for print, and 27 percent for radio. (Total "p&a" costs would eventually exceed $6.5 million.) Warner Bros., like other distributors, projects anticipated box-office performance, or quotas, to assess a film's performance. From April 23 through August 27, performance quotas for specific markets were revised, some upward and others downward. *Stand and Deliver* surpassed its quota in Boston, Chicago, Cleveland, Dallas, Denver,

Detroit, Kansas City, Los Angeles, Minneapolis, Philadelphia, San Francisco, Seattle/Portland, and Washington, D.C. (thirteen cities); and fell below the quota in Atlanta, Charlotte, Cincinnati, Jacksonville, New Orleans, and New York (six cities).

OTHER MARKETS

Homevideo · Distributed by Warner Bros.; 150,000 units were shipped.

Pay Cable · Warner Bros. has a premium cable deal with Home Box Office for first-window television release. The fact that the film was partially financed by "American Playhouse" required Warners to renegotiate with HBO for a later cable telecast and, in turn, cut its licensing fee. Subsequent to the HBO showing, the film has been telecast on the Showtime and the Disney premium cable services.

Television · PBS's "American Playhouse" has first broadcast television rights.

Nontheatrical · Handled by Swank. It negotiated in-flight deals with at least nine carriers, including American, Delta, and Air France. ARCO and Pepsi did special promotional outreach. ARCO and IMB are distributing cassettes to 350 Los Angeles schools.

Merchandising · Put together music video with RCA featuring Mr. Mister.

REVIEW

Stand and Deliver is one of the most successful independent films released over the last decade. Its success can be measured by many factors, including a $14-plus million box-office gross, financial return to the filmmakers, and the positive impact the film has had among both Hispanic and non-Hispanic audiences. An equally important measure is that Edward Olmos received a 1988 Academy Award nomination for best actor. For the filmmakers, their efforts with the next film, *Rubi Rosa*, would have been far more difficult had they not achieved such an impressive success with *Stand and Deliver*.

Perhaps equally critical to the longterm viability of independent filmmaking, the film's successful release convincingly demonstrated that a major Hollywood studio could effectively handle a specialty film. Warner Bros. may be an exception among the studios because it has handled some of the most acclaimed "indie" productions—among them *Chariots of Fire, The Mission, The Killing Fields, Local Hero, 'Round Midnight, True Stories*, and *Roger and Me*. (Universal's deal with Spike Lee for *Do the Right Thing* and his next film, and MGM/UA's release of *True Love*, may signal a continuation of this.) But the film's success, even if it carried what appears to be a modest theatrical loss, shows how other factors beyond the bottom line can be a part of corporate decision-making.

Looking back on his experience working on *Stand and Deliver*, Bob Hoffman sums up the filmmakers' achievement:

> Tom and Ramon's greatest achievement was the overall structure they created—in terms of the production and the execution of the story. It was their philosophic approach to staff the production with individuals on the brink of breaking through in their respective careers—rather than working with bigger-name talent who might bring a lot of baggage with them. This was particularly true with the cast: Eddie [Olmos], Lou [Diamond Phillips], Andy [Garcia] and Rosanna [DeSoto]. But it is also true with the crew: Tom Richmond, director of photography; Nancy Richardson, editor; and Iya Labunka, associate producer, to name but a few. It takes a lot of guts to give an actor the freedom to shape a character the way Eddie did.
>
> Throughout the process, everyone seemed to rise to a very high level of expectation placed on all our shoulders. But that came from the story, from Mr. Escalante. Raising the level of expectation is a major theme in Jaime's work, and this theme infused the project from development through the marketing process.

Tom Musca, reflecting on the singular importance of this film for his own life, makes it clear that his success was due to more than good luck. "When Ramon and I started on this we visualized what would happen . . . and then made it happen. We planned everything and through this planning we made it happen. We predicted what could happen if we played our cards right."

Acknowledging that he was surprised and appreciative of the enormous success the film has enjoyed, Musca stresses that *Stand and Deliver* was produced with a clear eye toward what was going to happen next. Each step was carefully thought through to reduce the number of problems that either needed to be solved after the fact or that couldn't be solved at all. He stresses that an independent filmmaker has to anticipate the unanticipated and plan as well as possible and within the project's budget limitations for every contingency.

In conclusion, Musca stresses that it was a surprise to him just how much work he would be personally involved with in the distribution process. A film producer who simply turns his or her film over to a distributor is culpable for whatever shortcomings occur in the distribution process. "Distribution," he emphasizes, "is part of the producer's job!"

THE WEAVERS: WASN'T THAT A TIME!

(March 1982)

"We felt that if we sang loud enough and strong enough and hopefully enough, somehow it would make a difference."

Wasn't That A Time!

The Weavers
Pete Seeger
Lee Hays
Ronnie Gilbert
Fred Hellerman

with Arlo Guthrie • Don McLean • Holly Near • Peter, Paul & Mary
Directed by Jim Brown   Written by Lee Hays
Edited by Paul Barnes   Associate Producer Ginger Turek
Produced by Jim Brown • Harold Leventhal • George Stoney
Original Soundtrack Album Available on Loom Records

PRINCIPALS	*Director*	Jim Brown
	Producers	Jim Brown, Harold Leventhal, and George Stoney
	Principal cast	Pete Seeger, Lee Hays, Ronnie Gilbert, and Fred Hellerman
DISTRIBUTORS	*Theatrical*	United Artists Classics
	Homevideo	MGM/United Artists
	Pay cable	not available
	Nontheatrical	Films Incorporated
	Broadcast	PBS
	Foreign	Ron Devillier
THEATRICAL	*Opening date*	March 6, 1982
	Total playdates	100 (e)
	Box-office gross	$250,200 (e)
	Total distributor costs	
	Advance	None
	Publicity	not available
	Prints	not available
ANCILLARY	*Homevideo*	$ 40,000 (e)
	Nontheatrical	15,000 (e)
	Foreign	75,000 (e)
PARTICIPANTS CONTACTED		Jim Brown
		Harold Leventhal
		George Stoney
		Ira Deutchman
		Tom Bernard
		Michael Barker
		Nathaniel Kwit
		Fred Hellerman
		Steve Seifert

e = Estimate based on uncorroborated data derived from *Variety,* other industry sources, and authors' calculations.

FILM SYNOPSIS

The Weavers: Wasn't That a Time! *details the preparations leading up to the reunion concert of the original members of the legendary folk group the Weavers. Pete Seeger, Ronnie Gilbert, Lee Hays, and Fred Hellerman are seen as they come together again after seventeen years. The activities are interspersed with interviews with Studs Terkel, Arlo Guthrie, Holly Near, and others.*

DEVELOPMENT

The Weavers are out of the grass roots of America. I salute them for their work in authentic renditions of ballads, folk songs, ditties, nice antiques of word and melody. When I hear American singing, the Weavers are there.

—Carl Sandburg

The Weavers—Pete Seeger, Lee Hays, Ronnie Gilbert, and Fred Hellerman—made their professional debut on the stage of the Village Vanguard in Greenwich Village, New York City, in December 1949. Harold Leventhal was their manager.

The American music industry at that time was dominated by Perry Como, the Andrews Sisters, Patti Page, and Eddie Fisher. Yet, within weeks of their debut, the Weavers' Decca recording of "Good Night Irene" moved into the number one spot on the hit parade chart, stayed there for three months, and sold over two million copies.

By 1952, the group was suffering from the McCarthy blacklist and public denunciations for their "anti-American" attitudes; the number of their engagements dwindled. They disbanded, then returned to the stage in 1955, and though Pete Seeger left the group in 1958, the Weavers performed until 1963.

Most observers of American folk-music history agree with Carl Sandburg's assessment of the group's importance, though Pete Seeger modestly describes them as "an important link in a chain" that passes America's folk-music spirit from generation to generation. The Weavers sought out folk songs from across the American countryside, and with their vigorous treatments, made them accessible to sophisticated postwar audiences. Furthermore, they revived public enthusiasm for America's folk-music traditions, and paved the way for the mass-marketing of the idiom in the sixties.

Jim Brown, a young documentary filmmaker and folk-music devotee, was a friend and neighbor of Lee Hays at Croton-on-Hudson, New York. He had always hoped to do a portrait of Lee that would involve the Weavers. Lee, however, "had always been cold on the idea." A graduate of New York University Film School, Brown had made more than twelve documentaries with veteran George Stoney, including the award-winning *How the Myth Was Made*, about the making of Robert Flaherty's classic documentary film *Man of Aran*, as well as several magazine shows for WNET, New York's principal public television station. Brown worked in advertising for a time and then formed his own production company, later called the Ginger Group, which specialized in documentaries. Stoney, whom Brown describes as his "teacher and mentor," was a full-time faculty member at NYU.

In early 1981, Pete Seeger joined Ronnie Gilbert and Fred Hellerman for a recording session, the first time that the trio had been together in ten years. Brown recalls that Lee Hays, who had lost both legs to diabetes, was "a little miffed that he hadn't been invited to the recording sessions. He began to think of ways to unite the group on his own turf."

Brown invited Stoney to discuss with Hays a proposal to film a reunion of the Weavers at a picnic at Lee Hays's house. Stoney offered to put up equipment and some money to start the project through his own production company, G. Stoney Associates. Lee called Harold Leventhal, still the Weavers' business manager, and a man whom Brown admired as "a legend" and "the godfather of my heroes." Leventhal's fifty years in music management had included frequent ventures into the cinema. He had coproduced *Bound for Glory*, the film biography of his late client Woody Guthrie, for which he received an Academy Award nomination. He had also been involved, as Arlo Guthrie's manager, with *Alice's Restaurant*. As Alan Arkin's manager, he was experienced at negotiating deals for major theatrical films. Leventhal was skeptical about the project, believing that it would create a lot of unnecessary headaches for his aging clients and that the end result would not reach much of an audience. Still, he agreed to support it.

The idea to film the picnic at Hays's house was supported by all of the Weavers. Fred Hellerman recalls his curiosity at the proposed meeting, seeing the project at this point as a cross between a home movie and a documentation of the Weavers. Stoney and Brown were able to assemble a volunteer crew; the Weavers received no compensation. At the picnic, in September 1981, the musical experience of performing together was so successful that Seeger and Leventhal proposed that the Weavers reunite in November at a concert at Carnegie Hall. The picnic became the first rehearsal for the planned reunion.

Everyone involved was concerned about Hays's physical condition. He had not only lost his legs to diabetes, but also wore a pacemaker. Hays himself sometimes questioned the practicality of the plan for the Carnegie Hall reunion. The reunion concert could not have been arranged without the extraordinary generosity of Pete Seeger, who, with Leventhal, had booked the hall a month earlier for Seeger's annual Thanksgiving concert. Seeger agreed to have the other three Weavers join him for the last half of the evening, with Hays participating to the extent his physical condition would allow. It was to be Hays's last public performance.

Following the concert, the producers brought a flatbed to Lee's house, where he reviewed the progress of the film and recorded voiceovers. He died nine months after the concert, just prior to the first public screening of the completed film.

The generous cooperation of the other Weavers on the project was primarily occasioned by their concern for Lee Hays. No formal agreement for compensation was drawn up until after the film was in roughcut and substantially funded by the Corporation for Public Broadcasting (CPB).

PRODUCTION

A voluntary crew with donated equipment was assembled for the Carnegie Hall reunion. Leventhal's friends in the folk-music community donated the $10,000 fee required to film inside Carnegie Hall. Fred Hellerman remembers the concert as a very moving experience:

> We looked out into the packed audience and saw two and three generations out there—kids, parents, and grandparents. Many of them weren't born at the time of our last Carnegie Hall concert in 1963!

Jim Brown was praised by the Weavers for his nonintrusive presence. According to Hellerman:

> The last thing we thought about was the film. We had more immediate concerns like, what song was up next? And how was Lee Hays doing? Jim and his crew did not intrude at all, yet in the pressure of filming a nonrepeatable event, there was no margin for error. When we saw the final film, we realized that he'd caught it all.

The Carnegie Hall concert became a media event. "Once we filmed Carnegie Hall," says Brown, "we had less trouble raising funds to complete the film. We put together a good sample reel. CPB made a commitment to fund it based on the sample reel. The initial grant was $40,000, though in the end they gave us close to $100,000." In return, PBS secured first exclusive broadcast rights for four screenings over three years.

The film was made for approximately $150,000, with most salaries and fees deferred. Funding sources, in addition to CPB, included the New York State Council on the Arts (NYSCA) and the NEH. There were no private investors.

As the film took shape, Leventhal asked Stoney and Brown to allocate 50 percent of any profits to the Weavers. He also asked to participate as a coproducer; Stoney and Brown were eager to include him because of his marketing and deal-making experience.

DISTRIBUTION

Making the deal · "We knew that we were on to something good during the editing process," says Brown, though the Weavers and Leventhal still remained cautious. "When we had a final cut," Brown adds, "George and I moved the editing room to Lee Hays's house and invited the Weavers and Leventhal to view the film. It got their enthusiastic approval." Fred Hellerman recalls that he was "very delighted" with the film:

> It wasn't a puff piece, and we wouldn't have gone for that. The Weavers were a product/victim/mover of a time. Jim Brown and George Stoney caught that. They made a movie about a time, as well as about a group called the Weavers.

Leventhal finally saw the first print of *The Weavers: Wasn't That a Time!* at the IFP's Film Market in New York in September 1981, where it received a standing ovation. According to Leventhal:

> The film itself overwhelmed us. Then, in the lobby outside, it became obvious that the whole Market had opened up. All the major art-house distributors approached us. We realized that we had more than just a film for public television. I now started to dream a little about theatrical distribution. On the one hand, we had a documentary film about a group that hadn't appeared in public for twenty years. On the other hand, there was no doubt that this was an exciting, moving film.

How much did he dream could be made from theatrical distribution? "A $200,000 profit! Maximum!"

During this period, the film was widely screened for theatrical distributors, but the producers decided to hold off making a deal until after its world premiere at the London Film Festival.

In the meantime, the producers negotiated a deal to sell exclusive foreign television rights to Ron Devillier, a Washington, D.C., agent. Devillier also renegotiated the PBS/CPB contract to include a one-year theatrical window and a substantial increase in funding. *The Weavers* received another standing ovation at the London Film Festival, leading to widespread media coverage, including a glowing review in *Variety*. Fred Hellerman was full of nervous anticipation before the London screening:

I knew that Weavers fans would like the movie, but this was an audience of movie people. They'd never heard of the Weavers. They would judge it only as a film. Their response was fantastic. If there had been a first prize, we would have walked away with it.

All of this generated momentum for the negotiations for United States theatrical rights.

The offers were very similar, the conventional 50/50 percent art-house deal. However, the producers leaned heavily toward United Artists Classics (UAC), which had recently been successful with the Oscar-winning *From Mao to Mozart*, another music documentary.

UAC was relatively new to first-run theatrical releases. The unit had had a long history with a significant library of repertory titles. In 1979, Nathaniel Kwit was appointed head of this and several other UAC ancillary businesses. He was eager to move into first-run release of foreign and independent American films, and since Classics was a small, low-budget operation within a very large corporation, Kwit possessed a great deal of freedom to experiment. Early in 1980, he broke new ground with the theatrical opening of Pasolini's *Arabian Nights* and *The Canterbury Tales*, two titles that were already in the UAC library. His first move to acquire an American independent was a 1980 bid for John Sayles's *Return of the Secaucus Seven* (see case study). Soon after, UAC rereleased *Cutter's Way*, which, under the title of *Cutter and Bone*, had fallen through the cracks of UA's major distribution system. The film did significant business for UAC. Among the releases that followed were François Truffaut's *The Last Metro* and Jean-Jacques Beineix's *Diva*.

UA Classics was not the only company distributing independent films but, in an industry where the lifespan of a distributor can be very brief, it was the first to be associated with a Hollywood studio. Nathaniel Kwit explains several of the considerations that guided the unit:

First, we had such a low overhead—about $500,000, and with a staff of only fifteen—that we were free of the pressure to pick up films just to maintain an expensive distribution pipeline. We were able to acquire films that might not make a lot of money, nor would they lose a lot if they were carefully handled.

Second, we developed a new economics by redefining the standard

United Artists studio distribution deal into a 50/50 deal net of costs. This meant that the filmmaker wasn't being hit with outrageous studio overhead charges. It also encouraged them to work hard with us to reduce costs, by making sure that every advertising dollar went further. In a sense, every cost was an out-of-pocket expense to the filmmaker.

Third, we would spend only the minimum amount on advertising and promotion that could be directly traced to increased box office. This forced us to be imaginative. For instance, after picking up *Diva* for only $25,000, we held our press party in a New York bowling alley where we served peanuts and beer for a thousand people at a cost of about $800. That week, MGM's party for *Pennies from Heaven* cost about $250,000, and we got all the publicity.

Kwit himself was instrumental in the acquisition of *The Weavers*:

I remember being emotionally overwhelmed by *The Weavers*. It brought back wonderful childhood experiences connected with the music of Pete Seeger and the Weavers with the force of a ton of bricks. I wept! I was convinced that an older audience would react very similarly. On the other hand, I recognized that as a documentary, it would be a challenge.

Jim Brown recalls thinking to himself that it was a very positive sign that a prospective distributor was moved to tears by the film. Kwit called his staff together for an unusual Saturday preview, and once again he cried. His former staff retains a vivid memory of his emotional commitment to the film.

Tom Bernard, then on Kwit's staff and now with Orion Classics, recalls several considerations that arose during the evaluation of *The Weavers*:

- The length of the film (sixty minutes) was a concern. UA Classics needed to create a way to package it for theatrical distribution. Bernard reviewed hours of shorts before choosing a film by Pete Seeger.
- The coproducers were locked into a PBS airdate, thereby limiting UAC's flexibility in scheduling the New York opening and national playoff.
- There were some expectations that *The Weavers* would receive an Academy Award nomination. Bernard was "very disappointed" that it

didn't, although Kwit insists that its Oscar potential did not influence the acquisition.

Ira Deutchman, then UAC's director of marketing and later with Cinecom International, saw in the film one plus and one big minus:

The Weavers arrived with a rare combination of qualities. It was very entertaining and very moving. We were confident that, if we set it up with the right expectations, it would deliver, leading to strong word-of-mouth. There was a loyal core of Weavers fans out there and they would be sure to see it. And we were confident of good reviews.

The big negative, according to Deutchman, was that "documentaries are notoriously difficult to bring to a large theatrical audience." Leventhal recalls the factors that attracted him to UA Classics:

First, I liked the people I had met at United Artists [Studio] due to my experience with *Bound for Glory.*

Second, in the absence of any offers of advances from any other distributor, my principal concern was for a reasonable contract that defined what we did and didn't share in distribution costs. Since the film was shot on 16mm, I was concerned that the distributor should meet the cost of a 35mm blowup.

Finally, we had to be confident that our distributor had the market power to reach the entire domestic market.

Terms of the deal · UA Classics proceeded to prepare an offer for theatrical rights for *The Weavers*, which included:

- No advance.
- No guarantee.
- No commitment to a national run.
- U.S. and Canadian theatrical rights for fifteen years.
- A stepped revenue-sharing split in favor of the coproducers as follows: 50/50 up to $500,000; 40/60 from $500,000 to $750,000; 35/65 over $750,000.

Kwit committed to a New York opening, to be followed by national playoff on a market-by-market basis. Kwit's expectations were modest, forecasting rentals in the $250,000–$750,000 range.

Only domestic theatrical rights were included in the deal. The producers were determined to retain all other rights, including television, foreign television and theatrical, homevideo, and 16mm nontheatrical. As Brown explains:

> We knew that the theatrical distribution of feature documentaries is a risky venture. We were therefore wary of engaging a distributor who might throw the film into theatrical release for a week or so, then sell it off to homevideo or television. By splitting the rights, we knew that if a distributor was talking theatrical, then they must have been confident that they could make money there.

Kwit reluctantly accepted a theatrical-rights-only deal. He recognizes that "the problem with cross-collateralization is that once you've relieved the distributor of strict responsibility for a theatrical release, he could get sloppy, and rely on the expectation that he can cover his mistakes on the other [ancillary] side." But Kwit feared that if UA Classics insisted on all rights, then it could lose some acquisitions. "My position," he says, "was that if I couldn't get all rights, then I would settle for the theatrical rights and make sure that the company didn't lose money on the theatrical run."

It is worth noting, however, that UAC was a theatrical-only unit of United Artists, where a separate division negotiated homevideo deals. Also, the *Weavers* deal was negotiated before it became apparent that there would be a boom in homevideo royalties.

MARKETING CAMPAIGN

Strategy · It was clear from the outset that the primary target audience was people interested in folk music. Therefore, UA Classics based its promotional efforts for the New York launch on

- the extraordinary publicity given the Weavers' final concert at Carnegie Hall in major newspapers and radio;
- Seeger's frequent promotions of the film during his concerts across the country, along with Ronnie Gilbert's availability for a promotional tour; and
- reviving the Weavers' songs on radio as a tie-in with the release of the film.

Promotion and publicity · News of the impending release of the film stimulated a great deal of press, radio, and TV coverage focusing on the phenomenon of the Weavers. Backup material for these stories was prepared by Brown and was included in the press kits issued by the distributors. Publicist Steve Seifert was engaged by UA Classics for the preopening and opening period.

Heavy advance screenings for the press and target audience were scheduled in an effort to build up word-of-mouth. Deutchman says:

> The challenge of the preview period was to convince critics and opinion-leaders that this was more than a little documentary, that it was a film which would work well as entertainment for moviegoers.

Critics were invited to view the film with preview audiences. "This," says Deutchman, "is always a risk, since critics feel that you're trying to manipulate them." However, the *New York Times* critic Janet Maslin responded favorably by stressing the entertainment value of *The Weavers*.

In addition, a special promotion linking the Weavers to the film was broadcast on WBAI, a publicly supported New York radio station.

Trailer and ad · A 16mm trailer was completed by a free-lance editor, Keith Gilman, whose fee was approximately $4,000. The blowup to 35mm posed some problems, but UA Classics was pleased that the trailer conveyed the entertainment values of the film and avoided the trap of making *The Weavers* look like a PBS documentary.

The image used for the ad presented a challenge. Deutchman says that it was his intention to "create an image that would make the Weavers look like icons rather than like four elderly people." His first attempt was to commission an artist's rendering based on a photo of the group, but it didn't work. Deutchman had artwork created that combined a current photo of the Weavers with another shot of the group taken in their prime. Deutchman calls the result "vibrant and effective." The coproducers were involved throughout this process; they selected the scenes used in the trailer and chose one of their still photos of the Weavers for use in the artwork.

THEATRICAL RELEASE

Strategy · UA Classics planned a medium-scale New York opening campaign, with $22,000 committed for preopening and opening week advertising. Most of this was for print media, principally ads in the *New York Times* and the *Village Voice*. Deutchman recalls that the only type of radio promotion that made sense for this film would be on local listener-supported radio stations, so Harold Leventhal negotiated with WBAI for the airing of a feature program on the Weavers.

UAC also considered a Greenwich Village opening in order to capitalize on the Village origins of the folk movement, but rejected the idea because it would narrow expectations for the film. Instead the Cinema 3 was chosen for the New York launch. This 200-seat theater was the right size to create the important sense of intimacy for the relatively small audience expected. Like the Paris, it is located just west of Fifth Avenue, thus providing the cachet of a prestigious East Side first-run house. This was important in positioning *The Weavers* as a major film rather than as a TV documentary or a fringe theatrical release.

Further, the Cinema 3 was relatively affordable; its weekly house nut was about $9,000, compared to the $10,000 to $16,000 nuts of the larger East Side specialty cinemas. Alternative West Side venues for first runs had not matured at that stage, though the house expenses of these cinemas ranged between $5,000 and $6,000. The high operating costs of the major East Side theaters place great pressure on exhibitors to bring in new business if a film does not perform quickly. Therefore, the affordability of the Cinema 3 gave *The Weavers* more time to find its audience.

Other advantages offered by the Cinema 3 were:

· It was part of the Cinema Five chain of specialty houses, thus allowing trailers to be cross-promoted at other Cinema Five theaters.

· It had been the site of successful recent runs for other specialty films, including Pasolini's *Arabian Nights* and *The Canterbury Tales*. *Meetings with Remarkable Men*, which the distributor saw as appealing to a similar audience as *The Weavers*, had also performed very well there.

Opening run · *The Weavers* opened on Sunday, March 6, 1982. The Sunday opening was dictated by the exhibitor's commitments and by the distributor's difficulty meeting the newspaper advertising deadlines required for a Friday opening.

Deutchman recalls:

> The Sunday launch was a compromise we reached with the exhibitor, and it was a mistake. The only advantage of a Sunday opening is that it minimizes the danger of bad reviews, which are printed in the news section of the *Times* rather than in the entertainment section. A bad review will not be noticed there, but a good review can be reprinted in full as an advertisement during the following week.

As it happened, *The Weavers* received an excellent review in the Sunday *Times*, which was reprinted during the following week in both the *Times* and the *Village Voice*. In hindsight, Deutchman conceded that the film should have opened on Friday. If Maslin's review had appeared in the *Times*'s Friday entertainment section, that would have encouraged a strong first-weekend performance.

Business at the Cinema 3 was decent. Box-office grosses for the first four weeks were $7,988; $12,070; $9,634; and $9,385.

The Weavers hit *Variety*'s list of the fifty top-grossing films, which sparked exhibitor interest in other cities. Although the film received great local publicity, it failed to receive extensive national publicity, for instance a review in *Time*, which is crucial for an art-house release. Deutchman feels that business was negatively affected to a greater degree than was anticipated by the lack of identity of Cinema 3. There was a great deal of confusion about its location. Cinemas I and II are four blocks away, and the Plaza is two blocks away, yet Cinema 3 is in the basement of the Plaza hotel. This problem contributed to the difficulties in bringing the film to the theatrical marketplace.

The Weavers ran for twelve weeks. Weekly grosses were above $8,000, and at times reached $12,000. However, the film lost $30,000 against the house nut and high advertising costs associated with a New York opening. Michael Barker, vice-president of marketing for Orion Classics, comments: "This was not a bad result, for we had attracted the attention of exhibitors with a twelve-week run in a good first-run house. In other words, we had ensured a national playoff."

National playoff · Despite, on balance, a disappointing opening in New York, *The Weavers* played successfully on three screens in Los Angeles, where it opened as a political fundraiser organized by Jane Fonda for her then husband, state Senator Tom Hayden. Fred Hellerman flew in for preopening promotions. He remembers that press interviews focused more on the McCarthy-era blacklist than on the Weavers themselves, confirming his sense that "this was what the movie was all about."

Disappointed with UAC's publicity, Brown and associate producer Ginger Tureck traveled to Los Angeles and San Francisco, where they were able to generate several interviews. "We felt UA was about to let the film die," Brown says. "We were opening on eight screens in Los Angeles and San Francisco, but there was little or no awareness of the film." Against UAC's wishes, Brown called critic Roger Ebert and told him of the situation. He asked Ebert to broadcast his review before the Chicago opening. Brown had watched the film with Ebert at the U.S. Film Festival in Park City, Utah, and knew he cared about it deeply. Ebert graciously aired his enthusiastic review on "Sneak Previews" during the West Coast run. As a result, ticket sales increased and *The Weavers* returned to *Variety*'s "top fifty"—which, in turn, created more bookings.

A major disagreement developed between the coproducers and distributor over the Chicago opening. UA Classics had distributed *From Mao to Mozart* there, and had been hurt by a trashing from Siskel and Ebert on "Sneak Previews." The distributor was wary of their attitude toward *The Weavers*, a caution that was compounded by the disappointment in New York. Again, theater availability was an issue, for Chicago lacked at that time a small first-run theater known for specialty films. However, *The Weavers* was booked into a small repertory theater, and a rave review from Siskel and Ebert (on their new show "At the Movies") generated national publicity that extended its theatrical run around the country. According to Brown, the two critics told audiences that "this is a great film which is getting a bad distribution deal. Everyone should see it!" They compared it to *E.T.* As a result, *The Weavers* went from a one-week locked engagement at a small repertory house to open-ended runs at several first-run theaters in Chicago. Brown recalls frustration dealing with UA Classics at a time when the distributor was undergoing rapid changes in personnel.

Approximately one hundred national playdates followed, though Tom Bernard recalls that the proximity of the PBS broadcast date made bookings very difficult in several markets. Pete Seeger used his mailing list, his contacts, and his connections with the folk-music community to promote the film throughout the country. However, nowhere was there a long run to build back the momentum lost in New York.

OTHER MARKETS

Homevideo · The producers closed a deal with MGM/UA because, Leventhal recalls, "they came to us, and I like a company that's really on." An advance of "approximately $40,000" reflected the novelty of the homevideo business at that time. "They were bidding high to secure product, but were uncertain of the returns." In fact, *The Weavers* hasn't earned back its advance.

Pay cable · A twelve-minute version was sold to Bravo to garner completion funds.

Nontheatrical · Most of the major distributors made a bid. The producers closed with Films Incorporated, based on their personal affection for owner Charles Benton. An advance "of more than $10,000" was considered "better than modest." Awards at the American Film Festival helped sustain an excellent performance in this market. *The Weavers* has recovered its advance.

Broadcast · PBS retained broadcast television rights as a result of its funding of the project. *The Weavers* has proved to be one of PBS's most effective documentary fundraisers, raising millions of dollars in its four showings in three years. The coproducers are now renegotiating this arrangement.

Foreign · Foreign theatrical rights were sold by the producers for territories including the United Kingdom, Australia, and Canada. All foreign television deals were negotiated by Ron Devillier. His fee was 25 percent of gross. Sales were concluded in Canada for "more than

$20,000," and in all European markets except Italy, France, Spain, and Portugal. Sales were made to both East and West Germany. Sales figures included the United Kingdom (Channel Four) for "more than $25,000" and the Republic of Ireland at "less than $5,000." In Australia, all rights were assigned for approximately $12,000.

REVIEW

The odds are stacked against the success of feature documentary films in theatrical release. This was recognized from the beginning by the makers of *The Weavers: Wasn't That a Time!*, who produced their homage to the legendary folk group for public television, without anticipating a theatrical release. They renegotiated a one-year theatrical window with PBS after theatrical offers were made. It wasn't until the first public screening at the IFP's 1981 Film Market in New York that the theatrical potential of the film became clear. Even then, the filmmakers' expectations were very modest. United Artists Classics was selected on the basis of its national market power, and for its familiarity with the producers. The deal, a 50/50 split of revenues after deducting distribution costs, was to become the standard deal for specialty films. The terms of the acquisition reflected the distributor's cautious approach to a documentary: there was no advance, no guarantee, and a limited commitment to a national run.

A three-month opening run in New York was followed by extensive national playdates, based largely on excellent reviews. The campaign was carefully planned to emphasize the film's entertainment value, and to minimize the perception that it was a PBS documentary. However, *The Weavers* was not reviewed extensively in the national press, which, in the producers' view, contributed to a disappointing theatrical release.

The producers retained foreign and all nontheatrical rights, recovering a significant portion of the cost of the film through advances and international sales.

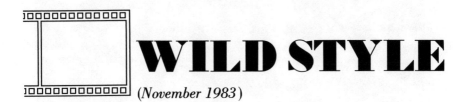

WILD STYLE

(November 1983)

PRINCIPALS	*Director/Producer/*	
	Writer	Charles Ahearn
	Musical Director	Frederick Brathwaite
	Original music	Chris Stein
	Principal cast	"Lee" George Quinones, Fred Brathwaite, Sandra "Pink" Fabara, and Patti Astor
	Producer's rep	Films Around the World
DISTRIBUTORS	*Theatrical*	First Run Features
	Homevideo	not available
	Pay cable	not available
	Nontheatrical	not available
	Broadcast	not available
	Foreign	Films Around the World
THEATRICAL	*Opening date*	November 23, 1983
	Total playdates	not available
	Box-office gross	$1,200,000 (e)
	Gross film rental	480,000 (e)
	Total distributor costs	
	Advance	25,000
	Publicity	not available
	Prints	not available
ANCILLARY	*Homevideo*	not available
PARTICIPANTS CONTACTED		Charles Ahearn
		Janet Cole
		Fran Spielman
		Peter Elson

e = Estimate based on uncorroborated data derived from *Variety,* other industry sources, and authors' calculations.

FILM SYNOPSIS

The story follows the exploits of Raymond, a master graffiti artist, as he defies danger and the law to spraypaint his visions on New York's subway cars. A trendy journalist, impressed with his work, tracks him down and brings him "aboveground" recognition that leads to promotion of his work by a Lower East Side art gallery. The dramatic conflict centers on Raymond's struggle to hold on to his outlaw identity and artistic integrity in the face of sudden acclaim by the art-world establishment.

DEVELOPMENT

Genesis · Charles Ahearn had been a participant in the New York avant-garde art scene since 1973, producing "art movies" that were shown at the Museum of Modern Art and the Collective for Living Cinema. In the late 1970s, he began to lose interest in the art scene and was attracted to the "really rich variety of life going on in the [public housing] projects" of lower Manhattan. Out of this experience, he made a super-8mm film, *The Deadly Art of Survival*, on the martial arts as an expression of dance choreography and style. The film was self-distributed, and shown at city art-house theaters and on public-access cable stations.

As Ahearn says,

> I was interested in the idea of free-form, underground film in the ghetto. Like what underground movies were in the Village: reflecting the people there, without a commercial base, close to what was happening . . . like Warhol, but in the projects.

244

In the summer of 1980, he met Fred Brathwaite [a.k.a. Fab 5 Freddy], an active participant in the "hip-hop" culture, who introduced him to this underground world of art created by young people in the South Bronx. He saw it as an affirmative alternative activity to the gang rituals that had brutalized his older siblings.

From its inception, *Wild Style* was conceived as a combination of documentary and narrative, but not, Ahearn insists, as a "docudrama." The film uses a storyline developed by Ahearn and Brathwaite, and a script written by Ahearn to hold the action and music together. Originally, the actors were encouraged to use the script as a starting point for their own improvisations in order to achieve greater authenticity; but ultimately the improvisational scenes were cut out and reshot according to a final script.

Financing · Ahearn initially approached PBS and its New York affiliate, WNET, but received "very negative reactions." However, in the summer of 1980, he successfully approached Germany's ZDF with the help of Joy Pereths, from England's Channel Four. Channel Four gave money up front, in cash, on the basis of a one-page story synopsis, a budget, and photocopies of graffiti-laden trains and breakdancers. Ahearn notes that "they were attracted to the idea that the film was a story and not a documentary."

The total 16mm production costs were $250,000. ZDF television contributed an estimated $60,000, Channel Four provided about $60,000, and NYSCA awarded a small completion grant. The balance was raised from private U.S. sources.

Anticipating an audience · Defining the audience for *Wild Style* was a problem from the beginning. As Ahearn says, "I wanted to make an art movie that would play to a ghetto audience." But as the film took shape, the definition of both film and audience became more precise: a "musical" art film for an "inner-city" youth audience. In Ahearn's words:

> I had a dream that the film would play on 42nd Street. I was hoping that *Wild Style* would be on the marquee and all the "B-boys" [i.e., breakdancers] would come and check it out. I thought the movie would be big, but never anticipated it being as big as it was. I was never sure if the film would play to a ghetto or to an art-house audience.

PRODUCTION

Film development and preproduction lasted over a year, from June 1980 to September 1981. While Ahearn wrote a story outline and working script, he never completed a final shooting script. Rather, he invested time and effort in getting to know the people who were to be the subjects of the film. He spent a lot of time hanging out with people on street corners and in dance clubs, and going to subway yards at night. Ahearn says this was "a lot of fun," and necessary both for script development and casting. Without records or videos for research, he had to form his own, first-hand understanding of the hip-hop scene.

The film was shot in 16mm, and was framed for eventual 35mm blowup. As Ahearn says, "I always knew we'd go to 35[mm]; I wanted it in theaters." As a low-budget art feature, the film was produced below guild minimums. Actors, for example, got $50 per day, while crew fees ranged from below $50 per day for production assistants to $100 a day for a camera person. Cast and crew worked on the film because they liked it, or wanted the experience and credit. All the talent (e.g., rappers, major actors, and dancers) received points.

Shooting took seven weeks. Ahearn used locations and people as he found them to achieve the desired authenticity and vitality, often shooting actors in front of their apartment buildings and wearing their own clothes.

The film was edited during the winter of 1981–82. In the spring of 1982, Ahearn reshot several scenes because of problems with the original sound recording and was able to add some new sequences. During postproduction he screened a three-hour roughcut for ZDF. Ahearn eventually cut out the more "sociological" parts of the version liked by ZDF in favor of a more musical tone and structure. He insists: "Everything improvised in the movie was finally cut out. Everything that remains was directed."

DISTRIBUTION DEAL

Making the deal · Ahearn screened the original version of *Wild Style* in 16mm at the 1982 IFP Market. Many distributors expressed interest. Paramount Pictures borrowed a print for review while their film *Flashdance*, the first Hollywood production to include break-dancing sequences, was in preproduction. Taking advantage of a favorable climate, Ahearn flew to Los Angeles and screened his film for other distributors. Reactions were mixed: distributors saw it as an original work but with limited commercial potential due to its low-budget, quasi-documentary style. In Hollywood, Ahearn faced a deeper problem: "I didn't know what to ask for or what to do."

Following the IFP Market, Ahearn was invited to premiere the film at the New Directors/New Films series sponsored by the Museum of Modern Art and the Film Society of Lincoln Center in New York the following spring. He met the late Irvin Shapiro, head of Films Around the World, a representative for foreign sales, who became the producer's representative in all markets. Shapiro invested money for a 35mm blowup.

Shapiro negotiated all deals for Ahearn, and sought to make upfront deals, i.e., offering concessions in favor of as large an advance as possible. This freed Ahearn from handling the tough negotiations with the distributors and, with upfront money, cut Shapiro's risks.

First Run Features was the only company to make a solid offer that included an advance and a contract. According to Janet Cole, First Run's former manager, the distributor pursued *Wild Style* for the following reasons:

- As a small distributor specializing mostly in political documentaries, First Run was seeking a 35mm feature for theatrical release.
- From the IFP Market and New Directors/New Films screenings, *Wild Style* had enough positive reviews (especially one in the *Village Voice*) to be assured of getting serious attention.
- The film was perhaps offbeat and eccentric enough to become a cult hit and make money.
- First Run felt *Wild Style* could heighten the company's profile.

Ahearn and Shapiro spent the spring and summer of 1983 looking for the most favorable deal, and finally came back to First Run.

Terms of the deal · According to Ahearn, the two most important elements of the deal were a cash advance estimated at $25,000 and a gross deal on a 30/70 percent split to the distributor.

Shapiro had paid for the 35mm blowup and one print; First Run paid the lab cost for each additional print struck. The contract also provided First Run some back-end protection through a percentage of homevideo and broadcast market revenues.

In addition to the advance, First Run was an attractive distributor for a number of reasons. First Run was known in the distribution world as an honest company, it was sympathetic to the politics of the film, and it wanted to reach a crossover audience. Ahearn originally wanted a distributor experienced in handling exploitation films for an inner-city audience, but none was willing to put up an advance. At the same time, he wanted to reach the art-house audience familiar to First Run.

MARKETING CAMPAIGN

Strategy · Both the distributor and the filmmaker recognized that *Wild Style* would be a difficult film to position in the marketplace. The following three factors significantly shaped First Run's marketing strategy:

· Time constraints.
· A desire to reach both the inner-city youth and art-house audiences.
· Financial constraints affecting distribution. First Run decided to work extensively with subdistributors in different markets. This led to the decision to secure a Motion Picture Association of America (MPAA) rating to help gain access to the youth market nationwide.

Because Ahearn and Shapiro kept looking for a more favorable distribution deal, the final contract with First Run was not signed until August 1983. Paramount released *Flashdance* in September, beating *Wild Style* into the marketplace. Ahearn says, "I freaked out . . . I was so upset. I was trying to do something experimental and here comes this commercial movie."

This posed a serious problem for First Run. *Wild Style* had been identified as a summer film, one to be seen while the weather was still warm. With the release of *Flashdance* and with publicity building about two other break-dance films in the works (Orion's *Beat Street* and

Cannon's *Breakin'*), First Run, in Janet Cole's words, "felt the foot-steps" of these more commercial films. They decided to open *Wild Style* in the fall rather than compete with these other films the following summer.

First Run attempted to counter what it anticipated to be uneven critical reviews by presenting "wild style" as a phenomenon, a descriptive term, in addition to the film's title. They also built on the *Village Voice* review, which presented the movie as the *first* rap musical, the first feature film dealing with the newest urban craze, the hip-hop culture. The *Voice* called it "easily among the best film musicals in the past half decade." Finally, as part of a campaign to target the film for a youth market, First Run applied to the MPAA for a rating, a necessity in many states. (This is discussed in the next section.)

Promotion and publicity · With a campaign strategy aimed at two distinct audiences—art-house filmgoers and inner-city youth—First Run recognized that its efforts had to encompass both conventional advertising and publicity as well as more innovative promotional outreach efforts. These two approaches can be further distinguished as follows:

- Advertising and publicity outreach: a reliance on editorial and advertising coverage in a variety of mass media (i.e., newspapers, magazines, TV, and radio) to generate awareness. For specialty distributors, this approach relies on both critical reviews and feature articles, and "selective" ad placements (as distinguished from studios' "saturation" approach). This is primarily a capital-intensive strategy.

- Promotional outreach: a reliance on more direct forms of outreach to generate word-of-mouth. This encompasses tie-ins, parties, targeted screenings, personal appearances, and other grassroots or street-level techniques to reach distinct market segments. This is usually a labor-intensive strategy.

Each approach has to be assessed on the basis of budgetary constraints and projected return. Ideally, these efforts overlap and reinforce each other.

First Run recognized that youth audiences, and especially those of the inner city, were not heavy newspaper readers, and, accordingly, did not follow the lead of critics in deciding which film to see. Traditionally, high-visibility television ads and, to a lesser extent, radio spots were the most important—and expensive—ways to reach the youth market. First Run concentrated on more labor-intensive promotional efforts to generate word-of-mouth interest among inner-city youth, in addition to carefully placed radio and newspaper ads.

First Run employed a number of highly imaginative and successful outreach efforts. The New York promotion and publicity campaign was handled by Janet Cole and local publicist Lauren Hyman. It included:

- The use of runners to distribute handbills and fliers advertising the film to every high school in the city. Cole says, "The real key to our success in New York [was] the outreach to the high-school kids through a massive handbill campaign." During the first two weeks of the New York run, First Run distributed 35,000 handbills. As Cole describes this effort:

  Charlie Ahearn and Fred Brathwaite handpicked team leaders for different sections of town . . . each of whom distributed handbills (while wearing *Wild Style* T-shirts) in the high schools, on street corners, in shopping centers, in dance/rap clubs. We also hit the clubs where break-dancing happens once or twice a week, and the places where [coexecutive producer Harry] Belafonte was casting *Beat Street*.

- Performances by the film talent, especially rappers, at many of the city's popular music clubs.

- Hosting a number of break-dance parties at music clubs and roller-skating rinks to stimulate word-of-mouth.

- The free distribution of *Wild Style* buttons and T-shirts.

- The postering of over 1,500 one-sheets throughout the city, especially in inner-city neighborhoods, where the film performers had an indigenous following.

- The displaying of one-sheets in record stores, accomplished, according to Cole, by sending First Run representatives to "sweet-talk the managements."

- The use of sound trucks for opening night promotion. Cole remembers:

  On opening night, we had a *Wild Style* van plastered with posters and equipped with a loudspeaker going through the neighborhoods distributing fliers, buttons, and invitations to the parties. We also had rappers with bullhorns at strategic locations.

In addition, prior to signing with First Run, some of the film's talent painted a giant wall mural of the film's title on New York's Riverside Drive. It drew considerable attention (not all of it favorable), and was used as an image for the poster art. A similar high-visibility stunt was planned for the Boston opening. The management of the Coolidge Corner Theater hired Brathwaite and Sandra "Pink" Fabara to paint a mural on the theater's outside wall. However, because of bad weather conditions, the effect was disappointing, garnering only limited television and print coverage.

Finally, in New York and a few other markets, First Run used radio ads and ran ticket giveaways on stations that cater to teen audiences. Cole recalls:

> Besides the obvious top-rated stations, there are some smaller, black stations that play more hip-hop music. We advertised on those, too.
>
> We advertised on the top two stations in New York and the top three stations in Boston, and did ticket giveaways with all of them. Had we had more time, we'd have tied in a fashion angle or something in addition to the "tenth caller will receive" ticket giveaway. One station offered its van to play the music, judge a rap contest, and give away buttons and tickets at different locations (shopping centers, street corners, etc.).

For its second-track campaign of reaching the art-house audience, First Run employed techniques common to specialty distributors:

- Targeted advertising, with newspaper ads for the opening and throughout the run placed in the *Daily News, Post, Amsterdam News,* and *Village Voice.* First Run did not place ads in the *New York Times* for the opening and ran them only for the occasional Friday (Weekend) and Sunday (Arts and Leisure) sections.
- Hosting a dozen press screenings for feature writers and radio, television, and music-club disc jockeys, the recognized opinion-leaders of the hip-hop music scene.

Cole describes this effort:

> In essence, we tried to find opinion-makers in these areas who would talk up the film in their circles, whether or not they could produce a

[published] piece. With the teen stations, we extended general invitations to *all* station personnel, as well as to TV personnel involved with music, dance, and teen shows. We also invited high-school and college newspaper and radio people.

These promotional efforts helped *Wild Style* gain broader visibility beyond the inner-city youth audience and were boosted by a good number of favorable reviews (see next section). Television coverage was, however, limited due to the appearance of other more commercial films, most notably *Beat Street*.

The filmmaker handled a soundtrack record album deal with Animal/Chrysalis records. The record was released on Jem Records, a small label from New Jersey. A properly released record can help overall theatrical promotional efforts, but according to Cole the record's release was accompanied by problems that limited effective cross-merchandising opportunities. First, the record did not come out until early January 1984, preventing effective tie-ins with music-video television programs. Second, Jem Records did not want to invest any money in promoting the record.

First Run also negotiated a second merchandising spin-off for "Wild Style"–brand sneakers.

The estimated marketing costs, exclusive of outside labor costs, were $15,000 for preopening and opening advertising in New York, and $15,000 for preopening and opening publicity and promotion in Boston.

Trailer and ad · The film's trailer was cut by the film's editor, Steve Brown.

Problems developed between Ahearn and First Run over artwork. Ahearn sought to exercise significant control over all the artwork for the purpose of establishing consistency. However, First Run worked with its own artist, producing results that Ahearn disliked. The filmmaker complains, "We ended up with a big mess, because every territory had a different poster . . . with only the logo for continuity." First Run points out that ancillary distributors created different artwork for their own markets. First Run had rights only to the U.S. theatrical market and, therefore, could not enforce the use of a uniform image. Ahearn, and some of the artists in the film, developed their own posters that were used in the campaign.

THEATRICAL RELEASE

Strategy · After defining their target audiences as both inner-city youth and art-house adults, First Run faced a series of difficult choices. First, they had to decide in which market to open and, in turn, at which theater. Second, they had to decide how to approach the national rollout. Speed in release planning was paramount, because the slicker, more commercial break-dance films threatened to scoop *Wild Style*'s potential target audience.

Because of the film's New York locale, First Run decided that the film should open in New York, and would have its primary appeal in urban areas where a hip-hop subculture existed. Having decided on a semicommercial release approach to attract an inner-city audience, First Run sent the film to exhibitors in five major markets for their assessments and bids.

Because a youth audience was sought, First Run submitted *Wild Style* to the MPAA for a rating. To their surprise, this strategy backfired. They had hoped for a "PG" rating, but the film received an "R," due to its language and a twenty-second quasi-pornographic cartoon sequence. Because this rating would exclude younger children from the theaters, it posed some trouble for the film's release. Two subdistributors, however, felt the "R" rating would be an asset.

Opening run · First Run originally planned to open the film at the Waverly Theater in Greenwich Village during early October, but its open-end booking policy eventually thwarted this plan. It was hoped that a Waverly launch would draw both inner-city youth and art-house adults. In addition, the theater was situated on a major thoroughfare across the street from several basketball courts where spontaneous break-dancing often took place, and adjacent to the entrance to a major subway station. Break-dance demonstrations and other promotional events were to be staged on the sidewalk and adjoining basketball courts.

Wild Style was signed to follow the film then running, *Liquid Sky*, and First Run looked forward to a successful opening. To everyone's surprise, *Liquid Sky* became a cult hit and the Waverly kept extending its run. First Run was finally forced to cancel its agreement with the Waverly and open at a Times Square theater.

First Run opened *Wild Style* at the Embassy 3 on Thanksgiving weekend, 1983, and it ran for three months. In Cole's words: "It was totally exhilarating, after all we'd been through, to see lines around the block. The film took off like a shot!" According to the theater manager, Peter Elson, the turnout was "totally unanticipated." The opening was so successful that the owners opened a second 300-seat screen next door for the midnight show. Elson explains that he offered First Run a larger, 540-seat screen, but they refused it, looking to build the street excitement by restricting the audience that could be accommodated. This strategy worked. Box-office grosses for the first six weeks were $42,965; $33,230; $25,377; $15,312; $18,444; and $24,365.

According to Elson, *Wild Style*'s run set a record; it was the highest-grossing film on Broadway at that time. "With a $7,000 house expense and a 90/10 deal," Elson points out, "it was profitable above ad costs." He further notes that "it's very unusual for a first-run movie to make money, let alone break even [in New York] . . . but *Wild Style* had over 53 percent in film rental." The only negative aspect was the commotion and damage caused by the youth crowd, requiring the theater management to hire additional security. According to Elson, the audience "was not a rough crowd, but did a lot of damage . . . they ripped out seats and graffitied the bathroom."

The thirteen-week run at the Embassy 3 grossed $216,000. Costs totaled $82,000 for ads and promotion, with the bulk spent on radio ads. But Ahearn was disappointed that *Wild Style* never opened in an established art house. Because of its appeal to the youth market, where it did so well, it never "crossed back" to the art-house audience. According to Cole, First Run, "wowed" by the New York run, made assumptions about the rest of the country. This enthusiasm proved premature.

During the run at the Embassy, First Run negotiated with sub-distributor Marvin Freedlander of Marvin Films for a "break" to second-run houses throughout the metropolitan area. Freedlander specialized in the release of exploitation films and approached First Run to handle *Wild Style* due to its strong youth appeal. As a subdistributor, he took a percentage (18½ to 20 percent) off the top of gross box-office receipts.

First Run provided twenty-five 35mm prints for the break. The film opened in twenty-one theaters in early January 1984, and ran one or two months at various venues. Most deals were flat fees for rentals. This rather modest break was attributed to the very successful run in Times Square, which already drew young people from New York's outer boroughs and surrounding cities. The film has also been shown extensively in midnight "cult" slots and as a second feature in drive-ins.

National playoff · The surprisingly successful New York run shaped First Run's initial assessment of how the film would perform in other markets. As the film began to play around the country, however, First Run was forced to reassess *Wild Style* and its chances for success. It proved to be a sobering experience.

In Boston, the first market after New York, the film had a disappointing run. First Run had anticipated a strong showing, but the film only achieved a minimal profit above breakeven. This surprised everyone, especially when the film received a strong review in the *Boston Globe*, which called it "an ode to joy, a quantum leap beyond the drug and gang wars with which the South Bronx used to kill time." First Run attributes this poor showing to the problems associated with securing the proper theater.

Fran Spielman, then head of distribution for First Run, attempted to secure a commercial theater in Boston that would best attract an inner-city youth audience. Of the likely exhibitors, no one was interested in booking the film. First Run could only place *Wild Style* in art houses, the Orson Welles and Coolidge Corner. As already discussed, film talent went to the Coolidge to put on a wall-painting promotional effort, but failed to draw extensive press attention owing to bad weather. The art-house audience didn't take to the film, and the youth audience, unfamiliar with the theater, didn't show up. In Cole's assessment the Boston run "was the first indication that the film might not make it. We made assumptions based on the New York response to hip-hop that weren't going to be borne out."

In Philadelphia, *Wild Style* performed better than expected, even in the face of a potential confrontation between the local exhibitor and the mayor's office. According to Ahearn, the mayor's office sent a letter to the local exhibitor requesting that they not run the film. The letter informed the theater owners that the city already had a serious graffiti problem and that the mayor was against showing a film that glorified it. Ahearn wanted the management to publicize the letter, but they thought it wiser to simply ignore the request.

While the movie opened to poor reviews, it drew strong audiences, largely due to a heavy promotional effort handled, in part, by a local music publicist hired by First Run. The publicist brought Brathwaite and Fabara to Philadelphia to make personal appearances at malls, record stores, and clubs.

The Chicago run turned out to be a disaster. First Run used a local subdistributor, Levy Films, and a Los Angeles publicist chosen by Levy with prior promotional experience with the black community. The publicist targeted all his efforts to the city's small black press, virtually ignoring the major critics and publications. Cole recalls, "I think it was Levy's hunch that the major press wouldn't like the film, so he decided to sidestep them." Only after *Wild Style* opened did critic Gene Siskel see it, responding with a positive review. Unfortunately, the film was dead by the time the review ran. The publicist brought film talent to Chicago for a week, but concentrated almost exclusively on developing word-of-mouth among inner-city youth, staging talent appearances at high school basketball games and in local clubs. Making matters worse, terrible weather conditions, including forty-below-zero temperatures and a huge snowstorm, conspired to ruin the opening. The film played in seven theaters but for only one week, grossing a total of $40,000.

OTHER MARKETS

Homevideo · Not available.

Pay cable · Not available.

Nontheatrical · Not available.

Broadcast · No sales in the U.S.

Foreign · According to Ahearn, the film has performed well in its foreign release:

> The first foreign release of *Wild Style* was in Japan in September 1983. We toured the country with a group of thirty-five people from the movie and created a big sensation. The film did considerable business. We made very little in England, but did very good business in Germany. There we got an advance from ZDF, [did well] in homevideo sales, and played months in the theater. We [also] received advances in Italy, Scandinavia, Spain, and Canada.

REVIEW

Wild Style was the first feature by New York film and video artist Charles Ahearn. This narrative film with a cinema-verité look was the first to explore the phenomenon of "hip-hop," which embraces the inner-city art forms of break-dancing, rap music, and graffiti. Competing against the much more commercial Hollywood films, *Wild Style* helped popularize and legitimize this black and Latin youth subculture that emerged in the South Bronx in the early eighties.

The film was produced for $250,000, with monies raised from European television, the NYSCA, and private sources. It was shot entirely in New York City, mostly the South Bronx, and used local, nonprofessional talent. The fact that these performers were leaders of the hip-hop culture contributed to the film's authenticity, a key factor in its appeal to specialized audiences.

Wild Style was originally shown in 16mm at the IFP's 1982 Film Market, and was then invited to appear at the New Directors/New Films series at the Museum of Modern Art. Following this screening, the filmmaker struck a deal with Films Around the World to represent the film in all markets, and the company underwrote the cost of cutting a 35mm blowup. A number of specialty distributors courted the filmmaker, but were unwilling to commit to a distribution deal or a guarantee. Most saw *Wild Style* as an intriguing documentary lacking commercial value. First Run Features, however, saw commercial potential and made a serious cash offer and release plan.

The distributor and filmmaker assess the overall marketing efforts quite differently. According to Janet Cole, former manager of First Run Features, the effort may have been far more than the film's final return was worth. According to Cole, these efforts were too labor-intensive and "took too much out of a small company." However, for Ahearn, the film "received incredibly good response . . . better than I expected." He adds, "Our roots were so deep in the community that [it was] like my dream come true."

Conclusion

SUCCESSFUL filmmaking in America is as much a crapshoot for the independent filmmaker as for the Hollywood studio. While cross-collateralization and stars can reduce the risk of high-concept studio fare, nothing can guarantee breaking even—let alone a box-office smash. For independent filmmakers, the chance of success is even less likely, compounded by risks often involving not only artistic vision and belief in oneself, but personal finances, friendships, and years of one's life.

THE VISION

Against this pessimistic assessment of the overall film marketplace, the 1980s have been a golden age of American independent filmmaking. A growing body of critically and financially successful films has resulted in an increasing number of "indies," as well as the migration

259

of accomplished independent directors, producers, and writers to Hollywood—and oftentimes back to off-Hollywood. Equally important for the longterm viability of independent filmmaking, these developments bespeak the emergence of a loosely knit network of aspiring filmmakers, alternative financing arrangements, distributors, exhibitors, festivals, and supportive critics.

Like those associated with the French New Wave, the German New Cinema, or recent Australian and British film movements, American specialty filmmakers, while a heterogeneous group, share a common humanism and broad aesthetic vision. Most are first-time filmmakers with no means to complete a feature other than their own hard work and personal initiative. They often seek to express an original vision or point of view significantly different from Hollywood's mass-market standards. This vision is manifest in these quality films, small films with high literary values and, often, equally high levels of craftsmanship. Above all, specialty filmmaking is a labor of love.

Because of this, personal sacrifice is often substituted for salary and profit; the filmmakers share their risks with cast, crew, and others (especially DuArt Labs) through deferrals. Two of the basic operating rules of the specialty market are: first, the lower the budget, the lower the risk; and, second, put every cent onto the screen. By nature, such ventures are often marked by a high degree of cooperative effort and more informal lines of authority. One frequently finds, for example, that the film's moving force is neither the producer nor director but the actors, writers, and others, as is evident with the roles played by Edward James Olmos in *The Ballad of Gregorio Cortez* and Wallace Shawn and Andre Gregory in *My Dinner with Andre*.

Given all the risk and sacrifice associated with making specialty films, why have so many people tried to make them? The most obvious reason is personal gratification, the sense of success that comes with making a movie. But success means different things to different filmmakers. It may be simply finishing a work that involved years of labor, or receiving festival or critical acclaim, or simply achieving breakeven and paying back investors. A first film effort often serves as a calling card to gain entry to the studio system. Success sometimes means a miniblockbuster degree of popular acclaim and financial reward. For such specialty films, this would mean achieving between $3 million and $5 million in box-office grosses; an exceptional indie like *Dirty Dancing* grossed over $50 million. At best, only a half-dozen independent specialty features a year top $10 million in grosses. Whatever the definition of success, it helps a filmmaker achieve what all filmmakers, Hollywood or specialty, most desire: to make another film.

THE UNIQUE OPPORTUNITY

The specialty films chronicled in this book were born out of a unique combination of factors unlikely to reappear in the near future. Four of these were identified in the Introduction: increased demand, available capital, a supportive audience, and entrepreneurial filmmakers and distributors. Each needs to be discussed in some detail so as to define the context in which the specialty market grew and to understand how changes in that context have created formidable constraints for independent filmmakers who now attempt to function successfully within the commercial marketplace.

Demand for movies · During the 1980s, demand for movies soared to meet the increase in both out-of-home and in-home viewing options. This was due to the significant increase in movie screens, the explosive expansion of homevideo, and the continued growth of cable and, to a lesser extent, broadcast television:

- Between 1980 and 1989 there was a 30 percent increase in the number of movie-theater screens—from approximately 17,500 to 23,000. This increase was due in large part to the proliferation of multiplex cinemas with fewer seats in their screening rooms and smaller house nuts.

- In 1980, only 3 percent of U.S. households had a videocassette recorder (VCR), but by 1989 nearly three-quarters of all households owned at least one VCR. Concomitantly, consumer appetite for prerecorded cassettes—whether original movies or library product—seemed almost inexhaustible. More than 25,000 local video rental shops sprang up across the country and they couldn't stock their shelves fast enough. Total revenue generated from prerecorded cassette rentals and sales skyrocketed from $76 million in 1980 to an estimated $7 billion in 1989.

- In 1980, fifteen million households subscribed to cable television; by 1988 that number had tripled. The number of exclusive cable programming services (for basic, premium, and pay-per-view) more than doubled from thirty-four to seventy-two between 1980 and 1989. During this period, the number of broadcast television stations increased by one-third to nearly 1,000, and the number of independent stations now stands at about 250. In addition, there are over 300 public television stations across the country. The average number of over-the-air channels received by a television set has also increased, from 9.1 in 1980 to 11.3 in 1988.

- In addition, increased sales to foreign territories (most notably Europe and Japan) for all media markets proved a further incentive to independent filmmaking.

These markets thrive on original programming. While movie classics such as *Citizen Kane* and perennials such as *Cinderella* have strong followings, new releases garner the greatest audience interest at the box office or in second-run ancillary markets.

The movie business is an oligopoly, with the Hollywood majors having controlled the marketplace for half a century. The majors include Columbia (including Tri-Star), Warner Bros. (including Lorimar), Disney (including Touchstone), Paramount, 20th Century-Fox, Universal, Orion, and MGM/UA. The rapid increase of demand during the early to mid-1980s temporarily destabilized the studios' control over production and distribution, and provided a unique opportunity for independent filmmakers and distributors—be they the minimajors like De Laurentiis, Cannon, Vestron, Hemdale, and New World or the numerous "micros," some of whom are discussed in this book.

The studios' inability to control programming for the new media of homevideo and cable was the result of a business strategy that restricts supply through increased production costs in the search for blockbuster hits (i.e., movies that gross $20 million or more). How the studios deal with the coming of a new, and potentially threatening, technology is evident in their response to the advent of television after World War II. Faced with a steep fall-off in movie-theater attendance, they panicked. Gradually, they were able to regain control and become the principal suppliers to the networks of non-real-time original programming as well as for their movie libraries, a relatively inexpensive and inexhaustible programming staple. They were similarly unprepared for homevideo, as shown by the failed suit MCA (with Disney) mounted against Sony to prevent off-air copying for noncommercial reuse. Ironically, the studios' wholesale selling of movies to the retail rental markets, as opposed to their customary practice of renting prints, fostered the anarchic homevideo specialty stores.

Historically, independents have always supplied a sizeable share of released movies. But between 1980 and 1988 the total number of feature films released in the U.S. increased by 50 percent—from 342 to 513. However, while the Hollywood majors and minimajors accounted for 40 percent of movies released in 1980, their share shrank to 26 percent in 1987; in 1988, the major releases had increased to 31 percent. (Table 1 presents *Variety* data on movie releases for the 1984–88 period.)

TABLE 1
U.S. Feature Film Releases, 1984–88

Film Source	*1984*	*1985*	*1986*	*1987*	*1988*
Major distributor	170	150	144	135	161
Independent distributor	240	304	333	380	352
Total releases	410	454	477	515	513
Indie releases as a percentage of annual releases	58	67	70	74	69

Source: *Variety,* January 4, 1989.

During this period, average negative costs increased from $9.4 million to over $20 million in 1988. By restricting output, a studio assumes that of the dozen or so movies released annually, half will lose money, a few will break even, and one or two will be blockbusters. This strategy has proven successful when measured by the phenomenal performance of such recent hits as *Star Wars*, *E.T.*, *Ghostbusters*, *Who Framed Roger Rabbit*, and *Batman*, to name but a few, and even more rewarding when revenues from all ancillary markets are accounted for. Nevertheless, while there were seventeen blockbusters in 1980, there were only twenty in 1987.

Available capital · The "Reagan revolution" was characterized by the longest sustained recovery since the end of World War II. It started in 1982 and only began to slow down during mid- to late 1988. However, the affluence generated from this recovery is somewhat illusory: it is based more on an enormous expansion of debt than real productivity gains. While much is made about the skyrocketing federal deficit, people often lose sight of the fact that total corporate and consumer debt is estimated at over $5 trillion. Consumer installment credit alone increased by over 118 percent between 1980 and mid-1988; it now totals over $650 billion—and this excludes home mortgages and bank loans.

The debt-based affluence of the 1980s provided two complementary finance sources for the specialty film market: it made available investment capital for film production and distribution, and it increased consumer expendable dollars, fueling the accumulation of a vast array of new home entertainment products and services as well as generating increased box-office grosses. From an investment perspective, independent film financing does not compare to studio operations. For both publicly traded majors and nonstudio independents (e.g., Cannon or New Line), large—and sometimes enormous—pools of capital are available; Disney's financing arm, Silver Screen Partners, has raised over $1 billion through a series of four separate public offerings.

Low-budget specialty investment, on the other hand, is more akin to high-risk "play" money—investors with money they can afford to gamble assess their opportunity less on conservative business terms (e.g., protected investment or high-return potential) than on intrinsic, qualitative factors (e.g., a belief in the filmmaker, an excitement about the film, or the appeal of being involved in show biz). A host of financial mechanisms (e.g., loans, grants, limited partnerships, public offerings, etc.) allowed filmmakers to take advantage of the increased availability of capital. Beyond one-shot investments in individual films, increased capital availability to small distributors, homevideo companies, cable networks, and even venture-capital groups (e.g., FilmDallas) provided an important new revenue stream in the form of presale, acquisition, and negative pickup arrangements. Abruptly, however, the October 1987 stock market crash signaled an end to play-money investing.

Supportive audience • Perhaps the most important single factor in the development of specialty filmmaking was the emergence of a supportive audience. Distributors, publicists, and exhibitors often refer to the art-house audience as a distinct filmgoing segment. Although we have found no systematic research analyzing this audience on a national level, certain broad characteristics can be clearly recognized:

- First and foremost, they are discriminating filmgoers. They seek out "films"—as distinguished from movies—that offer an exquisitely realized or unusual aesthetic or dramatic experience, perhaps including some psychological, cultural, or sociohistorical insight. They possess an informed, sophisticated film sensibility and are aware of new releases and the work of particular directors. They derive their film education from a variety of sources, including substantive discussions with friends, film courses, reviews, and repeated film viewing via homevideo or pay-cable services.
- Equally important, they are frequent filmgoers. While there seems to be no detailed analysis of art-house filmgoing, it can safely be said that such filmgoers attend perhaps three to five times more frequently than the average of once a month, which the MPAA defines as frequent attendance.
- As a demographic entity, they are essentially baby boomers, both the slightly older crest of the generation wave of post-1960s adults and the somewhat younger college grads. They seem divided between singles or childless couples and more affluent boomers with young children who regularly get a babysitter and go out to a movie.

A further distinction between this primary art-house audience and a secondary audience should be kept in mind. The core art-house audience is a relatively narrow segment of the film market. According to many informed sources, it accounts for no more than 5 to 10 percent of the market at any given time. When a specialty film attracts a non-art-house audience, it begins to broaden out in one of two ways. It can appeal to a distinct social subgroup—inner-city youth (*Wild Style*), white teenagers (*Old Enough*)—or it can cross over to a wider, more mainstream audience (*My Dinner with Andre*). Successful box-office performance for a specialty film depends on reaching beyond the art-house milieu.

Entrepreneurial filmmakers and distributors · Independent—i.e., nonstudio—filmmaking has been a part of the movie industry since Charlie Chaplin, Douglas Fairbanks, Lillian Gish, and their partners formed United Artists in the 1920s. It has provided an alternative environment for creative filmmaking, helped cultivate new talent for the studio system, and encouraged maverick entrepreneurs to create new microstudios to compete with the established Hollywood system. Not unlike the studios, the independents produce a wide range of film genres, including action-adventure and slice-and-dice, "X"-rated pornographic and cult, teenage and wilderness, Hollywood knock-off family flicks, as well as innovative or quality specialty features.

From the Depression to the early 1950s, "B" studios like Monogram, Republic, Grand National, Producers Releasing Corp., and American-International were the locus of independent filmmaking and distribution. In turn, they were followed by such legendary genre or exploitation filmmakers as Roger Corman (New World) and Russ Meyer as well as the more uncompromising art filmmakers like Stan Brakhage and Kenneth Anger. Together with the profound contribution of such foreign filmmakers as Jean-Luc Godard, François Truffaut, and Federico Fellini, to name but a few, these influences helped give birth to the more commercial American specialty film market.

The new breed of specialty filmmakers come from a variety of backgrounds. Many were political or documentary filmmakers drawn to narrative film because of its ability not only to tell a better story but also, potentially, to reach a larger audience. Some were film-school graduates grounded in technique through careful study of the classics. In addition, film and video professionals from the nonfeature worlds of advertising, corporate communications, and television migrated into the expanding market. All benefited from the pioneering work of John Cassavetes, Francis Ford Coppola, Martin Scorsese, Robert Altman, and others, who, as studio enfants terribles during the 1970s, began to develop a more serious and sophisticated narrative film style.

Like the filmmakers, the distributors were innovative mavericks drawn to the expanding specialty market from a variety of backgrounds. Some moved up from college repertory houses or ancillary distributors (like Films Incorporated). Others crossed over from publicity or film criticism. Some were able to extend 1960s grassroots political organizing skills into effective marketing techniques.

From whatever background, the filmmakers and distributors who were the basis for the formative period of the specialty market were, not surprisingly, nearly mirror images of their most supportive, core art-house audience. They spoke the same language, shared the same symbols, and faced many of the same life choices. This unique reciprocity of interests not only defined the artistic content or subject matter of the films produced, but was demonstrated by the willingness to support innovation at the box office.

SPECIALTY FILMS: FACING A CHANGING MARKETPLACE

The film business is notoriously cyclical and has now entered a cooling-off phase. This slowdown is causing structural changes that will result in an industry realignment and see greater consolidation among the majors and their tighter control over output. In essence, these changes are due to reversals of the very factors that were so important to the emergence of the specialty market during the early 1980s: decline in demand for product, contraction of available capital, shift in audience demographics, and greater conservatism among new filmmakers and distributors.

In addition, the success of specialty filmmaking led to Hollywood studio recruitment of many of the best independent filmmakers. It also led to the studios' producing films for the same audience that the specialty filmmakers and distributors had worked so hard to cultivate. Not only has Hollywood released a series of sophisticated comedies and dramas (e.g., *A Fish Called Wanda*, *Bull Durham*, *Married to the Mob*, and *Moonstruck*) targeted to a hip adult audience, but it has also released movies such as *Crossing Delancey* (Warner), *The Accused* (Paramount), *Bird* (Warner), *Madame Sousatzka* (Cineplex Odeon/ Universal), *School Daze* (Columbia), *Powaggatsi* (Cannon), and *Stand and Deliver* (Warner), which would previously have been relegated to specialty microdistributors.

For current and future specialty filmmakers, who are far more vulnerable to the vicissitudes of the marketplace, these changes should lead to a fall-off in the number of films produced and released and to the failure of many small distributors. It is possible, however, that as the business cycle reverses itself, there will be a group of artistically and commercially creative low-budget filmmakers not unlike those who sparked the initial specialty movement in the early 1980s.

Movie demand has been met · There has been a slowdown in the number of screens being opened. Theatrical exhibition has just about reached saturation. The national average screen performance efficiency is falling. While *Variety* and the MPAA never tire of touting annual increases in box-office grosses, such increases mask a deeper, disturbing fact: increased grosses are the result of rising ticket prices and not admissions. Between 1980 and 1987, the average ticket price increased by 45 percent while admissions increased by only 6 percent, hovering at about 1.1 billion a year; in 1984, admissions hit 1.2 billion, the highest in the postwar era. Closer scrutiny reveals that in 1980 each screen generated approximately 1,110 admissions per week; by 1984 this had increased 10 percent to 1,221 admissions; by 1987, per screen performance had shrunk by almost 25 percent to a weekly average of 922 admissions.

The decline in theater efficiency has occurred during a period in which the studios have regained effective control over the exhibition business. The Reagan administration, through its policy of deregulation, effectively overturned the 1948 Paramount decree that barred studios from exhibition as a violation of antitrust laws. Among the majors with exhibitor holdings are Universal (MCA's 50 percent ownership of Cineplex Odeon), Paramount (Paramount Communication's ownership of Famous Players), Columbia (through Loews and Loews-Star), and Warner Bros. (Time Warner's cable television holdings, including HBO and Cinemax). In addition, the nation's largest cable operator, Telecommunications, Inc. (TCI), owns the nation's largest theater chain, United Artists, with 2,677 screens; and National Amusement, owner of the Viacom media conglomerate (which includes television, radio, and cable systems, programming syndication, and such programming networks as Showtime/The Movie Channel and MTV), operates the eighth largest chain. Equally critical is the recent acquisition by Heritage Entertainment of independently owned theaters that have long catered to specialty product, like Seven Gables and Landmark. New Yorker Films and Laemmle remain holdouts. The outcome of this process is not simply that the majors control the *largest* number of theaters or screens, but also the *most strategically located* in the dominant film market. This development is part of a larger process of consolidation, vertical integration, and globalization that is redefining the entertainment business on a world scale.

These changes do not mean that a good new film, one armed with strong critical acclaim, won't find exhibition. Exhibitors are hungry for such a product; success sells itself. Rather, those films that need time to cultivate a following are more likely to face either more impediments to an exhibitor sale or, if released, a more difficult time holding a theater. The economics of the business are limiting exhibitor options; they simply won't take the risks that they used to.

In the past an exhibitor operating a larger (eight- to ten-screen) multiplex often plugged one or two screens with smaller, specialty or foreign-language films. Because of the nature of the agreement between distributors and exhibitors (e.g., the 90/10 percent split), the exhibitor is motivated to quickly drop a new release after the first or, at most, second weekend unless it develops "legs." With so much product available, the exhibitor can rapidly—almost indiscriminately—turn over films searching for a hit. But a hit is defined in part by the scale of dollars committed to the release. Given the studios' operating business strategy of pushing blockbusters, exhibitors will hold over "A" titles by moving them to the smaller screens, thus creating a vacuum cleaner effect for revenue accumulation.

By controlling both the number of big movies released and the scale of release (i.e., number of prints, opening playdates, and advertising and promotional expenditures), let alone the theaters themselves, the studios can more effectively manage, if not predict, performance. The fact that specialty film exhibition is principally limited to four market tiers means that approximately 80 percent of box-office performance for such films is derived from only the top eight cities. This combined shift in exhibition will result in reduced viewer choices and have a negative impact on independent filmmakers and distributors.

Equally consequential, the rapid expansion of homevideo has stopped. Defining characteristics of this development include:

- Slowdown in new VCR ownership.
- Flattening out of the number of rental or turns per VCR as the novelty effect wears off.
- Shift to "super A" and "A" titles (i.e., blockbuster hits with box-office grosses topping $100 million and over $30 million, respectively) driving rentals.
- Depth-of-copy (increased copies of hits) replaces breadth-of-copy (number of titles carried) as retailer purchasing criteria.
- Increase in number and dominance of video chains over mom-and-pop specialty outlets—with chains providing more efficient ordering, turns-per-cassette, and use of co-op advertising.
- Studio homevideo arms shifting from a two-step to a one-step mode of distribution.

With large inventories in place, the demand for product has slowed, resulting in less favorable presale and acquisition deals for the more offbeat specialty movies, the "B's" and "C's." This development is occurring at a time when investment in movies is declining, only making it harder for independent filmmakers, especially first-timers, to produce new works.

Capital contraction · The October 1987 stock market crash sent a shockwave not only through U.S. capital markets, but through the independent film marketplace as well. Money became harder to raise and had to be more carefully managed and protected with secured or guaranteed returns. While it is impossible to determine the total number of film projects that have sought financing, successfully or not, one can gather insight into the tightening money market from sources anecdotal and otherwise.

One of the key differences is the significant reduction of federal support for feature films from agencies such as the NEH. Without this support during the late 1970s and early eighties, such important specialty films as *Heartland, The Ballad of Gregorio Cortez, The Good Fight,* and many others not included in this book would most likely not have been made. (One notable exception was the National Science Foundation and ARCO support for *Stand and Deliver.*)

Specialty filmmakers continue to rely on the types of financing described in this book: partial self-financing, loans and deferrals, or presale deals with public entities like PBS's "American Playhouse," Britain's Channel Four, and Germany's ZDF. However, during the mid- to late 1980s filmmakers clearly became more professional in putting together their deals. The role of limited partnership and presale agreements is illustrated in *Old Enough.* Some filmmakers have sought to raise money through public offers, with little success. A number of venture-capital pools, like Pacific Film Fund and Boston Film Partners, have attempted to raise money to finance publicity and advertising as well as production. Numerous private placements have sought financing for multipicture development deals. As discussed below, specialty distributors became microstudios when they started to invest directly in production. In addition, the specialty market saw the entry of more conventional film companies, homevideo distribu- tors (like Vestron), and even television networks (NBC's financing of *Square Dance*) into the low-budget art market. The net effect was to make a presale agreement almost a precondition for production.

Specialty distributors have played a critical role in helping wean independent filmmaking from an alternative, fringe cinema to a viable market category. Specialty distributors are (with the exception of Orion Classics) small, independent companies. Among the leaders have been Cinecom, Goldwyn, Island, Skouras, Alive, FilmDallas, Miramax, and Circle Releasing; such larger independents as New Line, Atlantic Releasing, and Cannon occasionally handle specialty fare. Those running these companies are driven by a variety of motives that are not unlike similar second-tier operations in comparable in- dustries, such as publishing or recorded music. These include finan- cial return, a wish to control one's own company, or to move to a studio position, a secret desire to make movies, and a genuine love of specialty films. Whatever the reason, their expertise was crucial in helping develop the specialty market.

Specialty distribution is a labor-intense business, marked by relatively high overhead and tight margins. (See Appendix A, "The Economics of Specialty Film Marketing," and Appendix B, "Launching a Specialty Film," for a discussion of some of the financial aspects of doing business.) Small distributors have been hit particularly hard by the overall realignment in the film market. First, there was a marked escalation in operating costs. Increased competition for product often fueled price wars that drove the acquisition costs sky high. Many distributors complain that they have been forced to pay artificially inflated prices, simply to stay competitive and in business, for films that could not recoup the combined guarantee and marketing costs. Second, most deals were done on the basis of back-end protection—ancillary sales to homevideo and pay cable were required to offset losses from theatrical release. Third, as homevideo became a major component in film financing, homevideo companies (like Vestron, RCA/Columbia, and Nelson) established output deals with microdistributors like Cinecom, New Line, Goldwyn, and others to launch a theatrical release to leverage the homevideo performance.

The specialty distributors' move into film financing during the mid-1980s was a rational response to a precarious market. Cinecom International's cofinancing of John Sayles's film *Matewan*, Circle Releasing's multipicture deal with the Coen brothers, and Alive Pictures's commitment to Alan Rudolph are but a few examples. Despite the obvious risks, nearly all specialty distributors took equity positions in what they believed were quality commercial properties. They did this to guarantee a flow of product, to guarantee returns from all markets, to pick up the theatrical distribution fee, and, simply, to produce films. These microstudios, not unlike their Hollywood counterparts, thought they could pick winners. Unfortunately, many of the more recent films released by specialty distributors (and some distributors had significant financial stakes in many of them) failed at the box office, thus putting these smaller companies at risk. Among recent box-office disappointments are *Patti Rocks* and *Da* from FilmDallas, *The Deceivers* and *The Lighthorsemen* from Cinecom, *Mr. North* from Goldwyn, *Prince of Pennsylvania* from New Line, *Tokyo Pop* from Spectrafilm, *Pascali's Island* from Avenue, and *Patti Hearst* from Atlantic.

The tightening marketplace is beginning to take its toll. Successful specialty distributors of only a couple of years ago—Libra, Cinema

Five, United Artists Classics, and Fox Classics—are no longer in business. Hoping to avoid such a fate, a number of today's leading specialty distributors have sought greater financial security through recapitalization schemes: Cinecom was acquired by SBK Entertainment during 1988; Atlantic Releasing was sold; and Skouras failed in its 1988 bid to go public. FilmDallas, an innovative venture-capital pool, production company, and distributor (with Academy Award winners *The Trip to Bountiful* and *Kiss of the Spider Woman* to its credit) is the first casualty among the micros. Failing to deliver on an output deal with New World, they went bankrupt in December 1988. During 1989, Island Pictures and Vestron Pictures also failed. Unfortunately, they won't be the last.

Demographic realignment · In the most overstated terms, the 1980s witnessed the "maturation" of the baby boomers into couch potatoes. While the hardcore art-house audience is qualitatively different from the larger moviegoing universe, it does share many defining characteristics with its generation. First and foremost, the declining standard of living in the U.S. (as measured by purchasing power of real income, excluding inflation, income derived from a second income provider, and debt) has resulted in an increase in work time with a concomitant decrease in leisure time. This situation has contributed not only to the downturn of filmgoing but also to a decline in participation in many other out-of-home recreational activities. Like their contemporaries, the most avid art-house filmgoers are being pulled away by the increased responsibilities of building a career, increased household costs (e.g., paying off a mortgage), and childcare. Through the early 1990s, one can expect a continued rise of in-home entertainment (particularly beneficial for homevideo, pay- and pay-per-view cable television, and video games) as well as the likely rise of out-of-home recreation activities such as museum and live-music attendance.

Professionalization of filmmaking · Independent filmmaking is, in essence, an undercapitalized business venture. Like other high-risk undertakings that aim at a small, specialized part of the market, it has been characterized by remarkable inventiveness and personal commitment. This entrepreneurialism was a hallmark of the wave of independent filmmaking that occurred during the early through mid-1980s, and has been chronicled in the individual case studies profiled in this book. Much of this entrepreneurialism was motivated by more than simply economic or careerist self-interest. The populist sentiments of the 1960s and 1970s often fueled and inspired many of these earlier indie filmmakers.

However, as the market evolved, a noticeable change came over the character and motivation of the newer filmmakers. First, many more appear to be academically trained professionals from the dominant film graduate schools in New York (New York University and Columbia) and Los Angeles (University of California at Los Angeles and University of Southern California). Second, they seem less motivated by an alternative vision—either in terms of subject matter or aesthetics—than by landing a job at a studio or an established production company. They seem less inclined to take risks than to demonstrate professionalism. One can assume that if there is a noticeable slowdown in production during the early 1990s there will be a corresponding slowdown in film school attendance.

As discussed, successful filmmaking during the 1980s led to a considerable increase in independent film production. However, this resulted in a significant increase in films that failed to secure a theatrical release. As presented in Table 2, in 1983, one-third of the independent films produced failed to secure a theatrical release; by 1986—the most recent year for which data is available—that number had increased to more than half. The trend toward a higher proportion of films failing to find a commercial release probably continued (if not increased) during the 1987–88 period. The proportion of independent films failing to secure a commercial release is likely to taper off during the 1990s due to the fact that fewer indies are likely to be produced.

Since the early 1980s, the number of specialty films being released has increased dramatically. While no definitive total can be provided, this estimate is based upon films screened at the IFP's Film Market, increased film showings at U.S. film festivals that spotlight American independents (e.g., Telluride and U.S./Park City festivals), and anecdotal comments by people who have been in the field for a decade or more. In addition, MPAA and *Variety* data indirectly corroborates this finding. The films screened in the feature section of the IFP's annual market rose from twenty in 1978 to fifty-eight in 1984 to fifty-six (of ninety entries) in 1988* (and this does not include the fifty-six works-in-progress [of sixty-four entries] nor the sixty-seven short fiction/nonfiction documentaries [of ninety-seven entries] screened as part of the video sidebar).

TABLE 2
Independent Features Produced and Theatrical Releases, 1983–86

	1983	1984	1985	1986
Total U.S. production	334	363	351	512
Total U.S. indie production	242	271	251	390
Indie production set for release	161	164	147	183
Indies with no theatrical distributor	81	107	104	207
Percent of indies with no distributor	33	39	41	53

Source: *Variety*, February 25, 1987.

Another effect of the success due to the rapid market expansion was the demand for greater professionalism. Audiences and critics became less tolerant of amateurish aspects of specialty films, and distributors sought films with either more commercially competitive crossover qualities or with unique promotional aspects. All this conspired to burden independent filmmakers with heightened demands: a more polished script, greater production values, reliance on known talent and crew, more locations, etc. All this meant bigger budgets and therefore greater returns to cover investor risks as well as distributor costs.

Amidst this market sea change, some genuine low-budget specialty films have been produced and, more importantly, appreciated for their innovative, low-budget character. Prime examples include Robert Townsend's *Hollywood Shuffle*, Wayne Wang's $35,000 *Chan Is Missing* or Jim Jarmusch's *Stranger than Paradise* (which was made for $210,000 and grossed over $2 million). Unfortunately, these films

* As of 1986, the IFP's American Independent Feature Film Market Main Event is restricted to forty-two entrants to avoid overcrowding.

were the exceptions. The specialty market moved toward higher-budgeted product, such as the Coen brothers' *Blood Simple* and the Fox-released *Raising Arizona*, and crossover specialty films like *The Trip to Bountiful*, *Kiss of the Spider Woman*, and *Desert Bloom*; Warner's release of *Stand and Deliver* and Michael Moore's *Roger and Me* are the exceptions that proved the rule.

THE DISTRIBUTION STRATEGY

This book was written to provide information and insight to those interested in specialty filmmaking. While the market is and will continue to be beset by significant retrenchment and realignment, there will still be a need for independent films. Adversity often leads to new opportunities. In this environment, the successful making and marketing of more expensive independent films ($3 million–$5 million) will become more difficult. For such properties, distributors will look for money committed and stars attached; they will be less willing to take risks on first-time or more offbeat movies that do not seem to meet a prescribed formula of successful performance. This will force dedicated filmmakers to be more resourceful. They will have to return to the innovative, risk-taking, and lower-budget mode of filmmaking that characterized the early 1980s. While more challenging and probably less financially rewarding, these constraints will probably help engender a new wave of creativity and ingenuity, which has historically been the hallmark of independent filmmaking.

Given the vicissitudes of the specialty film marketplace, what concerns should a filmmaker bear in mind when maneuvering through this environment? First and foremost, the distribution process will likely be as arduous and time-consuming as making the film. Because specialty films are often made by first-time directors, are released with a modest promotional budget, and lack name talent, the filmmakers will be expected to participate actively in the film's marketing efforts. Many first-time filmmakers are surprised that, even before a film gets into release, they will have to launch their own marketing campaign to secure a distribution deal. Few prepare for the promotional efforts needed to attract industry attention, or budget adequately for the costs of stills, publicity, festival entry fees, extra prints, etc. Second, but still crucial, are decisions such as which festival to enter, not simply because some are mutually exclusive or more prestigious, but because premature exposure or overexposure can be harmful in securing a distribution deal.

Selecting a distributor—assuming that the film hasn't been presold—is the most critical decision. The signed contract is binding for years. It is a business partnership and a lot more. Key issues that all filmmakers face at this point are: the amount of the guarantee; how the distributor genuinely feels about the film; which rights are open to negotiation; the company's track record in theatrical release and, if appropriate, ancillary markets; its leverage with exhibitors to guarantee collections; its dependability in reporting the film's performance, and timeliness in making additional payments (many films end up in long and expensive audits and legal challenges); what other films the company is handling; how much will be committed to the opening for prints, ads, and other costs; and where and when the film will open and how many other cities the rollout will involve.

While preparing this book, we found that a successful distribution deal—whether or not the film scored high box-office returns—was characterized by positive working relationships and strong personal affinities between the filmmakers and distributors. The distributor not only appreciated the film, but both filmmaker and distributor concurred in the definition of its intended audience(s) and likely appeal. Filmmakers should know, even if only in a preliminary sense, how a distributor intends to market their film and the extent to which they will be involved in this process. The specialty film business is remarkably small, and everyone has tough skins and long memories.

In deciding on a distributor, a filmmaker must have a keen sense of priorities. This often comes down to a decision about whether to take an advance or to look at the film as a longterm investment. The need to pay off outstanding debts quickly or the desire to move on to another project may lead a filmmaker to sign with the first offer. As has been repeatedly stressed throughout this book, there's simply no right way.

There is a basic paradox inherent in specialty film distribution. The filmmaker must rely upon the distributors' expertise to mount a successful film release. Yet these very same distributors insist that there are no magic truths, no right ways, no predictable schemes to ensure a successful campaign. They insist every film is unique and must have its own marketing approach. Their experience with other films is, therefore, often irrelevant when deciding on such issues as ad design, the cut of the trailer, and the film's opening. Yet it is only their success with other films that keeps them in business.

Real expertise enables the specialty distributor to overcome this apparent paradox and to create an innovative and appropriate marketing campaign that fits the needs of each film. Hollywood studios that are seeking instantaneous name recognition for a new release opening in 600 to 2,000 theaters rely upon saturation advertising through TV, radio, and print. Specialty distribution seeks to create word-of-mouth recognition and thus employs a fundamentally different marketing strategy. First, a film is released by platforming it in a limited number of cities and usually only one appropriate theater per city. Second, the campaign is aimed at a segment of the general audience. Third, the launch strategy involves successfully assessing the film's particularities and audience appeal, and tailoring all subsequent activities to realize this goal—creating the proper identity for a film, positioning it in the minds of potential viewers, packaging it in an ad or trailer, and disseminating it through an organized yet flexible campaign. It relies heavily upon favorable festival performance, positive press attention, the right timing, and, all too often, simple good luck. To achieve visibility—let alone success—the marketing and promotional effort has to cut through the blanket of studio-film advertising, even as it competes with other quality programs from museums or art galleries; music, theater, or dance performances; classic film showings; and television programs.

Word-of-mouth is the great mystery of the distribution process. No one knows exactly what it is, but it makes a film a hit or a bomb. It is the serendipitous convergence of a great film, industry enthusiasm, an effective, well-handled campaign by a sympathetic distributor, favorable press attention, and a strategic release not undercut by competitive challengers or bad weather. But above all, it means the excitement of early enthusiastic viewers who encourage others to spend money to see it. When you've got that, you've got a hit.

Afterword

DEMYSTIFYING THE MOVIE BUSINESS

by Jivan Tabibian
The Sundance Institute

THE VALUE OF RESEARCH

RESEARCH and publications about the marketing and distribution of films are rather few. Rarer still are studies dealing with the business of independent films. This lack of attention does not reflect a lack of interest. The film community at large, and the independent film community in particular, could use some well-researched studies about film marketing and distribution, if such studies were available. Four of the more obvious explanations for the lack of such studies are: lack of data, the uniqueness of each film, market volatility, and methodological problems. I will consider each point separately.

Lack of data · Business, legal, and tax reasons often underlie the desire for secretiveness. The relations between producers and distributors and between distributors and exhibitors have long been adversarial: the gains of one are often seen as the losses of the other. In this context, the divulging of financial records is seen as potentially embarrassing and even damaging.

However, this reluctance to divulge information sometimes masks a more innocent, if no less frustrating, reality. Often, true and accurate records of the facts simply do not exist, or do not exist in useable form. Many people in the film industry prefer to claim the right to secrecy than to admit to ignorance, sloppy record-keeping, or primitive data-gathering capacity. Computerized record-keeping should help this situation.

The *Off-Hollywood* project was conceived in full recognition of this data handicap. Doubts about the availability of "hard" information often threatened to scuttle the project. It is gratifying to know that the authors persevered.

I want to reiterate here what I often told the researchers and their advisors over the life of this enterprise: all data is imperfect, all information is incomplete, no facts are unbiased, and a few bits of data are better than none. Moreover, I have tried to suggest to them that quite often the value of a particular figure (for example a $400,000 guarantee, or a 10 percent royalty, or a 50/50 split) is *in the range it may define, or a direction or a tendency it may establish.* Thus, even incomplete or specifically inaccurate numbers can be of some value when combined with other numbers. Without this attitude, all work about social phenomena either would be impossible to undertake, or would lead to grossly exaggerated claims.

Though the numbers gathered in this study are by no means ideally complete or totally accurate, I strongly believe that they have filled in many blank spaces. We should consider the precedent-setting aspect of the data-gathering and quantitative component of this book encouraging and commendable. It breaks the ice by daring to collect partial information and proves that the sharing of information will not lead to the collapse of financial empires or the irreparable loss of irreplaceable trade secrets.

The uniqueness of each film · The unique nature of each film, both as a work of art and as a commercial product, has often been used to justify the industry-wide belief in the inappropriateness or futility of undertaking marketing research. It is said, and generally agreed upon, that this condition is particularly true in the case of independent films, which are presumably even more unique. Here again, I consider this extreme position both indefensible and unproductive. Without questioning the fact that each film is in some way unique— just as is, incidentally, each and every person, cat, or book—it is nevertheless possible to discover common traits, identify patterns, and make useful generalizations about all these items. There is nothing demeaning in recognizing the market reality of the film *genre*. Not only do writers, directors, and producers think and work in a certain genre, but so do audiences. And not all genres are created or imagined by the bosses of the Hollywood film studios.

For instance, the *film noir* has had quite a respectable history without the help of Hollywood executives. As to specialty films, genre and subgenre are not totally outside a frame of reference either. But genre is not the only way to classify a film for purposes of distribution and marketing. Other dimensions and other criteria, in combination, yield a multiplicity of other categories with which to conceptualize release strategies. Content-based elements like politics, ethnicity, nostalgia, or regionalism may help identify theoretically clustered films whose audiences may be likewise clustered. Sometimes the elements common to a certain film have to do with form: documentary, or the pivotal use of music or a conscious primitivism of technique. In such instances, these elements combined with other categories may also suggest patterns that the distributor can identify and exploit.

Off-Hollywood explores and describes some of these situations rather well. After all, distributors and exhibitors do think analogically and historically, by precedent. They have dominant or operative models that they use in handling new product. It would, otherwise, be both ineffectual and grossly inefficient for them to treat each new film so uniquely that they would have to reinvent the wheel each time out.

Finally, they also know by experience that there are even greater patterns—structural, sociocultural, regional, ethnic, etc.—which tend to shape almost all *filmgoing*. The patterns that describe filmgoing are the other half of the proposition, and they invariably influence the patterns of film distribution. In this equation, we can see why it is frequently the producer/director who is most likely to espouse the argument for uniqueness. After all, for the producer/director, the film is his or her unique and singular creation. For any independent producer/director, this perception is even more pronounced.

Off-Hollywood provides quite clear and obvious information on this question. The distribution of independent films seems to benefit from simultaneous accommodation on the part of both producers and distributors. The latter should accommodate the former by being more attentive to the distinctive and distinguishing qualities of a given film. The producers/directors, on the other hand, should not totally resist the distributors'/exhibitors' attempt to position the film in ways similar to comparable films that may have been successfully marketed. Distributors should not be penalized unfairly for having or using a formula. It is only when they fail to adapt and to tinker that the formula goes stale. Similarly, producers/directors should not be blamed for passionately stating the novel qualities of their film. But they must also not transform that belief into an unenlightened and vain resistance to the idea that their film may be similar to other successful films as far as audiences or marketing may be concerned.

Market volatility · It is often argued that the attempt to predict audience behavior or reaction is essentially futile. Taste and preference are claimed to be highly variable; fads are, by definition, short-lived. And movie audiences are nothing if not faddish. Thus, it is further claimed that even the popularity of well-established genres or stars is not sufficient to allow robust predictions. The gurus of the gut-feeling school of marketing in Hollywood have long lists of star vehicles crash-landing in some script galaxy (Paul Newman in *Quintet*), or stuck in the mud of frontier badlands (Marlon Brando and Jack Nicholson in *The Missouri Breaks*), or out of steam in the adulterous romance of "now" people (Robert De Niro and Meryl Streep in *Falling in Love*).

The unpredictable successes are no less numerous or surprising than the failures, the skeptics continue. Since you never know what audiences want or will want, the surest way is exposure: thus, secure the largest media budget, the biggest advertising campaign, the widest opening, the most frequent TV spot. The rest, it's a crapshoot! You let the largest number of people hear about your film, and hope that some of them will go see it. At least enough to pay for the $6,000,000 release budget.

The films analyzed in *Off-Hollywood* do not have—nor, I propose, should they want to have—that luxury. Audiences are not as inscrutable and mysterious as that. These audiences are simply not a grab-bag, all-inclusive, one-size-fits-all segment of frequent moviegoers between eighteen and twenty-four years of age. Instead, these demographics more likely involve the steady, stable preference and profile of middle-age lefties, or urbane graduate students, or Sierra Club members, or pacifists, or ethnic pride advocates, or *New Yorker* readers, or Volvo drivers. Perhaps pinpoint targeting of some combination of these audiences or groups (through, for example, grassroots organizing or late-late-night talk shows) can stretch the few available dollars.

Methodological problems • Those questioning the validity of market research in film distribution often refer to serious methodological problems that go beyond the straightforward difficulties discussed above. They argue, with some merit, that some unpredictability of audience behavior, even data unavailability, is part of a much larger problem: *the complexity of variables* affecting the success or failure of the release of any film. These numerous variables, it is claimed, influence the fate of a film in the marketplace, and tie each product in its own Gordian knot.

Time of year, competition from other films, alternative leisure activities, weather and economic conditions, advertising, critical reviews, subject matter, network, pay and cable TV, theater location, and demographics all contribute to the level of a film's performance. Some of these variables affect, in particular, the opening phase, which in turn determines the next stage. Other variables have more of an impact on the longevity of a theatrical run, in spite of a healthy launch. In all cases, most of these variables cannot be predicted, at least not early enough to influence the release strategy. Some, in fact, can never be modified even when they become known: they are indeed independent variables. Without discounting either the complexity of the model or the independence of the variables, I will argue, however, that the conclusions one must draw from this situation are not obvious, at least not obvious enough to discount the validity of marketing research. Even unpredictable and independent variables can and should be taken into account. How these variables may have affected the release of films is definitely worth knowing.

Various combinations tend to produce different results. A blizzard in the inner city has less of a chilling effect on moviegoing than in the suburbs, where driving is necessary to get to the theater. A rash of successful, popular movies may stimulate all moviegoing and create a coattail effect that may carry along otherwise marginal films. Large TV audiences also deliver large targets for film ads carried on the tube. There are spillovers and crossovers. There are ripple effects, amplifications, and lags. There is synchronicity and synergy. What it all amounts to is that complexity essentially invalidates any kind of oversimplifying determinism, the kind of linear thinking that searches for the mechanistic if-then formula.

Modest though it may be in this regard, the lesson of *Off-Hollywood* is to demonstrate that there is a subtle if fragile web of circumstances in which no single decision or variable accounts for all success or failure. It helps us appreciate that complexity offers opportunities for those who are not trapped by reductionist assumptions.

Off-Hollywood provides us with descriptive and anecdotal evidence of both the complexity of the situation and the effectiveness of solutions that best recognize, and hence tackle, that complexity, and the failure of strategies that ignore it. At the very least it is a first attempt to identify and list in context some of the critical variables in the release of specialty films.

More research and more case studies may well lead to useful laundry lists, and maybe to annotated catalogs of trails and boulders strewn across the landscape of film distribution. Like any roadmap, the utility is not in duplicating reality, but in providing enough road signs and benchmarks to help one at least not get lost, even if one does not always reach one's destination. Fundamentally, all roadmaps are inaccurate and abstract, and they exclude more information than they include. Good roadmaps succeed because they represent (graphically, symbolically) relationships between variables. No matter how partial or imperfect, these relationships between elements (or places) define the value of a map. Similarly, good marketing research tries to describe some relationships. In this sense, *Off-Hollywood* is a very rough, very primitive navigational instrument, to be used with caution, but still worth using. Like its counterparts in other areas of market research, this study will be improved upon by the successive feedback, corrections, and refinements of navigators who follow precariously in its path. The history of cartography brilliantly illustrates the same building-block nature.

THE FILMMAKER: MYTHMAKER AND MYTH

The objections and arguments I have dealt with so far share a certain basic pragmatic and/or rationalist perspective. On the surface, at least, they are arguments that question validity, reliability, feasibility, and utility. As such, they are comprehensible, and answerable, more or less, depending on one's paradigms and standards of validation and utility. It is in this sense that they lead to an obvious debate.

I propose that the next set of obstacles to the study of film distribution, of independent film distribution in particular, is much less obvious in that sense. They are harder to pinpoint, and harder still to deal with. Instead of dealing with methodological or pragmatic issues, they derive more from ideological, psychodynamic, and cultural forces. They stem more from fears than doubts. They reflect hidden values more than articulate beliefs. They are the manifestation more of affective conflicts than cognitive contradictions.

This set of arguments against market research and analysis can be traced to the following broadly sketched polemical-rhetorical-problematic clusters: art vs. commerce (and both against science); threats to an auteur's integrity as he or she attempts to anticipate audience appeal and tries to cater to it; and finally the relation between knowledge and free will. Of course, these concerns are themselves related to each other and must be addressed somewhat simultaneously. It appears to me that these dilemmas are the remnants, the lingering manifestations, of old dualisms that still permeate our view of the world in modern Western civilization.

Abstract and elitist conceptions of art stem simultaneously from such things as mind/body dualism, class-based social structures, and unresolved narcissistic conflicts pitting the self against the other and the community. Within this framework, popular art comes to be perceived as vulgar art, and the search for audience appeal a sure way to compromise personal vision. The sociology of the film subculture in our larger culture has transformed filmmaking into the chosen vocation and has made filmmakers the mythmakers of our time. Besides the not-so-negligible rewards of power, fame, riches, and glamour, the very medium of this new mythmaking allows the mythmakers to populate their own myths. The director both is creator of characters external to him, and uses these characters to actualize him- or herself. Like shamans, prophets, and Homeric poets, writer/directors are tempted to define and represent the limits of the human experience. But unlike other mythmakers, the images they project are "real." Their creation of the world is more palpably manmade, hence the inevitable notions of the omniscient self, bounded by no more than a public's refusal to look.

Deriving the legitimacy of their vision from spirits, gods, or muses, shamans, prophets, and poets were secure in their own myths no matter who dared or dared not share the quest. For the filmmaker, on the other hand, the myths transmitted in a film can only derive their validation through their externalization, that is, from the viewer— from being viewed. It is this fragility, this dependence on the audience that is ultimately so threatening to the filmmaker. Unsure of its attention, and fearful of its rejection, the filmmaker mystifies the audience.

Eager to substantiate the legitimacy of the film as *independent* of the mystifying and mysterious audience, the filmmaker transposes the myth from the film to filmmaking. Thus, for the filmmaker, the mythology emanates from the process and not from the product, and is therefore liberated from the dialectic of confronting the world through its content. In this context, distribution, exhibition, marketing, research, analysis, audience preference and reaction come to be viewed as fundamentally subversive activities. They are subversive in that they challenge the filmmaker to rejoin the community, to complete the transition from narcissism to integration, from the manipulation of symbols to the creation and sharing of symbols, of stories, of values.

Unafraid of this challenge, and not unlike true prophets, the film-maker, conscious of his own mythmaking powers, can now take his story and his images not to his colleagues and to his coreligionists, but to the vulgar masses.

As a new mythmaker, the filmmaker can seek the multitudes of the mainstream *and* marginal audiences whose present pagan practices, tastes, and beliefs are both a provocation and an invitation. The filmmaker must adapt the myths to entice the audience's attention: embellish the tales, exaggerate the drama, magnify the fantasy. But to succeed further and displace the old myths, he or she must first and foremost love the audience and respect it, must gauge its mood, sense its needs, fathom its fears, and articulate its aspirations.

True prophets have always belonged to the people. They have not been reluctant to learn about the habits and the customs of those to whom they have chosen to speak. Learning to speak the language of the audience does not impoverish the quality of the discourse. Nor does it predetermine the conclusions of that discourse. *Off-Hollywood* demonstrates that a sensitivity to commerce is no indication of artistic compromise. Neither is the pursuit of a vision free from market concerns any guarantee for producing great art.

It is exactly because so many commercially inspired films ("Holly-wood" films) have been so effective in creating their mythologies that it would be a pity for American independent films to resign themselves to only a marginal social impact. Instead the idea is to outcommercial-ize "Hollywood." In order to do so, independent filmmakers must seek any and every tool in the arsenal of effective distribution. Rather than being a threat or corrupting influence, marketing is the indispensable ingredient for the growth and effectiveness of independent films. Unable to afford customized market research and audience studies, independent filmmakers must band together, and encourage, under-take, subscribe to, and even subsidize cooperative projects. The pooling of resources is essential. Instead of hiding behind ideas of uniqueness, collective interests and similarity of circumstances must be emphasized, examined, and supported. It is in this spirit that the *Off-Hollywood* project was conceived and the authors pursued the work. And it is in this spirit that I hope the independent filmmakers who consult this volume have read it.

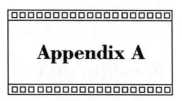

Appendix A

THE ECONOMICS OF SPECIALTY FILM MARKETING

INTRODUCTION

BECAUSE specialty films so eloquently combine communicative and artistic values, their economic character can easily be lost sight of. Hollywood film executives rarely confuse a movie's artistic and commercial dimensions. For independent filmmakers, the task is to preserve the artistic vision and passionate commitment needed to make the film while maintaining a clear view of the commercial challenges faced in bringing a film to an audience.

The thirteen films profiled in this book reveal that an individual film's value can be measured by sometimes conflicting criteria. First, is it a "good" film?—that is, did it fulfill the filmmaker's original vision? did critics like it? has it met industry standards of technical proficiency? is it "original"? etc. Second, is it a successful film?—what was its box-office gross? did it pay back investors? did it make money? etc. These values, while often distinct and easily identifiable, tend to impact upon and reinforce one another.

As a set of financial relationships, every film is subject to specific conditions of the production and distribution process. Production financing is the initial, and most critical, economic determinant. Financing arrangements have been described for all the films covered in this study; for greater understanding of film financing, the reader should consult accountants, attorneys, and other sources.

The charts and tables in this appendix dissect the distribution process as an economic phenomenon and clarify the bottom-line evaluation to which films are subject.

DEAL STRUCTURES

The films analyzed in this book were all produced and released at different times during the early through late 1980s and were, therefore, subject to changing market and contractual relations. These conditions are continuing to evolve even now. Over the 1980s the nature and terms, or structure, of deals have changed. Key features of this change include the shift from a 50/50 profit split deal to today's more common net deal. In the former deal agreed-upon costs are deducted from gross receipts before the filmmaker and distributor equally divide the net balance; this type of deal is common to many in projects covered in this book. The latter deal is characterized by the distributor taking a service fee (usually 30 percent) off the top from reported gross receipts before all expenses are further deducted, after which any remaining revenue is returned to the producer. Chart 1 presents a summary of three types of contemporary deals for theatrical releases; these are the profit split, net, and gross deals.

A second change in the basic economic character of deals has to do with the rights involved. During the earlier phase of the evolution of the specialty market, filmmakers were able to separate rights—i.e., to split the theatrical rights from, say, homevideo or pay cable. Today, it is more difficult to do this. Most theatrical distributors insist on either acquiring rights to all markets or securing back-end protection. Under an all-rights deal, the distributor either handles the ancillary distribution itself or negotiates with the appropriate subdistributors and receives an agent's commission for this service. Under a back-end deal, the distributor gets a percentage from ancillary sales, usually from homevideo, in order to cover risks associated with the theatrical release.

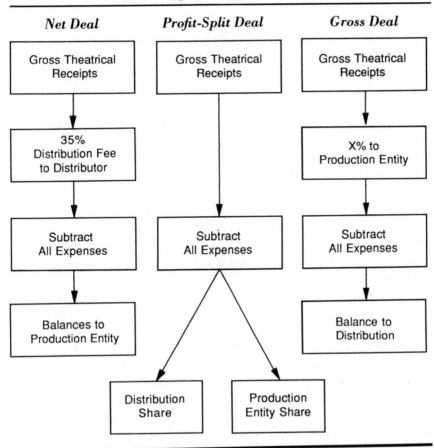

CHART 1
Three Types of Deal Structures

Net Deal	Profit-Split Deal	Gross Deal
Gross Theatrical Receipts	Gross Theatrical Receipts	Gross Theatrical Receipts
35% Distribution Fee to Distributor		X% to Production Entity
Subtract All Expenses	Subtract All Expenses	Subtract All Expenses
Balances to Production Entity		Balance to Distribution
	Distribution Share · Production Entity Share	

Note: Net deal most common; used by majors for negative pickup and in-house productions. Profit-split deal very common for pickups, especially when only domestic rights are involved or for foreign films. Gross deal quite uncommon, unless you are Eddie Murphy or Jack Nicholson.

Source: Ira Deutchman.

CASH FLOW OF THEATRICAL DISTRIBUTION

An individual film has the potential of achieving payback from a host of domestic and foreign media markets, including theatrical, homevideo, television (pay-cable and broadcast), and nontheatrical markets (e.g., libraries, museums, in-flight, prisons, colleges, etc.). Chart 2 presents a schematic overview of how money moves through the various steps involved before it finally gets back to the production entity and, from there, to the profit participants and/or investors who originally underwrote production financing. This chart reflects current distribution deals in which the filmmaker has not separated rights for the domestic market, but has done so for foreign markets. The following two charts provide greater detail on domestic theatrical and ancillary markets. Specifically, Chart 3 provides a broad outline of the financial return from a film's theatrical exhibition; and Chart 4 extends the outline of returns from the domestic homevideo, pay-cable, and broadcast television markets, and nontheatrical as well as all foreign markets.

The analysis of theatrical distribution revenue flow is based on a model 50/50 net profit split deal that characterizes many of the distribution deals included in the book. All deals, like all specialty films, are unique, and it must be stressed that the 50/50 deal, while common at any earlier phase of specialty film production, is less common today. With the critical importance of ancillary markets to the revenue potential, it is not uncommon to find distributors giving away the theatrical market to leverage a favorable ancillary deal. For example, a distributor may seek to recoup only 20 percent of box-office receipts from exhibition as gross film rental in order to ensure a sufficient theatrical run to meet the requirements of ancillary rights sales.

The information and data presented in Charts 3 and 4 are intended to illustrate the economics of the specialty film marketplace and not the performance of a particular film. There is no standard deal among distributors. For analytic purposes, Charts 3 and 4 assume a 50/50 net profit split. For the sake of simplicity, it is assumed that the theatrical distributor also acquires ancillary rights and that no presales have been made. Definitions and assumptions of the terms of Chart 3 include the following:

- Gross Box-Office Receipts [line 1]: This is the dollar volume of ticket-sale receipts that the theaters have collectively taken in at the door. From this, applicable state and local taxes (amounting to approximately 8 percent) are deducted.

CHART 2
Aggregate Cash Flow from All Sources, Domestic and Foreign

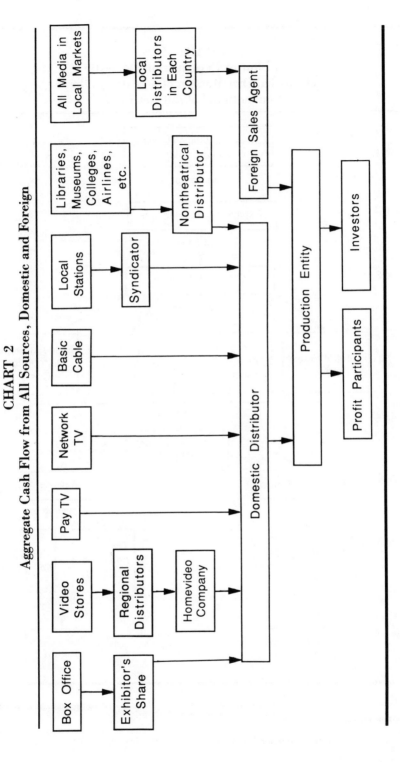

Source: Ira Deutchman.

CHART 3
Cash Flow of Return from Domestic
Theatrical Distribution of a Feature Film
(Conventional 50/50 Net Deal)

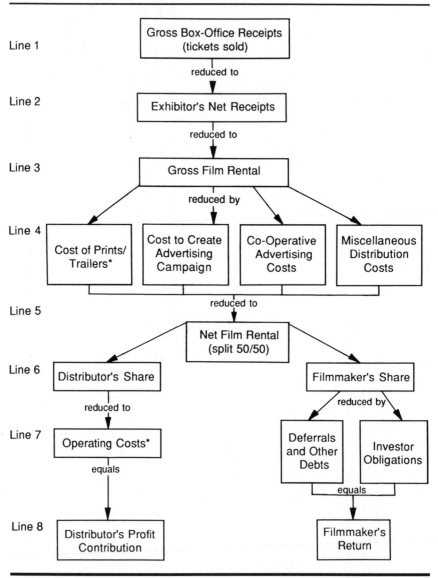

* Fixed costs and overhead charges applications vary with each distributor; can be applied to lines 4 or 7.

Source: Adapted from Independent Feature Project and Orion Classics.

- Exhibitor's Net Receipts [line 2]: Theater owners typically retain 25 to 75 percent of box-office receipts, but sometimes a deal is structured on the basis of deducting the house nut from first receipts with some percentage of receipts above that retained as the exhibitor's profit. For specialty films, exhibitors traditionally retain 60 percent of the receipts.

- Gross Film Rental [line 3]: This is equal to the box-office gross less the exhibitor's net receipts share, and is the amount returned to the distributor. While negotiable, specialty distributors usually receive approximately 40 percent of box-office receipts.

- Total Distributor Expenses [line 4]* normally cover the following four expense categories:

  1. Cost of Prints/Trailers: This is the duplication cost of both the 35mm prints and the promotional trailers.

  2. Cost to Create Advertising Campaign: This covers the cost of creative art and design work to fashion the promotional campaign material, including the slick one-sheet, press packet, trailer, radio spots, theater blowups, etc.

  3. Cost of Co-op Advertising: This is the cost of the media time/space that the distributor incurs when releasing the film in each local market. The distributor usually absorbs between 90 and 95 percent and the local exhibitor contributes the difference. Unlike Hollywood releases, specialty films are not usually supported by a national advertising campaign.

  4. Miscellaneous Distribution Costs: This includes the cost not included above and covers such things as publicists' fees, promotional travel costs, printing and shipping of posters, etc.

- Net Film Rental [line 5]: This is the amount left when all direct distribution expenses are deducted from the gross film rental. It is from this base that the traditional 50/50 split between distributor and producer is calculated.

- Distributor's Share/Filmmaker's Share [line 6]: From its half of the net film rental, the distributor deducts operating costs, debt services, etc. [line 7] in order to determine the net-net, or profit [line 8]. Likewise, the filmmaker (i.e., production entity) must deduct outstanding obligations [line 7], be they investor payments, deferrals, or other debts, before profit is realized [line 8].

* As noted above, most distributors today do not accept this 50/50 split but charge a fee for services rendered. This fee is often between 20 and 40 percent of the gross film rental. A detailed breakdown of types and ranges of expenses is presented in Appendix B.

CASH FLOW OF ANCILLARY MARKET DISTRIBUTION

Chart 4 reflects revenue flow through domestic ancillary markets, with appropriate deductions for the distributor's split and filmmaker's expenses. Foreign market sales, covering theatrical, homevideo, and television (pay cable, satellite, or broadcast), are usually handled by a specialized sales agent who, in turn, works through local subdistributors in each market (and sometimes for each medium within each market). Chart 5 provides a break-out of elapsed time when the various sequential release windows traditionally occur. It covers three time periods—1980, 1985, and 1990—to show how these windows have shifted as markets changed.

Independent filmmakers have been able to cut ancillary market presale deals (i.e., sell off the rights to certain markets or territories as a source of production financing), or sell theatrical and other markets separately once the finished film is in hand. For the purpose of this discussion, however, it is assumed that the theatrical distributor handles all ancillary market sales through specialized subdistributors for each market. The key features of each market are:

- Nontheatrical [line 1]: Traditionally, the sale of films in 16mm or videocassette to the nontheatrical market provided the major ancillary return to the independent filmmaker. However, with the advent of homevideo and the flattening out of school and library budgets, this market is providing less revenue. In addition to direct expenses incurred out of first receipts, the distributor traditionally receives a fee of 30 to 50 percent for domestic nontheatrical distribution, with higher fees for foreign nontheatrical and in-flight placements.

- Homevideo [line 2]: Unlike the major studios, independent distributors do not have a homevideo distribution arm. They sublicense the homevideo rights to a studio or independent homevideo distributor. Therefore, the chart assumes that the homevideo rights are sublicensed, and that the distributor receives a percentage of 25 to 35 percent of the homevideo royalty returns (including any advance against them) for selling the property to the homevideo distributor. Returns are contingent upon the terms of the deal, i.e., what expenses are applied against returns.

  The homevideo distributor will typically acquire a film by paying a minimum advance against royalties or a minimum guarantee paid off over time. The guarantee is usually calculated against the size of the

CHART 4
Cash Flow of Revenue from Domestic Ancillary Market Distribution of a Feature Film

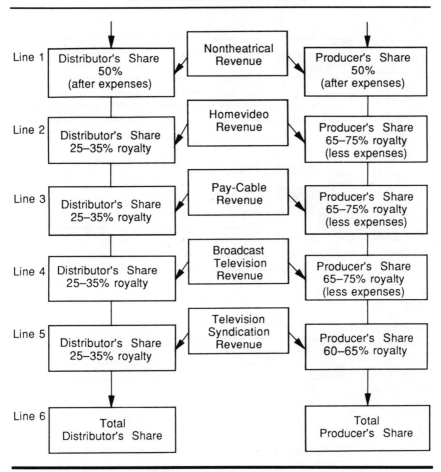

Source: Independent Feature Project.

CHART 5
Feature Film Distribution: Typical Release Sequence

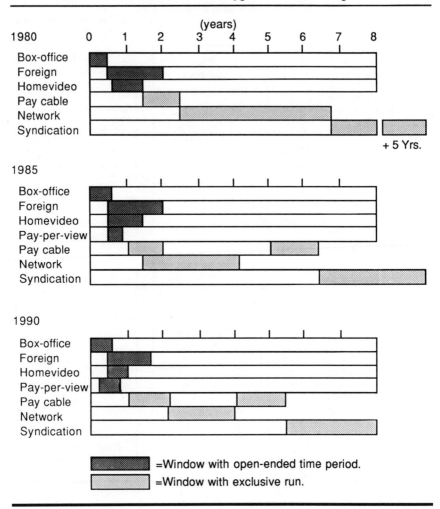

Source: LINK Resources Corp.

theatrical launch (i.e., total publicity and advertising expenses, cities opened, etc.) rather than simply box-office grosses. Offset against this payment are royalties accrued against the cumulative revenue generated; this payment is a percentage of the wholesale price of each cassette sold, and can range from 10 to 20 percent. The following formula is suggested as a model for calculating return:

A homevideo distributor pays an advance or guarantee of $100,000 against a 15 percent royalty. The wholesale price is $50 per cassette, with the royalty being $7.50. If the homevideo distributor sells 13,334 cassettes, the guarantee is recouped ($7.50 × 13,334 = $100,000). Above this breakeven, the licensee is paid $7.50 for each additional cassette sold.

The theatrical distributor receives a fixed-percentage fee of between 25 and 30 percent for making the deal with the homevideo distributor. This cut comes directly out of the guarantee and any additional royalty payments.

- Pay Television [line 3]: During the late 1970s and early eighties, the pay-cable market was supportive of independent filmmakers. As the market matured, Home Box Office/Cinemax and Showtime/The Movie Channel came to dominate the business and forced out a number of smaller services. These two programming networks (along with Bravo, Disney, and smaller networks) now have longterm, multipicture deals with Hollywood studios. As subscriber growth has flattened, independent films have come to command more modest acquisition or licensing fees. The distributor's fee for making the deal is usually between 25 and 35 percent, with the filmmaker's share being further discounted by direct costs (e.g., tape dupe and other distributor costs).

- Broadcast Television and Television Syndication [lines 4 and 5]: With rare exception, specialty films will appear only on PBS, either "American Playhouse," or another scheduled slot. If CPB, NEH, "American Playhouse" or other public money is invested in the production as a presale, then PBS will have as a grant or contract condition the right of first refusal in airing the film. If the film is acquired by PBS or another network, a licensing fee is paid for a set number of airings over the course of a set number of years, often four plays over three years. None of the films in this study has yet to secure a syndication or network sale and, because of their inherent quirkiness, few if any are likely to be bought for commercial broadcast television. Some recent specialty films of a crossover nature, like *The Trip to Bountiful*,

Desert Bloom, and *Stand and Deliver,* may secure a commercial television airing. With a syndication sale, the licensing term is normally three to eight airings over seven years. The distributor receives a fee of between 10 and 30 percent for a network sale and 30 to 40 percent for a syndication deal.

RETURN TO FILMMAKERS

Based on the preceding discussion of theatrical and ancillary market cash flow, we will examine the returns realized at different levels of box-office performance. First, we will examine a hypothetical best-case scenario and then apply the model to the films analyzed in this study.

Table 1 details specialty film revenue streams. Originally developed by Cinecom International some years ago as part of a promotional brochure, this table details market-by-market performance of a prototypical film they would have handled then. Cinecom assumes a 40 percent gross film rental. The reader should be advised that this table is being included for illustrative purposes only and to help filmmakers grasp the scope of financial relations involved in a multimarket release. Current conditions preclude the establishment of either specific financial relations between markets or the scale of projected returns. This table suggests interesting conclusions:

- Box-office gross [column 1] is the most critical factor in generating overall return to the filmmaker, impacting upon the relative strength of return from all ancillary markets (nontheatrical, homevideo, pay-cable, and free TV).

- However, even though box-office receipts increase 20-fold and net film rental jumps 300-fold, the filmmakers' absolute share of revenues increases 87-fold while their relative share of net revenues from all markets (producer's revenue share divided by total net revenue) increases by only about 3 percent, remaining roughly 50 percent of all revenues.

- When gross film rental increases with box-office receipts, distributor expenses decrease proportionally—i.e., there is a built-in cost-effectiveness of distribution tied to increased box-office grosses because as a film gains popularity, promotional expenses do not increase.

TABLE 1
Estimated Feature Film Performance in Domestic Distribution (in $000)

1 Theatrical Box-Office Gross	2 Gross Film Rental	3 Total Distribution Expense	4 Net Film Rental	5 Non-theatrical Revenue	6 Home-video Revenue	7 Pay-Cable Revenue	8 Free TV Revenue	9 Total Net Revenue	10 Producer Revenue Share*
500,000	200	200	0	50	0	25	0	75	42.5
1,000,000	400	300	100	60	50	75	0	285	167.5
2,500,000	1,000	540	460	90	200	225	0	975	572.5
5,000,000	2,000	880	1,120	140	500	425	100	2,360	1,400.0
7,500,000	3,000	1,000	2,000	190	750	750	750	4,415	2,670.0
10,000,000	4,000	1,000	3,000	220	1,000	1,000	1,000	6,220	3,710.0

* Excludes theatrical box-office gross.

Source: Used by permission of Cinecom International.

This last point is further analyzed in Chart 6. This chart shows the relative share of the financial participants at box-office grosses of $1 million and $5 million, with ticket price assumed at $5.00, illustrating the decrease in per-ticket expenses and resulting increased profit for distributors and film-makers at high levels of gross revenue.

FINANCIAL RETURN OF *OFF-HOLLYWOOD* FILMS

Table 2 provides a detailed breakdown of market-by-market returns for all thirteen films covered. As discussed in the Introduction, not all participants provided equally complete or comparable data, and many figures are estimates or not available. Thus, one can see that even with the sponsorship of the Sundance Institute and the Independent Feature Project, it is extremely difficult to get hard financial data on specific films and deals from either filmmakers or distributors.

CHART 6
Who Gets What from a Specialty Film Ticket Purchase
($5 Ticket Price)*

Example 1: Box-Office Gross of $1 Million

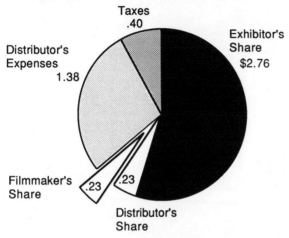

Example 2: Box-Office Gross of $5 Million

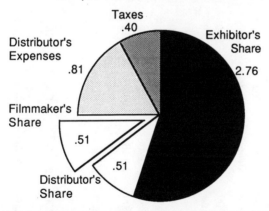

* Based on conventional 50/50 net deal.

TABLE 2
Financial Performance of Films in *Off-Hollywood* (in $000)

Film	1 Negative Costs	2 Box-Office Gross	3 Gross Film Rental	4 Theatrical Dist. Costs	5 Guarantee	6 Non-theatrical Sales/Pro. Revenues	7 Home video Sales/Pro. Revenues	8 Pay TV Sales/Pro. Revenues	9 TV/PBS Sales/Pro. Revenues	10 Foreign Sales/Revenues (all)	11 Pro-duction Return (all)
Cortez	1,174	909	429	1,424	500	118	350s	55s	140*	365s	NA
Cold Feet	250	100	40e	155e	0	5	25s	NA	0	75s	NA
Eating Raoul	508	3,600	1,500	1,400	350	NA	3,000s	1,300s	NA	200s	NA
El Norte	850	5,500e	2,200e	950e	200+	NA	100+r	NA	425*	45s	NA
Good Fight	245	265e	120e	85	0	30r	0	7+	245*	15r	NA
Heartland	1,048	3,500	1,148	556	15	NA	125r	63r	645*	167r	(58)
Hollywood Shuffle	150e	5,500	2,750	850+e	100e	NA	1,000	NA	NA	1,000	NA
My Dinner with Andre	525	5,250	2,100	800e	0	70e	100e	300e	0	150e	NA
Old Enough	635	650e	260e	310e	150+	NA	150e	100e	0	NA	NA
The Return of the Secaucus Seven	125	2,000e	800+e	NA	25	25r	100r#	#	50r	65r	425

Stand and Deliver	1,370	14,104	6,229	7,322	3,500	92	NA	800	500*	2,900	425
Weavers	150	250	100e	NA	0	15r	40r	10er	100*	75r	NA
Wild Style	250	1,200e	480e	NA	25	NA	NA	NA	0	120+	NA

Note: Financial information derived from filmmaker and/or distributor and includes (s) gross sales and (r) revenue returned to filmmaker/producer. Estimates (e) are derived from *Variety*, other sources, and researchers' estimates; a (+) indicates a sum in excess of that reported; a (#) indicates figures are combined; (NA) indicates that neither data nor estimate is available.

Negative costs include deferments: Gross film rental is estimated at 40 percent of box-office gross. Theatrical distributor costs include guarantee/advance. TV/PBS figures with (*) indicate grant monies from public sources (e.g., NEH, NEA, CPB, or "American Playhouse") have been included as a presales obligation of right of first refusal.

Appendix B

LAUNCHING A SPECIALTY FILM

BUYING media to support the release of a specialized film is itself a very specialized activity. Commercial films "break" in 1,000 or more screens and are supported by multimillion-dollar advertising and promotional campaigns. But the narrow profit margins and highly specific audiences of a specialized film require that a release receive very careful handling. A distributor will look closely at every dollar spent and every ad bought for periods lasting as long as eighteen months. The distributors do not follow a simple formula, except to minimize costs. Nevertheless, there are a few rules of thumb that can give the independent filmmaker insight into the decision variables that influence the distributor's media-buying decisions.

THE MARKETS

Underlying any distributor's budget decisions is the fact that nearly all specialized films will generate 80 percent or more of their total revenue from the top eight markets. Specialty film exhibition is organized along four market tiers, with the principal audiences coming from eight cities. They are specified in Table 3.

TABLE 3
Specialty Exhibition Market Tiers

Tiers	*Metropolitan Markets*
Tier 1	New York: for opening and for attracting the attention of the national press. A run of two to four weeks gives the film a chance to break out to outlying theaters in the metropolitan area as well as on Long Island and in Westchester.
	Los Angeles: for West Coast and film industry exposure. A two- to four-week run can lead to a breakout to theaters in San Diego and Orange County. Some distributors place Los Angeles in the second tier, considering it less important for press reputation and word-of-mouth recognition than New York.
Tier 2	Boston: a successful run can lead to a breakout to other parts of New England.
	Washington, D.C.: break out to Maryland and Virginia metropolitan area.
	Philadelphia: break out to other mid-Atlantic centers.
	Chicago: break out to Midwest.
	San Francisco: break out to northern California.
	Seattle: break out to Portland and other parts of the Pacific Northwest. (Seattle is considered a unique filmgoing city. With a population of approximately 500,000, its very loyal audience for specialty films makes it a more important market for these films than the larger cities of Boston, Washington, D.C., and San Francisco. Much of the credit for the cultivation of the Seattle market has been attributed to the innovative marketing efforts of Randy Finley, the former owner of the Seven Gables theater chain.)
Tier 3	These markets are defined by the presence of a more sophisticated audience segment that sustains innovative cultural activities. Such markets are usually associated with major universities or state capitals. They include: Atlanta, Austin, Baltimore, Cleveland, Dallas, Detroit, Houston, Madison, Miami, Minneapolis, Salt Lake City, and Tucson.
Tier 4	Includes a host of smaller cities such as Des Moines, Norfolk, Richmond, and Rochester. Split-week engagements are common.

New York is always emphasized in marketing strategy for independent films, for it is the home of the national press. Most distributors will try to open in New York and then move to other cities. There are circumstances, however, which lead the distributor to choose an "out-of-town" opening for a film. For example, if the distributor believes the film will be better received by the critics in Los Angeles or by audiences in Seattle, then it might open in those cities before coming to New York.

THE COSTS

What are the costs of buying media in these markets? To begin with, it is important to note that the key factor in determining advertising budgets is the cost of newspaper advertising. Television is generally considered too broad in reach to be cost-efficient in attracting the specialized film audience. Radio is used more frequently, particularly if there is a strong score or witty dialogue, but radio is generally inefficient in reaching the specialized audience. Thus, newspaper advertising is heavily relied upon as the most cost-efficient medium, with 85 percent or more of ad budgets for specialized films being slated for newspaper ads.

The cost of ad space varies significantly from city to city; from $300 per column inch in New York to $200 in Chicago and $150 in Los Angeles. Distributors are quick to point out that prices have skyrocketed in recent years, with average costs increasing by as much as 200 percent from 1983 to 1988.

The traditional size of an ad for a specialized film also varies from market to market (see sample). For example, in Los Angeles and New York, they can range from as little as seven column inches to as much as one-third of a page. Thus, in New York, costs for an ad can range from a low of $2,000 to a high of $10,000, depending on the distributor's advertising strategy.

Co-op advertising can offset a portion of this expense. The exhibitor reimburses a portion of advertising expenses to the distributor, based on a prenegotiated percentage. Ten to fifteen percent of the total ad cost is generally the rule. New York, however, is unique in that no house participates in co-op advertising. Even the directory listings, traditionally paid for by exhibitors, are billed to distributors in New York.

"**IMPRESSIVE DEBUT**

FOR WRITER, DIRECTOR MARISA SILVER."
—Jim Calio, People Magazine

"REMARKABLY POLISHED."
—Kathleen Carroll, N.Y. Daily News

"REAL MAGIC."
—Bruce Handy, Vogue Magazine

"FIRST RATE."
—Caroline Miller, Newsday

OLD ENOUGH

Production Designer JEFFREY TOWNSEND · Written and Directed by MARISA SILVER

PG PARENTAL GUIDANCE SUGGESTED SOME MATERIAL MAY NOT BE SUITABLE FOR CHILDREN

1984 Orion Classics An **ORION** Release CLASSICS

AD# 203   2 COL. x 5 = 10"

"REAL MAGIC."
— Vogue Magazine

OLD ENOUGH

PG ©1984 Orion Classics An **ORION** Release CLASSICS

"REMARKABLY POLISHED."
—Kathleen Carroll, N.Y. Daily News

OLD ENOUGH

PG ©1984 Orion Classics An **ORION** Release CLASSICS

AD #102   1 COL. x 2" = 2"   AD #103   1 COL x 3" = 3"

HOW MUCH TO SPEND

Given these costs, what factors will ultimately determine the size of the advertising budget? To begin with, budgets are estimated on the basis of the box-office projections made by the sales staff. Other factors relating to each individual market are then analyzed. These include the size of the ad traditionally run in that market, the type of theater, the size of the house, and the film's experience in other markets. Also important, and often overlooked by the filmmaker, is the agreement between distributor and exhibitor in each market. If the split of box-office receipts is particularly favorable to the distributor, then he will be more inclined to spend additional money to bring in the audience. For example, since Los Angeles is currently the most competitive market, box-office terms are generally more favorable to the distributor, thus this market is more conducive to additional advertising expenditures.

Another factor in determining an ad budget is the prints and advertising (P&A) commitment made by the distributor to the producer or the video-cassette distributor. Such commitments contractually require a distributor to spend a certain minimum amount in advertising prior to the opening. In the case of the homevideo deal, there may well be an escalator clause, meaning a larger guarantee for the distributor for every additional dollar amount spent on advertising the theatrical release.

One last factor to be considered is the strategy of "buying grosses," or putting more advertising dollars into a market (generally New York) than would normally be warranted in an attempt to squeeze out higher box-office totals. The expectation is that higher opening totals will give a distributor a stronger hand in negotiating terms with exhibitors in other markets.

Given the costs and variables to be considered in buying media, what can a distributor expect to spend in opening a film in the top eight markets? (Note that opening costs include the week prior to opening and the first five days of release.) Though the preceding discussion should make it clear that budgets will vary greatly from picture to picture, past experience has given specialty film distributors certain ballpark figures within which to work. Average opening expenses for the top eight markets are specified in Table 4.

TABLE 4
Average Specialty Film Opening Costs for
Top Eight Markets

Market	*Average Costs*
New York	$50,000–$150,000
Los Angeles	15,000– 40,000
Boston	10,000– 20,000
San Francisco	10,000– 20,000
Chicago	10,000– 20,000
Washington, D.C.	7,500– 15,000
Seattle	7,500– 15,000
Philadelphia	7,500– 15,000

Thus, a distributor can expect to spend anywhere from $117,500 to $295,000 on opening expenses alone in the top eight markets.

A detailed breakdown for a modestly released specialty film follows in Table 5. Costs are organized as one-time preparations, which are amortized for both the local and national release and for the New York City opening run (i.e., the first four weeks).

TABLE 5
Distribution Costs for Specialty Release

Activity	*Preparation*	*Week 1*	*Weeks 2–4*	*Total*
1. *General Materials*				
Key art (creative)	$ 10,000			
Posters (production)	3,000			
Ads (production)	4,000			
Stills	2,000			
Press kit	1,500			
Trailer (creative)	10,000			
Trailer (prints)	3,000			
TV spot (creative)	0			
TV spot (dubs)	0			
Radio spot (creative)	0			

TABLE 5 (*continued*)
Distribution Costs for Specialty Release

Activity	Preparation	Week 1	Weeks 2–4	Total
Radio spot (dubs)	0			
Fliers	3,000			
TV clips	2,500			
Misc. promo	0			
Subtotal	$ 39,000	$ 0	$ 0	$ 39,000
2. *Feature Prints* (20 prints)				
Interpositives/				
Internegatives	0			
Timing	0			
Answer print	$ 2,900			
Release prints	26,000			
Shipping costs	5,000			
Subtotal	$ 33,900	$ 0	$ 0	$ 33,900
3. *Nation*				
Publicity fees	$ 20,000			
Press junket	0			
Press tours	8,000			
Magazine ads	0			
TV time	0			
Subtotal	$ 28,000	$ 0	$ 0	$ 28,000
4. *New York*				
Newspaper ads	$ 0	$45,000	$42,000	$ 87,000
TV ads	0			
Radio	0	1,500	0	1,500
Ad production	0	3,000	3,900	6,900
Wild-postering	0	2,000		2,000
P.R. & screening	5,000			5,000
Opening event	3,000			3,000
Misc.*	4,000			4,000
Subtotal	$ 12,000	$51,500	$45,900	$109,400
Total	$112,900	$51,500	$45,900	$210,300

* Miscellaneous costs could include theater marquee ($2,000), flag ($1,500), and lobby display ($1,500).

TABLE 6
Preopening and First-week Media Costs for a Typical Specialty Film

Preopening Week and First Week	OD										COL. INCHES		RATES		TOTAL
	Sun.	Wed.	Thurs.	Fri.	Sat.	Sun.	Mon.	Tues.	Wed.	Thurs.	Sun.	Daily	Sun.	Daily	
New York Times — D			10	31.5	10[R]		4	4	10	4		63.5		269.37	$17,105.00
New York Times — S (¼ p)	31.5										10[R]			159.2	$ 1,590.20
News — D					10										
News — S											41.5		319.35		13,253.03
Post — D				G		G	G	G	G	G					149.25
Post — S					G										
Village Voice		600 lines										900		4.25	3,825.00
Wash. Sq. J				14								14		13.53	189.42
Baruch Ticker				14								14		9.60	134.40
Columbia Spectator				14								14		10.50	147.00
Barnard Bulletin			14	14								14		8.40	117.60
Hunter Envoy				14								14		10.01	140.14
															$36,651.04
														Est. Prod. Costs	3,700.00
														TOTAL	$40,351.04

OD = opening date; G = listing in *New York Post* entertainment guide; R = repeat; all figures in column-inches unless otherwise specified. D = daily; S = Sunday.

Source: Diener, Hauser, Bates, and Co.

Appendix C

GLOSSARY

Advance: Money obtained up front in anticipation of profits. It is refundable if film is not profitable, unlike a guarantee.

Advertising: All forms of paid media exposure (e.g., television, radio, newspapers, billboards).

AFI: American Film Institute.

AMPAS: Academy of Motion Picture Arts and Sciences.

Ancillary rights: Usually defined as all rights other than theatrical, and include homevideo, pay cable, syndicated television, foreign sales, and nontheatrical (e.g., sales to libraries, schools, in-flight). Theatrical rights are regarded as primary because: (a) they are the most potentially profitable, (b) they are the first in a sequence of "windows" or markets, and (c) advertising and publicity for the theatrical release enhances the value of a film in all subsequent markets. Ancillary rights may also be defined as the rights to any market other than that for which a film was originally produced. For example, a made-for-television movie may have ancillary value in homevideo or nontheatrical markets.

314

Art-house theater: Movie theater that shows specialized films (generally in exclusive engagements) rather than mass-marketed studio films.

Back end: Profit participation in a film after distribution and/or production costs have been recouped.

Blowup: Optical process of enlarging a film from its original format to another, most often from 16mm to 35mm.

Box-office gross: Total revenues taken in at movie-theater box offices before any expenses or percentages are deducted.

Break: To open a film in several theaters simultaneously in and around a single city or a group of cities, or on a national basis.

Break out: To break a film following an initial period of exclusive or limited engagement.

Broadcast television: Television that is supported by advertising and distributed over the air (e.g., networks, independent stations, and public broadcasting stations).

Cable TV: Television service delivered by coaxial cable. Includes advertiser-supported channels or services like USA and Arts & Entertainment networks, public access, and, for an additional fee, pay TV services.

Commercial distribution: As opposed to specialized distribution, characteristically aims at a mass audience with a large number of theaters playing the same film simultaneously in a given area or nationally, backed by extensive advertising expenditures with a heavy emphasis on television advertising in particular.

Completion bond: A form of insurance that, for a fee, guarantees completion of a film in the event the producer exceeds the budget and/or is unable to secure additional funding. Completion bonds are required by banks and financiers to secure loans and investments in a production. Should a bond be invoked, the completion guarantor will assume substantial control over the production and a recoupment position that precedes all investors.

Completion guarantor: The person or company who pledges the completion bond.

Contingency line: A line-item on production budget for unanticipated cost overruns, e.g., additional shooting days; usually no more than 10 percent of total below-the-line costs.

Co-op advertising: Advertising the cost of which is shared between the distributor and exhibitor. The specifics of the type of advertising and how costs are to be shared are not standardized and must be negotiated with the exhibitor on a film-by-film and week-by-week basis during the engagement.

CPB: The Corporation for Public Broadcasting.

Cross-collateralization: Legal and accounting practice by which distributors offset financial losses in one medium or market with profits from another, i.e., if theatrical expenses exceed income, homevideo revenue can be allocated to make up the balance (an unattractive but generally unavoidable deal point).

Crossover film: Film that is initially targeted for a narrow specialty market but achieves acceptance in a wider market.

DGA: Directors Guild of America (union for directors).

Day and date: The simultaneous opening of a film in two or more movie theaters in one or more cities.

Direct advertising: Mailings or fliers sent directly to consumers, usually targeted to a specific interest group.

Display advertising: Advertising that features artwork or title treatment specific to a given film, in newspaper and magazine advertising.

Distributor: Someone who promotes a film and negotiates licenses with various outlets including theaters, homevideo manufacturers, pay-cable services, broadcast television stations, etc. A distributor may distribute to all markets or may specialize in one or more markets.

Domestic rights: Rights within the U.S. and Canada only.

Exclusive opening: A style of release whereby a film is opened in a single theater in a major city, giving the distributor the option to hold the film for a long exclusive run or to move the film into additional theaters based on the film's performance.

Exhibitor: Owner or programmer of a movie theater that shows feature films.

Feature film: Full-length, fictional film (not a documentary or short subject) generally produced for theatrical release.

50/50 split: One of the possible revenue divisions between producer and distributor. Split is made after distribution costs have been recouped by the distributor.

First money: From the producer's point of view, the first revenue received from the distribution of a film. Not to be confused with profits, first monies are generally allocated to investors until recoupment, but may be allocated in part or in whole to deferred fees or services such as actors, technicians, or laboratories.

Floor: In a distributor/exhibitor split, a floor is the minimum percentage of the actual box-office receipts the distributor obtains, regardless of the theater's operating costs. Floors are a common part of a distributor/exhibitor agreement and will generally decline week by week over the course of the engagement. Floors will generally range between 70 percent and 25 percent, depending on the negotiations.

Foreign sale: Licensing a film in various territories and media outside the U.S. and Canada. Although Canada is technically a foreign territory, most domestic distributors acquire Canadian rights and (except for major film companies that have Canadian operations) use subdistributors in Canada.

Four-wall engagement: Renting a theater for a guaranteed flat fee that includes the theater staff. There is no split of the revenue with the exhibitor; fee is paid regardless of the performance of the film.

General partner: Management side of a limited partnership (the position usually taken by a film's producers) that structures a motion-picture investment and raises money from investors, who become limited partners. General partners control all business decisions regarding the partnership.

Grassroots campaign: Reaching your audience with a more intimate approach such as fliers, posters, and sticker endorsements from local organizations and community groups, and organizing word-of-mouth through special screenings.

Gross box office: Total revenue taken in at theater box office for ticket sales.

Gross film rental: The distributor's share of the gross box office before distribution costs (e.g., advertising, prints, promotion) are deducted.

Guarantee: A sum of money that is payable regardless of a film's performance in the marketplace. Guarantees can be payable up front in installments or in a lump sum at a specific date. Such sums are advance payments against the producer's or distributor's share of eventual profits, if any.

Homevideo: Distribution of a film via videocassettes or disc (or any device hereafter invented) that may be purchased or rented for home viewing on television.

House nut: The weekly operating expenses of a movie theater.

In-principle agreement: Nonbinding verbal agreement.

Key art: Artwork used in posters and ads for a movie. May be an elaborate pictorial approach or as simple as a logo or title treatment.

Key cities: Cities that are cultural and media centers and have larger and generally more lucrative markets.

License/licensing: Agreement between distributor and a second party that outlines profit split, rights, and limitations of uses of a film. It can refer to theatrical exhibition, homevideo, merchandising, or any other right. A license is generally characterized by a time limitation and conveys control but not ownership of such rights.

Limited partnership: Instrument of investment common to motion-picture financing. It consists of general partners, who initiate and control the partnership, and limited partners, who are investors but have no control over the partnership and no legal or financial liabilities beyond the amount of their investment. There are many subtleties and variations in structuring a limited partnership. Generally, the limited partnership will stipulate that limited partners will recoup their investments from first monies and a 50/50 split of profits between limited and general partners will take place thereafter.

Listings: In a newspaper or magazine, a paid entry in a regular list of movies playing locally.

Lobby card: Standard size (smaller than a one-sheet) poster used for display in a movie theater lobby or outside the theater.

Mainstream audience: A broad, general audience, targeted by most commercial releases.

Mass-marketing: Standard commercial approach that provides high visibility for film in all media and in many theaters.

Merchandising rights: Right to license, manufacture, and distribute merchandise based on characters, names, events, etc., appearing in or used in connection with a film.

Minimultiple: Method of release that falls between an exclusive engagement and a wide release, consisting of quality theaters in strategic geographic locations, generally a prelude to a wider break.

Move-over: Moving a film out of one theater into another.

Multitiered audience: An audience of different types of people who find the film attractive for different reasons and who must be reached by different publicity, promotion, and ad campaigns.

NABET: National Association of Broadcast Employees and Technicians. A union of film and television production personnel. Generally more flexible and less costly than IATSE (International Alliance of Theater and Stage Employees).

Negative cost: Actual cost of producing a film through to the manufacture of a completed negative (does not include cost of prints or advertising).

Negative pickup: Method of obtaining full or partial financing for a film. A distributor guarantees to pay a specified amount for distribution rights upon delivery of a completed film negative by a specific date. If the completed negative is not delivered on time, the distributor has no obligation or liability to the production. The negative pickup guarantee can be used as collateral for a bank loan to obtain production funds.

Net film rental: Revenue from theatrical release after distribution costs are deducted from gross film rental.

90/10 deal: Distributor/exhibitor split of box-office revenue, the sum left after the theater's nut has been deducted from box-office gross. The distributor obtains 90 percent of the remaining box-office receipts and the exhibitor 10 percent.

Nontheatrical distribution: Distribution to institutional users (as opposed to the general public); includes airline in-flight, ships, hotels, colleges, clubs, prisons, and military installations.

Nut: See House nut.

Off-Hollywood: A term used to define independently produced, relatively low-budget, quality, adult-oriented American films made outside the studio system (akin to off-Broadway).

One-sheet: A standard size (27″ × 41″) poster that is used for display at theaters and in other locations.

Opinion-makers: As opposed to reviewers and feature writers, opinion-makers are influential people from various walks of life (e.g., arts, media, politics) who will spread word-of-mouth about a film prior to its opening.

Output deal: Traditionally refers to an exclusive agreement between a film production company/microstudio and a homevideo or other ancillary distributor for the rights to the company's "output."

Outreach campaign: Another term for grassroots campaign.

Paid media: All forms of paid advertising.

Participation: A share in the profits of a film.

Pay-per-view: One-time payment for a special event (sporting, movie, etc.) on cable TV or over-the-air service to which consumer already subscribes.

Pay TV: A programming service not supported by advertising, for which consumers pay a monthly fee. Includes cable services such as Showtime and HBO as well as over-the-air services such as WHT and Select TV.

Platforming: A method of release whereby a film is opened in a single theater or a small group of key theaters in a major territory with the specific intention of widening the run to numerous theaters (either in one step or in phases).

Playoff: The distribution of a film after key openings.

Points: The percentage of profits given to a participant in the production of a film.

Preopening advertising: Advertising prior to the opening of a film or advance advertising of a film's opening date.

Press kit: Material made available to media representatives (editors, reviewers, etc.) including production notes, stills, bios, script synopses, prior reviews, and feature stories.

Prints: Copies of a film that are distributed to theaters.

Promotional activities: Activities geared toward gaining media attention and public interest, such as interviews, critics' screenings, public appearances by actors or by others involved in the film, sandwich-board advertising, T-shirts, comic books, opinion-maker screenings, sneak previews, fliers, interest group screenings.

Publicist: A person responsible for organizing and generating publicity. Also called a press agent.

Publicity: Media exposure (reviews, feature articles, interviews on TV, etc.) that is not paid for. Editorial content as opposed to paid advertising.

Quotes: Excerpted remarks from critical reviews used in advertising.

Regional release: As opposed to a simultaneous national release, a method of distribution whereby a film is opened in one or more territories with the expectation that the film will open in additional territories, in a preset or an ad hoc pattern, over a period of time.

Rollout: Distribution of a film around the country subsequent to key city openings or subsequent to opening in one city, usually New York.

Run: Length of time the feature plays in movie theaters or territory.

SAG: Screen Actors Guild (union for principal performers).

SEG: Screen Extra Guild (union of extras performers).

Secondary cities: As opposed to key cities, smaller, less lucrative markets, often satellites to key cities.

70/30 split: One of the possible revenue divisions between producer and distributor; distributor receives a 30 percent distribution fee on all revenues and producer receives the remaining 70 percent minus all distribution costs.

Slicks: Standardized ad mechanical printed on glossy paper that includes various sizes of display ads for a given film, designed to receive local theater information as needed.

Specialized distribution: As opposed to commercial distribution; distribution to a limited target audience, in a smaller number of theaters with limited advertising expenditures and a strong emphasis on publicity and critical reviews to reach a discerning public.

Stills: Photographs taken during production for use later in advertising and/or publicity.

Subdistributor: In theatrical releases, distributors who handle specific geographic territory for a film. They are subcontracted by the main distributor, who coordinates the distribution plans and marketing for all the subdistributors of a film.

Suburban venue: Suburban locality or theater.

Syndication: The distribution of motion pictures to independent commercial television stations on a regional or national basis.

Target market: The defined audience segment a distributor seeks to reach with its advertising and promotion campaign (e.g., teens, women over thirty, yuppies, Hispanics, etc.).

Test-marketing: Before committing to an advertising campaign, the releasing of a film in one or more small, representative markets. The effectiveness of the marketing plan can be judged and changed, if necessary, before proceeding with the key city and national release.

Theatrical release/distribution: The process of advertising, promoting, and physically distributing films to theaters.

Title treatment: A distinctive logo of a film's title used consistently in an advertising campaign.

Trailer: A preview or "coming attractions" advertisement that is exhibited in movie theaters prior to and during the run of a film; a component of an advertising campaign.

Unit publicist: Publicist assigned to a film during preproduction and production to generate publicity.

Wide release: The ultimate aim of commercial distribution whereby a film is played simultaneously in numerous theaters (800–2,000 theaters) nationally.

Window: Period of time in which a film is available in a given medium. Some windows may be open-ended, such as theatrical and homevideo, or limited, such as pay television or syndication.

Word-of-mouth: The positive or negative reputation a film gains through exposure to audiences.

World-wide rights: Rights in all markets and media throughout the world.

```
┌─────────────────────────────────────┐
│ □□□□□□□□□□□□□□□□□□□□□□□ │
│          **About the**              │
│         **Sponsoring**              │
│        **Organizations**            │
│ □□□ □□□□□□□□□□□□□□□□□ □ │
└─────────────────────────────────────┘
```

THE SUNDANCE INSTITUTE

THE Sundance Institute was founded in 1980 by Robert Redford and
other professional filmmakers out of two shared concerns: first, that
serious independent filmmakers were not getting enough opportunities to develop and present their work; and second, that an emphasis
on technology was beginning to overshadow the human dimension of
the filmmaking process, such as character, story, and acting. Located
in Provo Canyon, Utah, the Institute is a working community for
emerging artists to develop their projects, through collaboration with
resource professionals, in an environment free of financial risk.

Collaborative work at Sundance involves a number of different
programs: the Screenwriters Lab, the June Filmmakers Lab, the Film
Composers Lab, the Playwrights Lab, and the Dance/Film Lab. In
addition, Sundance presents the United States Film Festival in January and a Producers Conference at the Institute site in Provo Canyon

323

each August. The Feature Film Program, including the Screenwriters and June Filmmakers labs, is augmented by two initiatives in independent film support outside of the United States, the first represented by the Latin American program and the second by the more recently developed Soviet Union initiative. Similarly, the United States Film Festival is presented on a biannual basis in Tokyo.

The Feature Film Program, still the Institute's central emphasis, provides a continuum of services that:

- Support the in-depth development of projects specifically intended for production as feature motion pictures.
- Help locate financing for these projects through Sundance's extensive industry relationships.
- Provide assistance in obtaining distribution of completed films by arranging meetings with key executives, and through Institute-related programs such as the United States Film Festival and the Independent Producers Conference.

In each of the labs a group of eight to fourteen fellows are selected through a juried process. Manuscripts or videotapes, where appropriate, are submitted by prospective applicants either through the open submission process or through the additional solicitation of material by artistic directors. After selection, fellows spend three to four weeks at Sundance developing their projects with all the necessary resources and free of the financial constraints of tuition or board fees.

The Sundance Institute is the only organization in the country founded specifically to support independent filmmaking and work in the film arts. It offers state-of-the-art equipment and facilities and provides the highest caliber of industry professionals as resource advisors. Most importantly, Sundance has demonstrated since its founding a special commitment to the development of emerging film artists.

The Sundance Institute
132 West 21st Street
New York, NY 10011
212-243-7777

THE INDEPENDENT FEATURE PROJECT

SINCE its inception in 1979, the Independent Feature Project (IFP) has created a support structure for independent feature producers, offering a range of services and programs focusing on production, finance, distribution, and marketing. A nonprofit membership organization, the IFP maintains a unique and fundamental position within the film community—nourishing, educating, and promoting American independent cinema.

From the beginning, the purpose of the IFP has been to encourage quality films with fresh ideas and alternative viewpoints, and to support artists whose cinematic styles and content are not obviously commercial. The annual Independent Feature Film Market has been the main instrument in this effort. Past Markets have showcased such notable independent American films as *The Ballad of Gregorio Cortez, Blood Simple, El Norte, Northern Lights, Parting Glances, The Return of the Secaucus Seven, Stand and Deliver, The Times of Harvey Milk, Vernon, Florida,* and *Working Girls.*

The Market provides an opportunity for filmmakers to interact with marketing professionals in a lively working environment. Distributors, festival programmers, and foreign buyers come to survey each year's crop of independent films. Filmmakers come to sell. But beyond serving as a forum for the actual buying and selling, the Market is also a conference where industry professionals meet upcoming talent, filmmakers learn about market realities, and all involved make important contacts and initiate lasting collaborations.

Since 1979 the IFP Market has become a venerable institution in the growing world of independent cinema, a nexus for filmmakers on the rise and new talent on the brink of recognition.

In addition to the Market, the IFP offers high-quality and timely services that are designed to assist the independent producer at every phase of production—from the first draft of a script through financing and distribution. IFP activities include a monthly newsletter, seminars, publications, a resource program, screenings, and representation at key domestic and international film festivals.

In the future, the IFP will continue to provide innovative programming that is responsive to the changing needs of the independent filmmaker and shifting realities of the marketplace. The Independent Feature Project is an ongoing organization, informed by the energy, vision, and potential of today's independent filmmakers.

The Independent Feature Project
21 West 86th Street
New York, NY 10024
212-496-0909